Brute Reality

BRUTE REALITY

Power, Discourse and the Mediation of War

Stuart Price

PlutoPress
www.plutobooks.com

First published 2010 by Pluto Press
345 Archway Road, London N6 5AA and
175 Fifth Avenue, New York, NY 10010

www.plutobooks.com

Distributed in the United States of America exclusively by
Palgrave Macmillan, a division of St. Martin's Press LLC,
175 Fifth Avenue, New York, NY 10010

British Library Cataloguing in Publication Data
A catalogue record for this book is available from the British Library

ISBN   978 0 7453 2080 9   Hardback
ISBN   978 0 7453 2079 3   Paperback

Library of Congress Cataloging in Publication Data applied for

This book is printed on paper suitable for recycling and made from fully managed and
sustained forest sources. Logging, pulping and manufacturing processes are expected to
conform to the environmental standards of the country of origin.

10 9 8 7 6 5 4 3 2 1

Designed and produced for Pluto Press by
Chase Publishing Services Ltd, 33 Livonia Road, Sidmouth, EX10 9JB England
Typeset from disk by Stanford DTP Services, Northampton, England
Printed and bound in the European Union by
CPI Antony Rowe, Chippenham and Eastbourne

To my sister, Sharon Price

Contents

List of Illustrations

Acknowledgements

This book was completed during a short period of research leave, awarded by the Faculty of Humanities, De Montfort University. I also obtained practical support from a number of individuals. My thanks go first to Anne Beech at Pluto, for her good humour and patience. Karen Ross at Liverpool University and Georgina Gregory at UCLAN read the initial proposal, while Lucy Byrne read the final manuscript before it went to press. Within the Department of Media, Film and Journalism, Diane Taylor protected my time at the expense of her own. A number of colleagues and research associates helped to provide a supportive academic environment, including Helen Wood, Heidi Macpherson, Andrew Tolson, Simon Mills, Tony Graves, Stuart Hanson, Deborah Cartmell, Imelda Whelehan, Ruth Sanz Sabido and Rivers Barry. My sister Sharon, and my mother Jean, provided essential practical and moral support which helped facilitate the completion of the work.

The title of this book was first used in a public lecture delivered in 2003, and was intended to describe the apparent inconsistency created when rhetoric is employed to promote the realities of warfare; since that time, it has developed into the more extensive analysis of structure, power and mediation which follows. Some of the material it contains was presented within academic networks, including: the Media, Communication and Cultural Studies Association; the Media Group of the Political Studies Association; the British Association of American Studies; the British Film Institute; the International Visual Studies Association; Aston University's Centre for the Study of Language and Society, and events run by the University of Aveiro's Department of Language and Culture.

Permission to reprint illustrations and text has been obtained from the *Daily Mirror* (for 'Icon of Wealth'), the *Express* ('British Shoppers Defy the Terrorists') and the *Independent* (for Dave Brown's cartoon). The journal *Review of International American Studies* gave permission for the use of material in Chapter 5, which first appeared in *RIAS* 3.3–4.1 (2009), while Cambridge Scholars Publishing allowed me to adapt work from essays which were published under their imprint: 'Yo Blair!' in K. Ross and S. Price (eds), *Popular Media and Communication* (2008), and

'Brute Reality' in A. Barker (ed.), *Television, Aesthetics and Reality* (2006).

A note on the text: where attributions appear as: (Author, 1978: 1), this is the standard reference to a book, or a chapter in an edited volume (the Bibliography gives precise details). A reference such as (Author, 1 July 1978: 1) refers to a newspaper or periodical. The Bibliography covers only material referred to in the text, and therefore provides a complete list of references.

Transcription conventions used in the book:

[word]	Indicates authorial comment on content
(1)	Length of pause in seconds
(.)	Pause of less than a second
utterance	Indicates that emphasis has been placed on a term
uttera::nce	Indicates lengthening of vowel sound
=	Indicates speech that follows on immediately from previous utterance
[	Indicates overlap with previous utterance

Stuart Price
January 2010

Introduction
The Composition of the 'Terror War'

THE EMANCIPATION OF WOMEN?

'LIBERATION' – on 3 December 2001, this word appeared on the cover of *Business Week*, above the photograph of a smiling Afghan woman, her face clearly visible beneath a black headscarf. The caption alongside the picture declared that 'the US victory is a defining moment – for the Afghan people, for Western values, and for the cause of moderation in the Muslim world'. It was followed by the question, 'will we all seize the opportunity?' In this short passage, a basic technique of rhetoric – the compression of disparate concepts into the same discursive space – is perfectly exemplified. The accompanying image, meanwhile, was supposed to illustrate one of the central alibis for America's war: the emancipation of Afghan women. They were suddenly made visible, 'invested with freedom and agency ... by the grace of the American military complex' (Zine, 2007: 34).

The persuasiveness of this notion, that the female population had been set free, depended on the structural complicity of established or 'traditional' media forms. They were able to circulate a simple form of visual evidence to support the proposition, in the form of photographs and film that might arouse the curiosity of the western citizen-consumer: here were the faces of the oppressed. It is notable that *Business Week*, a magazine supposedly devoted to hard fiscal calculations, did not estimate the extent of this liberation by using economic indicators, like income, access to services, life expectancy and so on.

Although the magazine did make an attempt to analyse the prevailing conditions in Afghanistan as a whole, the major theme it had tried to animate on its cover seemed to be called into question by another illustration carried on its inside pages. Here, two women, their faces and bodies entirely concealed, are shown passing in front of an armoured vehicle. The caption reads: 'Khanabad – Burqua-clad women pass a Northern Alliance tank and soldiers as they flee US bombing on Nov. 18' (Walczak et al., 3 December 2001: 22–3). Perhaps this photograph and the accompanying explanation

1

should have appeared on the cover – women hurrying away from the bombs of their liberators.

Although it has since become painfully obvious that the declaration of victory in Afghanistan was premature, the fundamental question is not why the campaign was initially regarded as a military success, but how it was ever possible for it to have been presented as a *moral* triumph. In following this line, the caption writers at *Business Week* conflated the geopolitical ambitions of the US executive, first with the welfare of the Afghan people, then with an unspecified set of 'Western values', and finally with the hypothetical interests of a progressive tendency within the Muslim faith. The use of the image on the cover was meant to exemplify the worthiness of these goals, and even perhaps their actual attainment.

SECURITY AND FREEDOM?

The inside pages of *Business Week* also gave space to Bruce Nussbaum, who took up the theme of liberation with his assertion that 'the scenes of joy in the streets of Kabul evoke nothing less than the images of Paris liberated from the Nazis' (Nussbaum, 3 December 2001: 18). Allusions to the Third Reich in this period were not uncommon, and allowed the leading powers of the west[1] to reprise a familiar role: that of beleaguered allies who, faced with an implacable enemy that must not be 'appeased', are forced to conduct a war for the future of democracy.[2]

That, at least, was the original narrative. As the conflict developed, the pretext for western involvement began to alter, moving from high-minded talk of freedom and equality to a more modest conception. The United States and its allies began to settle for the creation of a viable state and 'effective governance' in Afghanistan, to be achieved through reconstruction and the creation of a 'secure' environment. The pursuit of security, however, rationalised on the grounds that it was the prerequisite for all other forms of progress, became an end in itself. It seemed above all to require violent intervention, ostensibly directed against those who would bring chaos (or, alternatively, the wrong kind of order in the form of repressive laws) to the country.[3] The death of civilians in the course of such operations, *guaranteed* within military practice as the result of inevitable 'error', would seem to challenge the ethical foundations of western policy.

Besides the accusation that the use of force has a tendency to produce disorder rather than security, the invaders had to cope with the fact that support for the Karzai government in Afghanistan[4] might associate the west with the values it was supposed to be fighting against. When President Karzai put his signature to a law suggesting that women should seek permission from their husbands to pursue even the simplest course of action, its provisions were described by one female senator as being worse than those enacted by the Taliban (Boone, 31 March 2009). In fact, the legislation did no more than formalise practices that already existed.

In December 2001, at about the time *Business Week* published its article, Sarah Chayes, a National Public Radio correspondent based in Kandahar, described how local women's lives were controlled. While little girls were free to roam around in the open, as they approached puberty their movements were restricted. Referring to one 13-year-old, Chayes noted that 'she was no longer allowed outside' (Chayes, 2007: 109). In essence, despite formal protests against the government's actions, women's rights were low on the west's political agenda. Yet, at the beginning, it had been this simple idea that women should experience freedom and equality which had been used to confirm the sincerity of the coalition's commitment to 'liberty' in general. It would appear, therefore, that any interest in women's rights was no more than a tactical manoeuvre. It resembled a form of 'embedded feminism' (Hunt, 2007: 5) in which references to female emancipation were intended to make the actions of the Taliban appear as the antithesis of the kind of 'Western humanist values' celebrated in *Business Week* (Nussbaum, 3 December 2001: 18). Once they had served their purpose, progressive discourses were relegated to the background. The chief aim of western intervention became – in the words of the British grandee Lord Ashdown – 'the protection of citizens and the improvement of their lifestyles' (Ashdown, 29 April 2009).

Although this sober appraisal might appear more realistic than the original conception of rights and freedom, it is in fact just as much of a fantasy. The terms used by Ashdown, where 'citizen' is a full member of a state or commonwealth, and 'lifestyle' refers to social standing achieved through consumption, suggest that the real social and political status of Afghanistan's ordinary inhabitants had not been understood. This kind of formulation is not unusual: ultimately, all official descriptions of western goals are couched in a mixture of humanitarian concern, condescension and martial resolve.

SOURCES OF INFORMATION AND THE PROPAGANDA WAR

Besides the formal alibis offered for western intervention, a number of other accounts of war and terror have appeared in the public realm. These include academic monographs, the work of war correspondents, 'citizen journalists' using the internet as a platform, narrative fiction (films and novels), and anti-war campaigns operating within a greatly expanded 'information environment' that have worked to create their own media outlets (Gillan et al., 2008: 26). Alternative perspectives have also been composed within that genre of story-telling known as the 'combat' narrative.[5] Each of these practices, whatever their origin, contributes to the discursive context within which the 'terror war'[6] must be understood, and no single element, however informative, can be seen in isolation.

While, for instance, a serious piece of journalism published in an established media format (newspapers, magazines, and their associated websites) can provide a detailed insight into events, this itself may have been shaped by the contributions of informants (diplomats, military officers, spies) who may have a particular case to make. So, for example, although standard accounts of military operations produced by government sources are treated with caution, even reports that offer more considered explanations must be seen in the wider context of the propaganda war and the discursive *space* that different interventions are allowed to occupy.

The following case may illustrate this point. In July 2008, the *Independent* carried a story suggesting that 'Taliban factions may be using British forces to assassinate rival commanders' (Sengupta, 25 July 2008). Though he did not name his sources, the journalist was careful to note that they included intelligence officials. The substance of the report dealt with the suspicion that some Taliban leaders were alerting 'western forces' to the whereabouts of fellow insurgents, so that these competitors could be eliminated in ambushes or air strikes. This article offers an interesting perspective on the realities of war, and testifies to the cynical manoeuvres carried out by all those involved in the conflict. Yet, in mentioning the nature of his sources, the reporter demonstrates that British officials are reluctant to make open or honest interventions, and that the media in general is often used as a conduit for the 'subterranean' dissemination of strategic information. A month after this article was published, the *Guardian* carried a report highlighting the work of a 'Whitehall counter-terrorism unit' which was 'targeting the BBC' and other media outlets in an attempt to 'taint the al-Qaeda brand' (Travis, 26 August 2008).

Sticking with the marketing jargon that has soaked into the heart of the political process, a secret Home Office report cited by the *Guardian* went on to note that al-Qaeda was trying to 'feed its new franchises with propaganda to keep the "brand" alive at all costs' (Travis, 2008). The idea, of course, was that the British authorities could diminish the impact of this material by providing their own stories. Information would be placed in reliable sources, to be used later as 'evidence' which could reinforce the original perspective favoured by the propagandist (see Davies, 2008a). Besides the attempt to influence mainstream channels, another way of countering the perspective of al-Qaeda was to 'channel messages through volunteers in internet forums' (Travis, 2008).

Although western politicians argue that the terror war is fought to prevent the subversion of democratic institutions, they appear to use tactics that are supposed to characterise the behaviour of their sworn enemies. At the practical level, the process of negotiation reveals the pragmatic attitudes that lie beneath ideological posturing. So, for example, during periods of dialogue, the relentless 'terrorist' is encouraged to undergo a transformation into an ally of democracy. Hence the invention of that uncomfortable category 'moderate Taliban',[7] applied to an individual or a group that might be inclined to embrace a more enlightened outlook, usually consisting of a willingness to stop fighting or to change sides. In all such processes, the key to understanding the motivations of the main actors is their common allegiance to hierarchical modes of rule: the leadership of each side negotiates only with opponents of equal status, while each set of subordinates is meant to do no more than carry out orders.

'NO ONE TOLD US ANYTHING': SEPTEMBER 11th 2001

'No one told us anything' – this utterance summed up the experience of one of the functionaries referred to above, in this case a military pilot whose F16 jet was scrambled from Langley Air Force Base on the morning of 11 September 2001. In testimony offered to the 9/11 Commission, the airman recalled flying above Washington and wondering what had caused the devastation on the ground below. Deprived of any guidance from his controller, he fell back on the military paradigm of the Cold War and 'reverted to the Russian threat', believing that cruise missiles had been fired 'from the sea' (9/11 Commission Report, 2004: 45). 'You look down and see the Pentagon burning and I thought the bastards snuck one by us', he said (*ibid*).

Civilians in New York also used existing frames of reference to understand the events of that day, again without any firm sense of assurance. A business reporter for *Newsday*, called S. Mitra Kalita, had watched a morning news bulletin which revealed that 'a plane had crashed into the World Trade Center' (Kalita, 2002: 53). Assuming that a light aircraft had been involved, she had dismissed the incident and switched off the television. From her previous experiences as a journalist in New Jersey, Kalita recalled that such accidents 'seemed as common as car crashes' (*ibid*). Later, as she sat in a dentist's chair two blocks away from her apartment, she first heard the event described as a terrorist attack. She began to question her assumptions: 'two planes? ... that's not what the morning news had said ... there had just been one plane a few moments ago' (*ibid*). Her dentist brought in a radio and she began to hear the first confused reports from the scene. For this individual, the shape of the event was gradually composed through the fragmentary evidence provided by conventional media forms.

Not all witnesses and participants, however, felt uncertain about what to think or how to respond. Standing in the grounds of the Pentagon on the same fateful day, a British journalist encountered a naval officer who declared that 'somebody's nation, somebody's cause, somebody's damn religion has just declared war on us, and we are the greatest war fighting machine the world has ever seen' (Fenton, 12 September 2001). Here, there is a dual meaning at work: both that the offender is not yet known, and that someone (anyone) must pay in blood for the attack. The reporter noticed that, in the course of this outburst, the officer covered up his name badge.

These three reactions were produced at moments when information was both scarce and inaccurate. The most significant feature of the first two testimonies is their dependence on authoritative sources for the formation of a provisional opinion. Despite the separate and quite different environments they inhabited, both had to rely on established modes of communication in order to make sense of their experiences. The third example reveals a rather different perspective – the determination of those at the centre of US power to pursue a military response.

EARLY WARNINGS

While the initial lack of direction and clarity may be attributed to the suddenness of the strike against the US mainland – the 9/11

Commission claimed that the authorities had at best nine minutes notice of the first hijacking and no warning at all of the other three – information about the general nature of the threat had not only circulated within the intelligence agencies but had also appeared in the public domain. Two examples will suffice to illustrate this, though a number of other sources have been identified.[8] In a *Newsweek* report at the beginning of January 2000, for instance, two journalists had identified 'the bin Laden threat' (Klaidman and Thomas, 3 January 2000: 31).

A year later, another *Newsweek* feature, entitled 'The Future of Terror', noted that 'top officials of the FBI and CIA believe there is a loose network of Islamic extremists planning terrorist attacks on the United States', and argued further that 'scary headlines' on this issue 'were not a media contrivance' (Thomas and Hirsh, 3 January 2001: 35). The article described America as 'the strongest, most dominating nation' yet one which was characterised by 'freedom and technology', and a 'mobile, open society' (*ibid*). 'Most frightening', according to Thomas and Hirsh, was 'the threat of ... weapons of mass destruction (WMD) falling into the wrong hands' (*ibid*); in the right hands, of course, such weaponry undergoes a category shift and mutates into a 'deterrent'.

The *Newsweek* article also carried an illustration of the 'terrorist network', showing three types of structure. With the aid of stylised figures, representing individual combatants, it drew attention to the organisational development of the terror cell, from the 'traditional' mode (the 'hierarchical framework'), to 'more efficient, networked models of organisation', supposedly learned from 'the example of business' (*ibid*). This remark was not, presumably, intended to suggest a moral parallel between the two practices, or to draw comparisons between their destructive capacity. The article also dealt with the question of security, arguing that 'for the FBI and the CIA, used to fighting hierarchical, monolithic foes like the Mafia and the KGB, chasing the "new terrorism" is frustrating': it ended by noting 'we will find out soon enough if they failed' (*ibid*: 39).

This appraisal of the authorities is notable for its prescience, but also for the reproduction of some familiar themes. America is presented as capable of projecting military power, while at the same time suffering from the disadvantages of being an 'open' society. Freedom, according to this perspective, leads to vulnerability; political innocence and strategic naivety must therefore be abandoned. This represents the confusion of martial and cultural qualities, a common form of mystification designed to make any struggle 'righteous'. The

Newsweek piece, as noted above, also gave credence to the uncertain proposition that determined opponents wanted to obtain 'weapons of mass destruction'. The expansion of this theme to include the idea that hostile states actually possessed such weapons, and were prepared to use them against US targets, became a central factor in the subsequent development of American policy on Iraq.

AN 'INITIATING EVENT'?

The representation of the 9/11 attack as an 'initiating event', the marker for an epochal disturbance that redirected the course of history, has appeared time and again in the commentaries produced by journalists and academics. Early observations drew attention to the magnitude and significance of the assault. 'The world changed forever', according to one writer (Rashid, 2001: vii), while another recalled that 'the familiar, known world seemed to disappear' (Schell, 2002). The cultural theorist Jean Baudrillard wondered if it was 'the absolute event', and noted that it had disrupted 'the whole play of history and power' (Baudrillard, 2003: 4). Astonishment at the scale and force of the attack gave way to speculation about the consequences that would follow: an American author identified 'an age of radical insecurity and post-state conflict' (George, 2002: 155), and a British academic listed a host of likely outcomes and effects, from western use of military force to the 'psychological aftermath of violence and insecurity felt in all societies' (Halliday, 2002: 32).

The early reports of shock and apprehension conveyed in many sections of the media, together with the gradual emergence of more considered analysis, stand in marked contrast to the polemic of national leaders like Bush and Blair. Apart from Bush's hesitant start, when he referred to the attackers as 'those folks who committed this act' (Woodward, 2002: 16), most of the formal speeches made by the two leaders were characterised by an expressive clarity. They declared their determination to overcome the challenge of terrorism, and offered an apparently simple distinction between their own values and those of their enemies.

Three days after 9/11, the British Prime Minister made a statement to the House of Commons in which he referred to 'the hideous and foul events' in America, and declared that the attacks were not simply directed against people and buildings, or even 'merely upon the USA', but represented an assault 'on the basic democratic values in which we all believe' (Blair, 14 September 2001b). Here, the physical materiality of lives and structures are made to represent a set of principles that must be defended by the mysterious and flexible collective designated by the inclusive term 'we'. The persuasive force of this proposition would have some impact in a social order that had, largely through concepts circulating within the phenomenal world of advertising and politics, become familiar with the principle that solid things could exemplify emotional qualities.

A POLITICAL OPPORTUNITY

As the world struggled to comprehend the magnitude of September 11th, political leaders tried to show that they could rise above partisan divisions by aligning themselves with public sentiment. Beneath this parade of compassion, however, the bourgeois[9] political class saw an opportunity to consolidate their hold over the moral and political orientation of the social order. This could not be achieved by continuing to pretend that the political process had been deferred: displays of grief had to be followed by calls to action.[10] The groundswell of revulsion against terror was not, however, used to renew a commitment to peaceful civic values. In this, the vengeful attitude of the authorities was not far removed from the reactionary impulse often found within the public realm, except that the official mode of expression had to observe certain forms of protocol. Right-wing commentators, not yet fully conversant with the still underdeveloped practice of blogging (Rettberg, 2008), gave vent to their opinions by using the internet to post often scurrilous visual propositions about the new enemy, with particular reference to the supposed sexual preferences of Osama bin Laden.[11]

The powerful, meanwhile, dedicated themselves to the general cause of an armed and belligerent modernity. As they rushed to make declarations of support for the United States, they found that, instead of having to justify their own pre-eminence by making a tired and offensive distinction between 'advanced' and 'developing' economies, they could promote their interests by reinforcing a new demarcation – between 'enlightened', sophisticated democracies and a barbarous network of terrorists, supposedly dedicated to the defeat of human progress. The west and its allies had now identified an implacable enemy that could be represented as its polar opposite – al-Qaeda.

The rhetorical call to arms that washed over the ranks of the international political elite did not, however, satisfy some commentators on the Right, who were not convinced by the show of solidarity made by some of those allies who had rallied to America's cause. One such commentator, writing for *The European*, declared that most of the 19 countries that had expressed their support 'can only offer words of comfort', because the long decades spent 'sheltering under a US military umbrella have emasculated their power' to provide any practical assistance (Almond, 2001: 5). This remark, using the concept of a sexually neutered nation, inverts the issue of moral responsibility, because the hosts are blamed for their dependency. The purpose of the American presence – to keep minor nations in precisely the state of impotence described – is turned into an act of paternal benevolence.[12]

Other mainstream writers believed that September 11th would make the west more tolerant of any abuses of power committed by their foreign collaborators. In an assessment of Pakistan's position, an anonymous *Newsweek* writer addressed its repression of internal opponents, imagining the new confidence the authorities would gain from their alliance with the Americans: 'Human rights? Who's going to carp about crackdowns on dissidents at a time like this?' (*Newsweek*, 8 October 2001). When the early show of unity began to fade, bourgeois politicians could still take advantage of the deliberately ambiguous project known as the 'war on terror', not because they all intended to make a serious material contribution to the wars that were to follow, but because an international campaign against terrorism could provide a major rationale for reinforcing authoritarian modes of *domestic* governance.

ORGANISING A 'STATE OF TERROR'

It seemed to various world leaders that the utilitarian discipline inherent in the production of armed force could be replicated within the domestic realm. The notion of hierarchical efficiency was especially attractive to governing parties: an authoritarian form of public regulation could be introduced through bureaucratic processes, without having to abandon the endless repetition of 'progressive' discourses, devoted to notions of fairness, freedom, compassion and other favoured concepts that pose no actual threat to the hierarchical state and the *patriarchal and capitalist*[13] social order upon which it is founded.

Within the borders of those countries that, like the US and UK, had declared themselves 'at war', the armoury of the state was reinforced through legislation (Hewitt, 2008), executive measures (Bonner, 2007) and the development of *worst case scenarios* (see the Conclusion), that posited an internal terror threat which must be met with organised 'paramilitary' force. Recalcitrant individuals, particularly amongst established Muslim communities in the west, were now supposed to make declarations of loyalty to a set of national/democratic values which politicians themselves struggled to identify, let alone observe.

Meanwhile, opposition to public policy could be drawn into the discourse of terror and security by the application of anti-terror laws to a range of low-level activity. 'Terrorism' became one of the preferred descriptions of any agitation that could be represented as a threat to national security. Peaceful protests outside arms fairs, economic 'sabotage' by environmental campaigners, and any demonstration where the right of assembly could be altered by the executive initiative of the police or gendarmerie, could be dragged into the category of 'terror threat'. In widening the conceptual net, two effects could be achieved: *i*) psychological and physical pressure could be applied to the subject-citizen in general, who had to avoid becoming a victim of the state's definition of terror, and *ii*) the state itself could *substantiate* the risk of terrorism by organising 'security events'. Unable to anticipate the exact behaviour of the unreliable 'Islamist terrorist', the security state could reinforce its argument that terrorism constituted the most serious hazard to the public, by making arrests and staging theatrical interventions in public life. In some cases, the threat might only 'materialise' because of such activities, while unnamed and unseen individuals might suffer the consequences of the whole charade.

PURPOSE OF THE BOOK: POWER, FORM AND STRUCTURE

Although this book began with references to September 11th, its main focus is not the terror or security 'event' *per se* (though many such incidents are analysed within the text), but rather the various *explanations* that have been offered for its commission. This requires an analysis of those formal attempts, made by prominent social actors, *to present a rationale for the existence and exercise of coercive power.*[14] A note of caution should, however, be introduced. The expression of any rationale for human activity is *i*) by its very nature inconsistent, is *ii*) often subjected to forms of critique, and *iii*) can appear in a number of forms, including for example oppositional discourses that are excluded from mainstream media, influential fictions generated by commercial organisations,[15] and public protest.

The period chosen to illustrate the key characteristics of this contradictory and fractured enterprise, extends from the state of 'war' created after the 9/11 attacks, to the strategic adjustments begun during the nadir of the Iraq adventure; it also includes reference to the modifications in policy made under the auspices of the Obama presidency. The overall aim is to offer a critical insight into a number of influential structures that have helped to shape contemporary attitudes to warfare.

In simple terms, the concept of structure is based on the notion that human affairs, whether cultural, political or economic, are underpinned, enabled and conditioned by a framework of practices, rituals, material assets and physical circumstances. These qualities and procedures enable individuals and groups to apply energy to what Jessop calls 'the production of significant effects' (Jessop, 2008: 29). When the 'projects entertained by [human] agents' are pursued (Archer, 1995: 200) they take place within (and entail the re-creation of) structures, which include informal alliances as well as more durable institutions.

An interest in '*dominant*' structures or centres of power should not suggest that bureaucratic organisations are so monolithic that individual or collective agency is irrelevant; in fact, bureaucracies depend on the dynamic operation of internal factions for their own renewal. Nor should it be imagined that the symbolic function[16] is entirely monopolised by orators and their officious minions: the opponents of war, for instance, often compete within the same mediated field of activity (Gillan et al., 2008: 29). In addition, public representation is not the only way in which those in responsible positions try to attain their objectives, because they have recourse to a number of other effective mechanisms, many of which bypass media forms entirely. In centres devoted to policy or governance, 'public diplomacy' or communication is necessary not because it is deemed effective, but because it demonstrates the 'goodwill' and public spiritedness that these organisations wish to project. This is sometimes regarded as more important than the goal of persuasion.

STRUCTURE OR CONSPIRACY?

Using structure as a model for human exchange can of course give rise to the suspicion that the analyst has created a mysterious world of subterranean influence, hinting at the existence of a private conspiracy or the composition of an abstract human subject. Latour, for example, in his study of human association, argues that the idea of an 'underlying hidden structure' determining activity is unhelpful (Latour, 2005: 196). He opposes the use of generalisations in the study of social interaction because he feels that they may reinforce the idea that a structure is 'simply an actor-network [about] which there is scant information' (*ibid*, 2005: 202). The analysis of influential organisations, however, has to meet precisely this challenge; not only are certain types of data inaccessible, but it also seems that powerful collectives are anxious to disguise the process through which they arrive at decisions.

If the ordinary business of government is indeed conducted in a conspiratorial manner, it is not unreasonable to ask questions about the internal life of these institutions. Once we acknowledge that much of the 'evidence' we have about the workings of executive authority, is *the publicity generated on its behalf*, it is possible to wonder if the contemporary fascination with language and the symbolic has led, in some cases at least, to the study of ephemeral material specifically designed to burn up critical energy (see below).

THE MANIFESTATION OF AUTHORITY

This is not to deny that the study of official rhetoric is essential, but that it is also important to take into account other forms of evidence, such as mundane or bureaucratic types of communication, gaffes or inconsistencies produced in contested situations (see Chapter 4), and the host of practical effects that make themselves felt in everyday life. It is clear, for example, that practical *manifestations* of authority (like pre-emptive raids against 'terror' suspects) are usually provided with timely alibis. Yet in many other cases similar events are given only a retrospective justification or else occur without *any formal explanation* at all.

There are three potential scenarios to consider when studying the commission of an act carried out by any authority: first, where an enterprise is accompanied by an official commentary or narrative; second, when some justification is offered after the event; and third, when an incident occurs and no information is provided. Where no reasons are offered for the commission of an act, then the meaning has to be guessed at through knowledge of context, past experience of similar actions, and any visual or aural evidence which makes up the communicative signs that accompany the incident (in the case of the terror raid, the word 'police' emblazoned on a vehicle, the uniforms worn by officers, the stances they assume, the equipment they display, etc).[17]

The kind of human projects Archer describes, are therefore only partly composed of acts of representation, but where this process is a *key* activity, it can be defined as both *i*) an attempt to portray or exemplify various phenomena (issues, events or persons) and *ii*) as a political appeal made on behalf of supposedly distinctive groups, perspectives or causes. The appeal can take various forms, such as petitions or demands, and may feature 'expressive displays' that involve some form of 'claim-making and collective production of identities' (DeLanda, 2006: 60/87). The main focus of attention will remain, however, those types of (largely representational) *behaviour* produced when some contentious project is conceived, and when those who occupy positions of legitimate authority offer the public (imagined as a largely passive collective), an account of the activities pursued in its name.

WAR, PASSIVITY AND MORAL PARABLES

Although McNair argues that the expectations of 'liberal democracy' demand that war should be 'legitimised in the eyes of the people' (McNair, 2003: 201), this does not mean that a formal procedure, such as a vote or referendum, will be offered. The electoral process is designed to provide governments with a broad mandate, not specific consent for every endeavour, however momentous. In fact, the political class has little interest in encouraging expressions of public spirit, even in support of government policy. No independent collective activity, even the impulse to volunteer for combat, is therefore an absolute prerequisite in preparing a 'democratic' nation for war. The aim is not to *persuade* the citizen (see below), but to 'soften up' public opinion, even if this produces a number of deleterious effects on the social order.

The prevailing attitude to the public role in war, was exemplified during the early period of the 'war on terror', when George W. Bush made a speech to Congress in which he referred to the role of US citizens in the forthcoming struggle. He noted that 'Americans are asking: what is expected of us?' and, in time-honoured rhetorical fashion, provided the answer. The response, however, was hardly a call to arms: 'I ask you to live your lives, and hug your children' (Speech to Congress, 20 September 2001). This subdued appeal, essentially to carry on as normal, reinforcing the sanctity of domestic existence, demonstrates the contradiction inherent in an authoritarian conception of civic responsibility.

It is worth noting that such a feeble punch-line, after such a grand rhetorical appeal, is to be expected in a society that encourages its citizens to pursue only approved activities. The falling cadence was not simply a symptom of G.W. Bush's famous incoherence. In 2006, for instance, Barack Obama delivered a rousing address in which he declared that 'I've had enough of being told that we can't afford body armour for our troops and health care for our veterans' and insisted that 'I've had enough of our kids going to schools where the rats outnumber the computers' (Russell, 2009: 53–4). Warming to his theme (i.e. following the contours of his script), he said 'I've had enough of being told that all we can do about this is sit and wait' (*ibid*: 54). He carried on in this vein before turning to his audience and saying 'if you've had enough too then we got some work to do' (*ibid*). His listeners, presumably ready at this stage to drag the bourgeoisie into the street and beat them senseless, were then given a less than rousing call to action. They were provided with a list of approved activities: 'we got some checks to write, some calls to make, and some doors to knock on' (*ibid*). Such is the nature of contemporary activism.

War in particular is presented in a contradictory manner, as both an urgent challenge to be met, and as an opportunity to conform to routine expectations. It is described as a struggle for survival, requiring some form of public participation, and yet as an enterprise best left to the discretion of the executive and its unelected subordinates. Public action is therefore confined to respectable activity, which is then reinterpreted as defiance in the face of the terrorist threat. An early headline in the *Daily Express*, for example, announced that 'BRITISH SHOPPERS DEFY THE TERRORISTS', noting that there was 'at last some good news' after the September 11th attacks, because consumer spending had risen (Fletcher and O'Grady, 19 October 2001: 1).

Consent is therefore conceived in paradoxical terms, as an 'act' of passivity, in which conformist behaviour is supposed to characterise the inclinations of individuals determined to pursue 'private goals for most if not all' of their lives (Yunis, 1996: 7). Instead of a genuine national debate, a campaign of public diplomacy is conducted by the authorities, which does no more than imitate the process of persuasion, concentrating on the production of *a broadly plausible scenario*. This model of communication emerges from the belief that governance, rather than the production of democratic exchange,

Figure 1   The public's contribution to 'the war on terror'? *Daily Express*, 19 October 2001.

is the primary task of public authority. As a result, the public as a whole (temporarily 'constituted' by the address) is called upon to witness the articulation of a moral parable, in which imperial[18] powers embark upon a mission to redress some terrible injustice.

Too great an enthusiasm for any one aspect of this narrative would be counter-productive, because it might impede the reception of a fresh rationale for war produced when an original alibi begins to collapse (see Chapter 1). In the meantime, critics are invited to pour their energies into answering the illogical propositions of the belligerent powers. The composite referential category 'weapons of mass destruction', for instance, provided one notable example of official rhetoric. Seized upon because it gave the Bush administration the opportunity to reach a 'bureaucratic compromise' in its effort to find the most suitable justification for invading Iraq, references to 'WMD' failed to make the case for war more convincing, but helped to draw the fire of opponents. This tactic was not an isolated case; when examined closely, the whole narrative of war is made up of a confused amalgam of practical and ethical perspectives, in which an enemy attack is presented as an initiating event (see above), rather than as one more incident generated within a cycle of reciprocal violence.

THE RULE OF INCOHERENCE

Despite the apparently easy transmission of authoritarian policy into the public sphere, major contradictions occur in the production of meaningful communication. This can be seen in the occasionally schizophrenic combination of the various categories that are supposed to prop up the case for aggressive intervention in the affairs of 'failed states'. Although the advocates of war have ample opportunity to lie, deliberate misrepresentation provides only a limited explanation for the disorder that often accompanies the exercise of power. While the advantage of being in a position to describe events, is that any formal representation need bear only a tangential relationship to the full practical and discursive range of the activity, this is not the only factor to consider. Of greater significance is the fact that the occupation of a dominant structural position means that a political project does not even need to be entirely coherent; the essential requirement is simply to make regular public announcements in the spirit of managerial oversight.

Although, as explained above, it is not the primary intention of the powerful necessarily to *persuade* the subaltern of a particular case, the process of assembling and refining specific ideas is actually of considerable benefit to bureaucrats and functionaries. As an exercise, it provides factions within organisations with some degree of practical and ideological cohesion (Abercrombie et al., 1980). Nonetheless, it is important to know why even a *genuine* attempt to achieve communicative consistency is likely to fall short. Some of the reasons for such failures apply to any intentional effort to compose a meaningful act of communication, while others relate more specifically to institutional procedure.

The first consideration is that any position must be composed with reference to its discursive alternatives, suggesting that an argument is forced to rehearse its own negation; this is why politicians avoid the real strengths of an opponent, preferring to fabricate a set of perspectives they can attribute to an enemy, and which they can then take pains to refute. The second significant impediment is that each authoritative institution is composed of competing divisions, requiring the imposition of a unitary perspective to secure a settlement; when, for example, external consultants are brought in to publicise the values of the organisation, one major purpose of the exercise is to force an end to internal argument.

The third barrier to the creation of a successful message, is the need to take account of rival bodies, which are bound to advocate their own perspectives. The fourth element to consider is the fact that a proposition must pass through the hands of a number of mediators, who may treat it as no more than raw material for the production of their own agenda. The fifth difficulty is that the intended audience, habitually neglected so that it can follow the 'normative' paradigm of consumption, may not be listening to anything that emanates from the political realm. The sixth challenge lies in the move away from unitary forms of media, to a more disparate set of practices in which individuals talk to one another without taking their lead from formal institutions. Together, these elements explain why public explanations, as a *formal* necessity, remain provisional. The end result of this process of composition is usually a temporary *configuration of meaning*, but this is more than adequate for the purpose: a timely intervention is usually all that is required to achieve a particular outcome, since the whole point of an executive decision is that it can be made without consent.

None of the reservations expressed above, however, should suggest that executive power is not serious about important issues. The point is that it reserves its strength for the most crucial matters, which are protected while a public façade is presented for attack.

So, for example, although the invasion of Iraq was never blessed with a convincing alibi, the ideological practice of making a firm distinction between democratic principles and the values supposedly espoused by the 'terrorist', was definitely not negotiable. As a result, the world is still forced to tolerate an embarrassing pretence: that those forms of armed opposition commonly known as terrorism or insurgency have first, nothing to do with the expansion of the security state in belligerent democracies and, second, that terrorism really does represent an acute threat to the continued existence of western values or ways of life.[19] First aired in the early days of the 'war on terror', this narrative has not disappeared. In 2009, for example, the British Defence Secretary John Hutton was asked if the Afghan war was worth the cost in soldiers' lives (the total number of British troops killed had just reached 150). Hutton argued the case for renewed effort in the conflict by declaring that the armed forces were trying 'to turn the tide of international terrorism and extremism', and were meeting 'a fundamental challenge to our way of life' (BBC Radio 4 News, 15 March 2009). It was not, he said, 'a conflict we have sought' (*ibid*).

1
From the 'War on Terror' to 'Overseas Contingency Operations'

Within the contested fields of rhetorical utterance and public policy, two supposedly interchangeable terms have received a great deal of attention. These are *the war on terror* and *the war on terrorism*, which are both, on occasion, enlarged by inserting the adjective *global*. The broad range of meaning suggested by these alternative descriptions can be expressed, therefore, through a composite formula: *the (global) war on terror/ism*. This concept proposes the existence of a transnational (para)military campaign, conducted against a number of possible circumstances or threats, which might include a deliberate policy of coercion (political terror), the promotion of extreme fear (psychological terror), a disreputable form of political violence (terrorism as technique), or an ideology (terrorism as 'belief').

An obvious question therefore, is to what degree it is possible to direct an armed struggle against a political condition, a state of mind, a method of coercion, or an ideological conviction. If such goals are difficult or impossible to pursue, then it is worth asking what kinds of activity *the (global) war on terror/ism* is meant to indicate, or whether in fact it was ever intended as a rational description of a set of practices. Behind this particular issue lies a more fundamental problem: the questionable integrity of any descriptions of warfare produced, not for the purposes of enlightenment or analysis, but as an integral part of a military campaign.

The impact achieved by the multiple versions of *the (global) war on terror/ism*, which circulated as a form of conceptual shorthand, was considerable. The various forms of the statement do not, however, lead to a set of principles or any further explanation. They seem to function more as a *brand* than a guiding principle. The linguistic structure of *the (global) war on terror/ism* seems to confirm this suspicion. It is a phrase, rather than a complete sentence or a full proposition. Although it is grammatical, in the sense that it deploys an adjective, nouns and a preposition in a valid sequence, it displays only a limited semantic value. *The war on terror* lacks the sense of action necessary for the attribution of meaningful activity. Terror appears as the object of the concept 'war', yet no real effect is produced, and the whole perfunctory phrase hangs in suspended animation, removed from any material or temporal context.

The 'war on terror/ism', however, does more than merely offer an assumption about the nature of armed conflict: as a *formal sequence* it also manoeuvres the reader or listener into a position in which 'war' is the determining, normative factor, the core term that recurs in other contexts, such as the 'war on drugs'. In fact, *the war on terror* most closely resembles an idiom, a form of utterance peculiar to a specific culture, territory or social group. The attribution of a parochial quality to the concept may seem surprising, considering its widespread use, but its popularity proves only the correlation between an influential utterance and the successful transmission of themes within the public realm. It was actually the product of a small, predominantly male political cabal, and thus based on a narrow social and political consensus – at once idiomatic and *productively* idiotic.[1]

THE 'WAR ON TERROR': FIRST USE AND PURPOSE

The phrase 'war on terrorism' made its initial public appearance on 16 September 2001, in remarks uttered by President George W. Bush (Woodward, 2002: 94; Graham *et al.*, 2004: 199). Although the term seemed to indicate a formal military response to the '9/11' attacks, the scope of the policy which lay behind it was much more extensive. From the earliest moments of its conception within the Bush administration, 'the war on terrorism' was used as a catch-all for a variety of manoeuvres, including diplomatic, economic and intelligence activities (Woodward, 2002: 113). Central to the initiation of this war was a particular conception of gendered relations; it seemed to provide an opportunity for the 'performance of masculinity' (Enloe, 1989, cited in Hunt and Rygiel, 2007: 2). War was framed, as the Introduction notes, within a particular subterfuge: the proposition that military action was intended as a humanist intervention on behalf of women's rights. This was supported by the wide currency of a particular kind of conception, described by Zine as 'representations of backward, oppressed and politically immature women' who were supposed to be 'in need of liberation and rescue through imperialist interventions' (Zine, 2007:

27). In some cases, the recomposition of masculinity was made into an explicit cause (see Faludi, 2008).

The US President had made some elements of this agenda apparent on 20 September 2001, during his address at the National Cathedral, Washington (McClellan, 2008: 107). In private, the new campaign included the implementation of 'lethal covert action', which would 'keep the role of the United States hidden' (Woodward, 2002: 101). Despite the secrecy surrounding this decision, Bush may have drawn attention to the possibility of assassination and dirty tricks when a reporter asked him if he wanted bin Laden killed. He replied to the effect that posters 'out West' had once called for the capture of outlaws 'Dead or Alive' (Woodward, 2002: 100; Frum, 2003: 141). This response, Bush later explained, was one of those comments that 'just ... pops out' (Woodward, 2002: 100).

Fairly soon after its inception, attempts were made to widen the already broad scope of the conflict by *re-classifying established practices*. In 2002, for instance, then US Secretary of State Colin Powell declared that Colombia's anti-drug operations were part of the Bush administration's global campaign (Gareau, 2004: 214). In a sense, this kind of re-positioning reveals one of the enduring facts of the whole enterprise: the degree to which the 'war' has always been a flag of convenience, hoisted over a considerable number of long-standing but highly divergent practices.

The 'global war on terror', as the operation became known, was presented as a wide-ranging response to September 11th, in which every resource of the state was to be mobilised in an effort to eradicate a serious threat to US national security. Closer examination of the strategy reveals, however, certain elements that suggest that overall policy was dictated by more specific goals. These included *i*) the desire to exploit what Bush called an 'opportunity' to recast relationships with rival states (see Woodward, 2002: 32), demonstrating American 'pre-eminence', through the spatial and temporal extension of unilateral US power; *ii*) an internal manoeuvre dedicated to the re-validation of an assertive masculinity (see Faludi, 2008) played out in a 'theatre' of war and mobilised through the distinction between male warriors and the trope 'women and children' (Shepherd, 2008: 41), which was in turn designed to: *iii*) *settle the argument about those contested patriarchal values* operating in the domestic social/economic sphere, made manifest in issues like abortion, equal pay, childcare and so forth.

The *formal* political project, associated with the *Joint Vision 20/20* policy (Joint Chiefs of Staff, US Government, June 2000), was always concerned to maintain the pole position of the US, and in this sense was part of an unbroken tradition. The 'war on terror' was therefore an alibi, a form of shorthand for a whole range of activities. It has come to be associated with one political faction in the US core executive, though this perception needs to be treated with caution. The supposedly dominant faction, most commonly described as *neo-conservative*, certainly used the opportunity provided by the September 11th attacks to follow a course of action it had long intended to pursue. Yet it was only the 'opportunistic convergence' of interests between assertive nationalists (Holloway, 2008: 36), who did not believe in spreading democracy, and the neo-conservative Right, that allowed the extension of an aggressively voracious capitalist interest to be dressed up as democratic humanism.[2] The actual practices of the individuals who aligned themselves with neo-conservatism seem to confirm the suspicion that they took advantage of its precepts for the purposes of personal advancement.

WAR ON TERROR AND THE 'IDEOLOGY' OF TERRORISM

A *war on terror/ism*, as indicated above, does not make sense unless certain conditions can be fulfilled. The most important is that a definition of terror can be established in which it is portrayed not as a vague possibility, but as an enduring (and immediate) threat, constantly renewed by sporadic incidents of terrorism which testify to its permanence. Terror, as the subjective apprehension of fear, and terrorism, a method of combat, are clearly separate concepts, but are drawn together as though they constitute a system of belief.

The supposed existence of an ideology of terror is helped into existence by the attachment of the suffix 'ism', which completes the bogus transition from instrument or circumstance into a system, comparable with other established 'ideological' structures, such as environmentalism, conservatism and so on. While terrorism is turned into an intransigent foundational practice, the terrorist is presented as an individual who follows an 'ideology' of terror. Only terrorists (by definition) use terrorism as a means of advancing their interests, and only terrorists truly 'believe' in terror.

Suddenly, from a technique that is available to any organisation, state or 'non-state', which has access to the means of coercion or intimidation, terrorism becomes something entirely alien to democracy. This marks a retreat from older British definitions of terror, based on the notion that its most virulent forms can emerge from the exercise of state power: a terrorist for example was 'one who favours or uses terror-inspiring methods of governing or of coercing government or community' (*Concise OED*, 1964).

The associated notion, that terror (as a state of mind) can be inspired by symbolic actions, leads to the conclusion that terrorists may also ply their trade through the creation of fear, rather than simply through the production of practical effects such as explosions. The trouble with this conception, is that states are also capable of engendering such nervousness; some commentators, in fact, assign this sort of 'insubstantial' activity to the circulation of media content (see Hoskins and O'Loughlin, 2007).

A state of 'terror' may, according to this position, be achieved through the production of fear. A 'war on terrorism' suggests therefore a struggle against a practice or method that is geared towards producing this condition. If this is the case, then any activity which might scare people, including particular kinds of news reports, might fall into the realm of terrorist activity and find itself subject to repression. The utility of the 'war on terror' thus becomes apparent: in declaring the existence of an imprecise and limitless struggle against an invisible foe, the intention is to demonstrate the need to escape two forms of *temporal constraint*.

The first assault on the temporal order can be observed in the refusal of the belligerents to imagine an end to the war. The second form of evasion is their hostility to the governing norms of the secular (temporal) world, particularly restrictions on the use of indefinite imprisonment and torture. The 'war on terror', an attempt to establish a broad alibi for the economic, political and military activities of a dominant faction within the US core executive,[3] now seems to operate as a more general instrument of compulsion. It follows the principle of 'low intensity' warfare, in two closely related forms: imperial aggression at the periphery, and interminable governance within the domestic heartland. Meyers provides an insight into this condition, when he argues that '*real* war is not immediate violence but rather a form of politics' (Meyers, 2008: 7).[4] Military operations become, in this scenario, an 'auxiliary fact' within a dominant paradigm, described by Myers as the continuation of the Cold War (*ibid*: 7), and by others as the creation of boundless repression – the era of the Long War.[5]

Once it was established, this form of repressive governance was 'sold' like a franchise, and taken up by subordinate powers in an attempt to legitimise their own projects. In some cases, the formulation 'war on terror' is still employed to describe the various forms of opposition (external and internal) encountered by the 'neo-liberal' west, its allies and client states. It usually appears when authoritative speakers wish to suggest some correspondence between their own activities and the prevailing values of powerful sponsors. In following this course, they may not, however, appreciate the extent to which the basic proposition has become (in rhetorical terms at least) counter-productive (see below). So, for instance, the Israeli foreign minister, Tzipi Livni, refusing to countenance a ceasefire during the Gaza offensive of 2008/09, described her nation's actions as 'an ongoing, long battle, war, against terror' (Livni, cited in McGreal, 6 January 2009: 1). On the same day that Livni's remark appeared in the press, another report drew attention to an argument put forward by the lawyer Helena Kennedy. After the attacks of 9/11, Kennedy said, 'a lot of nations called their dissidents terrorists' (Kennedy, cited in Campbell, 6 January 2009: 15). The 'war on terror' thus provided an opportunity for the rebranding of established practices: regional conflicts, civil wars and border disputes, for example, could all be represented as an integral part of anti-terror policy.

THE WAR IN THE 'WAR ON TERROR'

A more intractable problem, however, is the perception that 'war' is still regarded as an appropriate term for an attack conducted by an advanced technological power, in which it attempts to impose a model of economic life on social or political collectives that occupy a subordinate position within a global system of capital relations. War should not be regarded, therefore, as the unmotivated or neutral concept within the phrase 'war on terror', as though 'war' has been contaminated through its association with 'terror'.

Wright's definition of war provides a useful point of departure, because it focuses on the question of parity in military encounters. He describes war as 'an extreme intensification of military activity, psychological tension, legal power, and social integration' which is only produced if the enemy is 'approximately equal in material power' (Wright, cited in Gupta, 2002: 41). Undoubtedly, many large-scale conflicts have taken place in which the forces aligned on each side are not at all proportionate; but Wright's perspective serves to underline the point that many contemporary campaigns undertaken by powerful states, do not fulfil the standard notion that combat should take place between comparable adversaries.

As Black notes of the clashes which took place at the beginning of the twenty-first century, '"developed" states tended not to fight each other, but rather to employ their forces against the "less developed"' (Black, 2001: 5). This, of course, was one reason for the emphasis on imaginary 'weapons of mass destruction' during the invasion of Iraq; it served as a spurious means of evening out the odds and also helped to distract attention from the pitiful condition of Iraq's armed forces. As a consequence, the 'coalition' could pose as an heroic combatant. Yet in such encounters, the destructive power of the technologically advanced state is vastly increased, because 'the battlefield is horizontally extended by the use of long-distance weapons', so that, if only one force should possess these resources, 'the inevitable result is a massacre' (Sofsky, 2002: 81).

The challenge, therefore, is not only to examine the conceptual difficulty presented by the notion of terror, but also to question the routine appearance of the term 'war'. A particular difficulty is the way in which war is placed in opposition to terror/ism, suggesting the existence of a qualitative difference between two modes of combat. If war stands in contrast to terror, the assumption appears to be that it represents a morally superior form of violence, expressed in the misleading notion of 'the rules of war'. So, for example, a popular conception which circulates amongst the champions of counter-insurgency is that the 'overwhelming conventional military superiority' of the United States has forced non-state actors to adopt 'insurgency and terrorism' as their only viable strategy (US Army/ Marine Corps, 2007: li).

This position can prepare the ground for an extensive analysis of 'asymmetric' struggle (*ibid*: 3–102), but depends for its rhetorical impact on the idea that conventional warfare does not resort to the methods of terrorism. The asymmetry *begins* with the 'disproportionate' use of force by the technologically superior aggressor. The weak may of course adopt ingenious and odious means in order to combat the strong, but the categories underpinning this perspective are presented as mutually exclusive. The inclusion of 'insurgency', as a parallel condition linked to terrorism, is simple to explain: without this association, counter-insurgency could not provide an overarching rationale, leaving the military with no choice but to refer to their policy as one of 'counter-terror', with all the negative connotations that implies.

Despite the continued insistence on a moral distinction between forces, definitions taken from history reveal the inherently malevolent nature of most warfare directed by formal authority.

So, for example, when Sun Tzu, the strategist who composed 'the Art of War' in about 500 BCE, described the principles of organised combat, he observed that 'in war, the way to avoid what is strong is to strike what is weak' (Sun Tzu, 2002: 62). This principle has merely been extended from its application to vulnerable points on the battlefield to a more general rule that the opponent as a whole should be relatively powerless, just as the Israeli armed forces made a point by following the US principle that a (largely) civilian enemy should not only be weak but should also be shocked by the ferocity of the assault. At one point, Sun Tzu refers to the importance of dividing plunder taken from the countryside between the invading soldiers. This anodyne remark conceals a universal truth about war – its despoliation of civilian existence. The female population often suffers the worst excesses of an invading army. Although not the universal practice of all armies, rape can be employed as 'an explicit terror tactic to clear an area and make people flee' (Slim, 2007: 61–2).

Where the opponent is another state or an *external* political entity, then a mediated demonstration of military power is enacted, underpinned by a series of incantations about the difference between the terrorist and the 'security forces'. Where the enemy is *internal*, or sufficiently weak, or removed from the due process of the law, the secret exercise of coercion will occur. When McCulloch observes that 'the military capacity of nations is being turned inwards' (McCulloch, 2002: 58), it is worth noting that armed formations have always been on hand to suppress dissent. Internal as well as external enemies were (and continue to be) nominated in this global realignment of power: the essential cowardice of this process is revealed in the fact that civilians are the most numerous victims and the enemy is usually relatively weak.

A distinction should therefore be made between a number of different levels of activity: the formal policies which contribute to the conduct of 'war'; the various innovations made by those engaged in fighting it; the use of the conflict as a disguise for behaviour that could be placed in other categories; and the numerous positions adopted in creating a coherent narrative from the various events and arguments which make up its complex public appearance. The 'war on terror' and its associated practices represent a contested field in which the 'official' position is inconsistent and unofficial commentaries have encouraged the development of alternative arguments. These alternative perspectives, not all of them politically progressive, have ensured the fractured character of the overall condition.

Contemporary warfare is nonetheless presented within the established discourse of crisis and moral resolve, based on a simplified paradigm drawn from a particular reading of the Second World War – in which, for example, the existence of sexual violence is attributed only to the undisciplined combatant, whether enemy or friend, rather than to the 'honourable' allies (see Burds, 2009: 35). The actual character of contemporary war waged by 'civilised' forces nonetheless resembles a form of violent regulation, in which the US and its allies intervene to manage or reinforce what Scraton calls 'endemic structural inequalities' (Scraton, 2002: 8).

Wars are still 'declared' but many of the activities they encompass, particularly the use of air power and tactics associated with counter-insurgency, do not depend on the formal announcement (or indeed cessation) of hostilities. War remains an instrument of governance; in its domestic manifestation, it is used to implicate the citizen in 'the widening social fact of war' (Meyers, 2008: 125). 'Civic war' – Meyers' term for the current policy – mimics the conditions of *total war*; instead of a general mobilisation, however, everyday activity is reinterpreted in light of the prevailing condition, yet also becomes removed from the actual consequences. Civilians continue to 'go to work ... to the movies, to bed at night', and at the same time 'are at war' (Meyers, 2008: 122). It is this sense of unreality, of a national mobilisation that requires no effort at all on the part of most of the population, that confirms the hollowness of public engagement with the conflict, and the near irrelevance of 'citizenship' under these conditions.

POLICY AND MORAL CONTEXT: THE 'SURGE'

The mutation of linguistic categories is inextricably linked to changes in practical and discursive activity. One vital factor in determining the overall direction of public discourse, is the degree to which particular depictions of social phenomena can provide actors with useful tools in the struggle to attain their goals. One of the most useful illustrations of this process can be found in the crisis faced by the Bush administration from 2005 to 2006, as it came under increasing pressure to change course in Iraq. Essentially, the argument was split between those who wanted to pursue the existing policy, which relied on training the Iraqi army to assume the duties of American troops, and another group which argued that the war could only be won if the military followed a variant of counter-insurgency theory, saturating Baghdad with US soldiers who could then establish bases in the heart of insurgent territory (Mansoor, 2008; Ricks, 2009).

The first vital question for anyone involved in the argument was how the situation in Iraq should be characterised. If supporters of the established policy could demonstrate that their approach was producing quantifiable results (a decline in deaths, or an increase in basic services), then there would have been no reason to change direction. If, however, their opponents could prove that the dominant model was inadequate, then the new strategy might stand a chance of being implemented. Both sides depended on the same range of symbolic and practical resources, and had access to similar types of evidence (e.g. statistics, battle reports, personal testimony, academic studies and opinion polls).

The two camps had also to follow the same basic procedures, which could include private lobbying, writing position papers, the use of friendly journalists and sympathetic academics, and the organisation of formal meetings. The goal in each instance was to make a case strong enough to persuade the 'principals' (the core executive) to support their point of view. The problem for the old guard was that the prevailing view of reality had altered since the early days of 2003, when Bush had declared victory. A rift had opened up between 'senior commanders in Baghdad and their bosses back in Washington *about how to see the war*' (Ricks, 2009: 38, my emphasis).

Once this shift in perception had taken place, it was not just a matter of wondering if the situation was deteriorating, because the *same* incidents could now be interpreted in different ways. So, for example, the announcement that a large number of insurgents had been killed in a US operation, might be used to reinforce the view that the official tactics were paying off. To the critics, however, this same event would illustrate a narrow obsession with punitive action, at the expense of their *declared* priority – interacting with civilian leaders who might be weaned away from the insurgency.

After many months, the balance of the discussion began to swing against the established position, which lost traction for one simple reason: it had become *impossible to deny failure* in Iraq, no matter what arguments were mobilised. Ultimately, the controversy was settled when all available 'indicators' began pointing to the same conclusion. This provided the counter-insurgency specialists with their opportunity. The military and civilian champions of the new policy seemed to imitate the precepts of philosophical realists; they appeared to be convinced of the existence of a fundamental condition, one that developed in ways that were, to some degree at least, separable from the means used to describe it. They were certain, for example, that the picture of the insurgency painted by their opponents fell short of a more disturbing reality.

They were also persuaded that a more exact association between circumstance and description was possible, revealing a belief in a material link between utterance (arguments, orders and requests) and outcomes in the field (security, reconstruction, victory). This does not mean that the advocates of the 'surge' – often highly experienced senior officers who had obtained doctorates – were willing to present a complete critique of the situation, one that might move beyond their limited objectives. They would never extend their critique to larger controversies, such as the historical role played by the US military in repressing the sovereign rights of smaller nations (Gareau, 2004; Ivie, 2005). In effect, they had functioned as an alternative centre of power; in the words of one writer: this 'small group of individuals, none of them elected or holding appointed office' had 'pulled off a quasi-coup' (Bacevich, 26 March 2009: 21).

TWO SIDES OF THE COIN

Despite their superior conception of the circumstances in Iraq, the champions of counter-insurgency (known by its acronym COIN) should not be mistaken for liberal humanists. Their pragmatic open-mindedness did not indicate the existence of a progressive worldview. Indeed, one of the leading proponents of the surge, General Odierno, had previously earned a 'reputation for being overly aggressive' in his use of the 4th Infantry Division during the period from mid 2003 to early 2004. One anonymous general described the Division's activities as 'a crime' (Ricks, 2006: 232). In Baghdad in 2007, Odierno became General Petraeus' essential ally as the latter assumed the command of US forces.

In this role, Odierno's belligerence was an asset because, in the words of one intelligence official, he was 'extremely good at using the force to execute what Petraeus wanted to do' (Ricks, 2009: 132). Here, then, is one simple structural explanation for the triumph of the more 'sensitive' approach to the Iraqi conundrum – the leader could afford to play good cop if his subordinate was ready to assume the less savoury role. The goal of the Petraeus faction – a military victory through the use of counter-insurgency practices – depended on the exploitation of existing power structures, not the liberation of the oppressed. Petraeus' commitment to 'secure and serve the population' included the establishment of 'local governance' (Petraeus, cited in Ricks, 2009: 369), which meant cutting deals with tribal leaders, rather than the development of independent, non-sectarian forces. It could hardly have been otherwise; the intention was not to encourage grass-roots democracy, especially as many Americans became convinced that the political soil was just too barren to allow their own social model to take root.

The practical measures taken to assist the surge included, therefore, some cynical ploys. Journalists began to notice that 'Sunni dissidents', previously characterised as the enemies of American interests, were to be armed by US forces in order to isolate al-Qaeda. Questioned about this decision, Major-General Rick Lynch was credited with declaring that 'there are good guys and bad guys and there are groups in between' (*Times* Foreign Staff, 12 June 2007: 31), a remark that revealed a willingness to maintain a basic set of divisions but to depart from his President's moral rhetoric of good and evil, if it was at all possible to recruit collaborators.

The US troop surge, in its initial phase from January 2007, pushed American casualties to an unprecedented level, before a marked decline in fatalities became evident in 2008, dropping further to a relatively small number in the early part of 2009; the minimum estimated number of Iraqi deaths since the beginning of the invasion six years before was calculated at anything between 100,000 and a million individuals (Steele and Goldenburg, 19 March 2009: 6). Some observers attributed the eventual diminution of violence to the impact of other factors, including 'the Shia victory over the Sunni in an extraordinarily savage civil war, a reaction against al-Qaeda, and the ceasefire called by the Mehdi Army' (Cockburn, 26 February 2009).

Some officers within the US military also shared this perspective. Colonel Gentile, the commander of a battalion in Baghdad in 2006, argued that the lessening of insurgent violence in 2007 'had more to do with the decision to ally with our former enemies to fight al-Qaeda', combined with 'Sadr's decision to stand down attacks' (Ricks, 2009: 216). Gentile was criticised by another senior officer, Colonel Mansoor (see below), who noted that Gentile's own practice had been to conduct patrols from a large compound, rather than place soldiers within local areas; this ran counter to the practices of the counter-insurgency enthusiasts. The latter, however, despite their excellent grasp of military necessity, political expediency and public relations, nonetheless operated within a highly restricted ideological environment.

Their underlying beliefs are, in some cases, difficult to distinguish from established 'master discourses' such as 'full spectrum dominance', which advocated the absolute pre-eminence of US military power, using soldiers 'ready to deliver victory for our Nation' (Joint Chiefs of Staff, 2000). There is no real incongruence between the creative flexibility of the counter-insurgency expert, who has a professional interest in military efficiency, and a deep attachment to the governing values of an imperial democracy. To the inhabitants of a nation where military leadership is exalted as one of the highest and most selfless forms of public service, such a position does not seem contradictory. The fact remains that the beliefs expressed within the ranks of the US armed forces underline the difference between technical insight and political enlightenment.

Peter Mansoor, for example, Petraeus' executive officer from 2007 to 2008, served as a Brigade Commander in Iraq, and described the achievements of his soldiers in the following terms: 'they established and maintained law and order and a secure environment that helped to defeat Global Terrorism' (Mansoor, 2008: 354). In an earlier passage, he used another familiar trope from the lexicon of US warfare – a reference to the 'long war'.[6] Castigating the attitudes of America's cultural elite, he warned that their reluctance to back the military 'could in time lead to ... defeat in the long war against Islamist extremism, and the eventual collapse of Western civilisation' (*ibid*: 352).

Another former battalion commander, Robert Cassidy, rejected the paradigm of the 'long war' but presented a view of American purposes that seemed to fit the ideological template of the 'war on terror', describing the 'war against al-Qaeda' and other groups that followed the 'banner of radical Islamic fundamentalism', as 'a global counterinsurgency' (Cassidy, 2008: 2). The role of the United States 'and its coalition partners' was therefore to try to 'eradicate an overlapping network of nasty nihilists' who seek support from 'the ungoverned periphery and in failing states' (*ibid*).

According to Lieutenant Colonel John Nagl, a participant in both invasions of Iraq, the US faced 'a long struggle against enemies who fight freedom with the ancient art of insurgency' (Nagl, 2002/2005: xxi). The United States, therefore, was 'working diligently in Iraq, as it did in Vietnam, to improve the lives of the people' (*ibid*, xiii). Ultimately, the task was to build Iraqi security forces that could 'defend Iraq against both internal and external threats' (*ibid*, xv).

There is no sense here that the American military might itself constitute an external threat to other sovereign powers; instead, any doubts expressed by these writers are essentially apolitical and immune to irony, and are focused entirely on the relative merits of different tactics. The rehabilitation of Vietnam as a moral cause, for example, might prompt some degree of incredulity. It is pursued in this case because military authors need to use it as an example of counter-insurgency, and cannot therefore allow any doubts about its ethical status to emerge.

Besides serving as a reminder that the possession of a doctorate does not guarantee the existence of a critical perspective (both Mansoor and Cassidy gained PhD's from military institutions), these accounts may also emphasise the fact that counter-insurgency is not simply a weapon but an outlook, one that can be *mapped onto the larger political assumption* shared by all factions within the US military and political establishment: that the American state should exercise its power to lead the 'free' world. It is this position, after all, which guarantees that any opposition to US power is conceived as an assault on freedom, or as anti-democratic. Only those elements of the local armed patriarchy, bought off by American cash or offered some other means of collaboration, are exempt from this charge; this exclusively masculine group is then safely reconstituted as a reliable and representative fraction of 'the people', an amorphous concept that never suggests an independent political capability, because this may run counter to American interests.

When the Obama administration called for more international effort in the Afghanistan campaign, mainstream opposition to US policy seemed to become relatively muted. Indeed, much of the sharp criticism directed at the policies of the Bush era (Ricks, 2006; Bobbitt, 2008) seems to stand confirmed as a simple aversion to failure, having little to do with taking a principled stand against imperial adventure *per se*. There is always a faint echo of this position whenever any commentator, however enlightened, laments the fact that 'we' do not seem to have a clear policy in a particular theatre of war, or that 'we' are using tactics that can only alienate a local population; this is, in part, a consequence of sharing the same broad outlook as the supposedly 'enlightened' elements of the armed forces.

In the US in particular, combat leaders who re-enter civil society as academics, professional analysts and politicians, are anxious to maintain their influence over public debate. As Mansoor argued, when describing the deficiencies in the education of military officers, 'engagement in civilian graduate programmes' gives soldiers the opportunity to 'interact with civil society, thereby narrowing the gap between the military and the people it is sworn to defend' (Mansoor, 2008: 14). Once again, the use of coercive force is not regarded as an attack, but as a defence of values: the issue is therefore what these principles really involve. If they are in fact a collection of techniques designed to intimidate and repress civilians while killing the intractable and turning established patriarchal authority into a partner in this process, then it might be argued that they are hardly worth defending.

Counter-insurgency, meanwhile, appears as a pragmatic attempt to *rationalise* the struggle to assert US power. Various forms of military action will be pursued in the name of democracy, national interest, regime change or indeed under the auspices of any other cause designed to secure the interests of a national elite. The point about the US approach to war is that its military is accustomed to fighting its enemies *with a degree of latitude*; it is not afraid to use 'overwhelming force' even where this may appear to contradict more incremental approaches. Tactics are interchangeable; the use of groups previously regarded as enemies may be the hallmark of counter-insurgency, and the deployment of heavy artillery in urban areas that of the more traditional proponent of the 'fire mission', but both characterise their efforts as necessary measures to defeat some essentially implacable enemy.

Attachment to some larger moral cause, meanwhile, is a vital ingredient in supplying the one thing that an invader often lacks – the ability to 'match the insurgent's concept with an appropriate government one' (Rufus, cited in Nagl, 2002/2005: 27). In other words, if the guerrilla has a discernible cause, the occupying power needs one too. The occupiers might say they are 'building democracy' or 'providing security', which takes care of that aspect of the fight; the point is that military activity is given a moral façade so that soldiers are allowed to pursue whatever tactics are deemed effective in each situation as it arises.

The counter-insurgency position is intended, of course, to be flexible, and is designed to take account of local circumstances. The precepts which determine it may therefore alter according to the demands of the hour, encompassing at once the methods advocated by Petraeus, and the kind of measures described by Colonel Jan Horvarth. In remarks made in November 2004, Horvarth described the challenge faced by the US military in suppressing the revolt in Fallujah, arguing that 'we must still root out the counter-state infrastructure in Fallujah' using the technique of 'population [and] resource control', employed most effectively by 'the Nazis' Gestapo and the Eastern European communists' (Herring and Rangwala, 2006: 178). The replication of such processes, he noted, should not imply that the Americans had become 'tainted or infected by their methods' (*ibid*).

STRUCTURAL COMPLICITY: WAR, MEDIATION AND POWER

An ongoing, long battle, war, against terror.
(Tzipi Livni, Israeli Foreign Minister, in McGreal, 2009: 1)

Our nation is at war, against a far-reaching network of violence and hatred.
(Barack Obama, Inauguration Address, 2009)

On 6 January 2009, Livni tried to recalibrate her definition of the Israeli campaign against Palestinian opponents, to take account of the US move to the notion of the 'long war'; yet Livni still got her semantic wires crossed, producing the hybrid term 'long battle'. On the 18 January 2009, after its 22-day assault on the impoverished enclave known as the Gaza strip, the Israeli government declared a ceasefire. In effect, it announced the conclusion of a war that had more closely resembled a punitive expedition directed against a largely civilian population. Unwilling to allow foreign journalists to send reports from inside Gaza, the Israeli authorities orchestrated an information campaign (Fisk, 10 January 2009) which presented their incursion as a just response to an intolerable situation. The war, they argued, had been designed to prevent rocket attacks launched by the militant group Hamas. Then, two days after the end of hostilities, as Barack Obama took office as the 44th President of the United States, Israel announced the final stages of its withdrawal from the ruined territory. Well over a thousand Palestinian lives had been extinguished during the campaign, while three Israeli civilians and ten soldiers were killed (Black, 19 January 2009: 20); half of these military deaths were attributed to 'friendly fire'.

Israel's political executive, operating as though it possessed a special dispensation provided by the United States government, had refused all external calls for restraint. The extent of the collusion between the two states was most clearly demonstrated when the US abstained from a major UN resolution – which American diplomats had themselves helped to draft – appealing for an immediate cessation of hostilities (Wheatcroft, 11 January 2009: 39). Without the support of the US, the demand for a ceasefire collapsed, and the ground offensive continued until the Israelis declared that their military objectives had been fulfilled.

The timing of the withdrawal, however, scheduled to end before the mandate of the new President came into force, suggested to some commentators that the Israelis were anxious to finish the operation because Barack Obama might have objected to their 'disproportionate' use of violence (a term used defiantly by the Israelis on 1 February 2009, to describe their projected response to renewed firing of rockets from Gaza). The belief that Israel had attempted to disguise the human cost of its war by calling a halt just before Obama's ascension, seems reasonable enough, as media attention was inevitably taken up by the events in Washington. The notion that this betrayed some trepidation about the attitude of the new administration is less convincing. International concern about Obama's attitude to the new Palestinian crisis started to emerge when the bombardment of Gaza began in December 2008. Asked to comment on the early stages of the conflict, Obama had initially refused to do so, on the grounds that there should be 'only one President' at a time (MacAskill, 29 December 2008: 7). Eventually, he announced that he had been 'disturbed' by civilian deaths on both sides. The absence of any substantial utterance on the subject was, however, picked up by a number of journalists in the press and online. One writer, for example, identified the new President's 'silence on Gaza' as 'startling' (Bromwich, 29 January 2009: 5). The same publication carried a similar observation from another contributor, who argued that '[Obama's] silence during the Gaza war speaks volumes' about his attitude to the prospect of future Israeli misconduct (Mearshimer, 29 January 2009: 6). Focusing on the Israeli side of the equation, Noam Chomsky produced a long article which appeared online on 20 January 2009, arguing that the Israeli withdrawal had been timed to 'minimise the (remote) threat' that Obama might take a critical stance on the issue (Chomsky, 2009). The veteran reporter Robert Fisk interpreted the end of the Israeli assault as a diversionary tactic; the ceasefire, he declared, had come 'just in time for Barack Obama to have a squeaky-clean inauguration' while the world's attention was turned upon 'the streets of Washington rather than the rubble of Gaza' (Fisk, 19 January 2009).[7]

Fisk, like Chomsky, had drawn attention to the political motives of the Israeli leadership, but his words contained a hint of the more complex structural relationship that underpins the manoeuvres of individual states. In noting that the ceremony in Washington had to be 'squeaky-clean', he seemed to provide more than a simple condemnation of Israel's strategic intentions; his remark can be read as a critique of the priorities of the American executive. This, in turn, may lead not only to the conviction that Israel had manipulated the circumstances, but also that some form of deliberate alignment between US and Israeli interests had taken place.

This conviction may be reinforced by Obama's assurance to the media, given over the weekend of 27–28 December 2008, that he had been fully briefed on the Gaza conflict by the outgoing Secretary of State, Condoleezza Rice. The first conversation they had on the subject was said to have lasted eight minutes (MacAskill, 29 December 2008: 7). This short exchange could not have provided much serious information. It is more likely simply to have confirmed a legitimate element of US protocol, namely that the President Elect would not interfere in foreign affairs.

Such a convention would therefore have coincided with Obama's instinct to avoid making pronouncements on issues that could not generate any substantial political benefit. Maintaining silence, on the other hand, would ensure that his standing with the Israeli leadership would not be damaged. This form of discretion would also ensure that the Israeli military had enough time to complete its operation. The important issue here, however, is not simply the degree to which bourgeois politicians can be relied upon to conform to prevailing political circumstance, but how collusion between established political forces is actually achieved.

The temporal 'coincidence' of an Israeli announcement and the US inauguration emerges from the dominant paradigm that guides Democratic Party attitudes to Israel. Democrats did not express serious reservations about Israel's conduct. So, while it is true that the Israeli government engineered their publicity to take account of the event in Washington, this does not prove that they were primarily concerned about provoking a *negative* reaction from President Obama. Equally, it would be perfectly correct to argue that the Israelis took advantage of the 'window of opportunity' offered in the last days of the Bush era, but this behaviour did not reflect any substantial uncertainty about Democrat sentiment. The end of the war actually resembled a gesture of goodwill, ensuring that the new executive would not be placed in the position of having to express *support* for, rather than criticism of, Israeli actions. Secretary of State Clinton, Chief of Staff Emanuel and President

Obama himself are all firm believers in the right of Israeli forces to act in 'self-defence'.

Clinton, in her first news conference at the State Department, declared that 'we support Israel's right to self-defence' and described the Hamas leaders as having chosen to 'provoke the right of self-defence' (in MacAskill and McCarthy, 28 January 2009: 16) by their actions. This statement is quite extraordinary, and fits into the paradigm that blames the victim for bringing on the wrath of an aggressor; except, of course, that Hamas as an armed group does not easily fit the profile of an innocent target. All that was required, in rhetorical terms, was to extend the status of the belligerent group to the civilians who had supported it.

A further indication of the close bonds between Israel and the US came on 8 January 2009, when the US Senate, led by a Democratic majority, passed a resolution expressing solidarity with the Israeli state (Wheatcroft, 11 January 2009). During the debate, the Senate Majority leader, Democrat Harry Reid, referred to Hamas rocket fire, asking his colleagues 'to imagine that happening here in the United States', while his Republican colleague Mitch McConnell claimed that 'the Israelis ... are responding in exactly the same way we would' (Reuters.com, 8 January 2009). It is worth noting in passing that the record of the US military in Iraq might support the idea that McConnell had spoken the truth.

The crucial point, however, is that while it is clear that the timing of the ceasefire was designed to benefit Israel's leaders, it also presented an advantage to the Democrats, ensuring that the Obama administration did not have to face, in the first days of its existence, a crisis in the Middle East. As a consequence, the new US leadership was able to preserve the high gloss of its moral veneer. This outcome had been underwritten by George W. Bush, who had performed the function of 'sin eater', taking the blame for following a course of action to the same pitiless conclusion that any US President might have been forced to consider. Once broad American support for Israeli policy had been decided upon, the logic of this long-standing commitment meant that 'disproportionate' aggression would not be condemned.

Israel's leadership, meanwhile, had worked hard to insulate its own population from world opinion, by magnifying a communal sense of moral indignation. When Tzipi Livni announced that Israel was 'going wild' in its attacks on Gaza (cited in Sengupta and Macintyre, 13 January 2009) her statement tried to give the impression of an enraged state, barely able to contain itself.

The whole campaign, however, was the product of dispassionate calculation. The operation in Gaza thus revealed a great deal about the position of the US core executive (whatever its formal political composition), the priorities of the 'international community', and the tactics of the Israeli Defence Force (IDF). Hamas – inefficient, brutal and ill-disciplined – had provided the rationale for an attack that seemed to have received tacit approval from a number of major states, though these nations had not perhaps anticipated the extent of the destruction that would ensue.

CONSPIRACY OR COMPLICITY?

When political analysts speak of an understanding between states, this does not necessarily mean that a detailed, explicit accord is an essential prerequisite for such collaboration. The existence of confidential, informal agreements is not in doubt, but the shadowy character of these private settlements creates a problem for those who describe them, because the whole idea is sometimes denounced as a form of 'conspiracy theory'. Although a great deal of confidential or covert activity does indeed underpin the foundations of formal authority, the identification of 'conspiracy' within international relations can be reformulated in order to make a more substantial argument about the exercise of power.

This is the notion that, while particular outcomes may well be the result of secret agreements, these must be framed within the context of long-term institutional commitments. These 'inter-state' obligations produce and in turn are produced by 'structured' behaviours, forms of conduct which occur as the natural by-product of the individual and collective will to 'achieve results' on behalf of a particular alliance. The active performance of certain functions, though voluntary in the sense that they will certainly be deliberate, nonetheless typifies the habitual conduct of a transnational political class devoted to the establishment, consolidation and projection of its own social and economic power. This power depends on the continued existence of a fundamental agreement between allied states that they, their associates and subordinates, do indeed exercise sovereignty over their own territory and, therefore, that they have the right to pursue their own interests, however morally objectionable. When it is difficult to deny that a close ally has perpetrated an outrage (as in the case of Israel and Gaza), then the animation of a humanitarian discourse and the provision of aid to the victims is used in an attempt to make up some of the moral deficit created by the initial period of collaboration.

Rather than search for direct evidence of some particular agreement between the Bush administration, the Israelis and the new incumbent of the White House, which may never be forthcoming, it is worth noting in the meantime that American support for the assault on Gaza was the inevitable outcome of an already firmly established commitment to the state of Israel, and is just one specific instance of mutually beneficial collusion. Ultimately, the capability of the Israeli state to mount its attack depended on the billions of dollars in military aid received from the US (see Chomsky, 2009).

Where an alliance is not in force, or where some supra-national agency like the United Nations is involved in passing judgement on individual states, then there is a greater likelihood of a critical stance being taken. So, for example, on 5 December 2008, at its 64th plenary meeting, the UN General Assembly adopted a resolution based on the work of a Special Committee which had studied the effect of Israeli practices on the human rights of Palestinian and other Arab occupants of the occupied territories. It observed that 'occupation itself represents a gross and grave violation of human rights' and went on to express 'grave concern about the continuing detrimental impact of the events that have taken place since 28 September 2000', including 'the excessive use of force by the Israeli occupying forces against Palestinian civilians' (UN online, domino.un.org, 18 December 2008). Strictly speaking, of course, there should be no use of force against civilians at all, 'excessive' or otherwise.

MEDIATION AND POWER

The fact that the Israeli ceasefire and the Presidential inauguration appeared within the same news bulletins, helped suggest that the conjunction of the two events was significant, and illustrated the operation of a number of routine functions associated with the production of effects within sophisticated, hierarchical social orders. These processes include the *conception* of public events, both in the sense that certain occasions are *initiated* by specific interest groups, and because they are simultaneously presented in a certain light, positioned for ideological consumption so they can be 'thought about' within existing frames of reference. Incidents like the bombardment of Gaza are thus enacted and presented *in the anticipation* that they will be represented by established media institutions devoted to the (intermittently critical) treatment and circulation of the narrative material generated by authoritative sources. The mediation of announcements, activities and behaviours that emanate from these sources testifies to the capacity of media forms, not simply to create widespread awareness of momentous occasions, but to contribute to their public character.

The idea that the ceremony in Washington and the end of the Israeli invasion were in some way linked was therefore created by two closely associated fields of activity: first, by conscious political interventions, initiated by national leaders in the knowledge that their point of view would come under scrutiny; and second, through media management of sources, conducted in the expectation that the information received had already been modified for public consumption. Although such an analysis may reinforce the argument that media organisations display a structural or ideological dependence on authoritative informants, the more urgent question concerns the degree to which one can speak of a form of *structural complicity*[8] between powerful social actors (see above).

This can be described as the tendency of certain general interests of powerful agents to coincide, without necessarily requiring an exact correlation between the values or intentions of the actors concerned. *Structural complicity* is therefore a state of (publicly) unacknowledged (and sometimes unknowing) collusion between various social and political forces. This recalls Weber's description of power as a quality dependent on the existence of a social relationship between individuals, in which goals and conduct are 'mutually adjusted and oriented towards each other' (Berenskoetter, 2007: 3). This suggests that these aims and behaviours are in agreement, and are mutually regulated by having to take account of the motives and tactics of the other person, group or *operational centre*. This foreknowledge of other competing activities affects, in turn, the strategies adopted by each interested party.

In the Gaza example, the desire of one executive authority to draw attention to a specific act (a suspension of hostilities), took advantage of an editorial process devoted both to the provision of timely information, and to the observation of established events in the international calendar. The mediated overview of these agendas created an inevitable comparison between the political process in the US and the disposition of the government in Israel. In this sense, therefore, the role of the media fulfilled one requirement of powerful executive forces: to repeat, in however critical a light, the original designation assigned to events by government operatives and representatives.

Given their inferior structural position, media outlets cannot ignore or dismiss these sources, since the whole rationale of journalism depends on taking the word of those in power seriously enough to make these utterances the point of origin for further (more or less critical) reference. The media are, from the perspective of the state, junior partners in the composition of meaning, but in the eyes of the audience they take on the role not merely of the source of information but as *moral originators* of certain positions. The public's sensitivity to this attitude allows journalists, in turn, to anticipate their reaction by assuming the role of moral interlocutor (see Chapter 4).

The coincidence of certain interests can, therefore, be explained not as conspiratorial agreement, but as the inevitable outcome of pursuing goals in a competitive field where other actors may have similar interests. From the perspective of authority, the media are vital, since without them, the messages produced by politicians would resemble unadulterated (unmediated) propaganda. There is no guarantee, in this or any other case, that a particular outcome will be achieved just because significant social forces attempt to secure specific goals; but propaganda tends to become counter-productive whenever its source becomes transparently obvious.

In the political realm, the production of any effect depends on the occupation of an institutional position that provides an opportunity to act. *Structural complicity* in this case is therefore not necessarily a consciously cooperative activity, since political leaders and journalists might very well see their relationship as antagonistic; the point is that forms of affiliation are often formed through strife. At the point at which social actors have to present a model of events to a third party (the 'public'), they are united in the process of representation, whatever their subsequent attitudes to the end result of their labours. The simple reality facing powerful actors is the necessity of having to accept a partial attainment of aims, rather than the complete fulfilment of any purpose; this 'shortfall' is not just created because subordinate groups occasionally possess an agenda which may not coincide with that constructed by authority, but rather because all *particular* strategies are the product of structural, institutionalised differences in the social purposes of, on the one hand, those authorities *allied* in pursuance of an aim and, on the other, media organisations and other centres that process data.

An apparently consistent ideological perspective may be presented to the world through media forms, but this is always the product of internal positions that settle on an agreement in order to achieve specific and limited aims. These disagreements may eventually emerge under pressure – tensions between different political positions within Israel, for example, led to competing descriptions of the objectives to be achieved in Gaza. In addition, influential actors always inherit constraints they must recognise but, in adapting to these strictures, they may also invent new modes of conduct that force the institutions in which they operate to evolve.

When some of these insights into structure, authority and competing centres of moral authority are applied to the behaviour of Barack Obama, it is possible to understand why bourgeois politicians and careerists are not necessarily driven by an evil animus; instead, any pathology they might display is the consequence of having to align their activities with the *general* orientation of dominant forces. Their personal success, even relevance, depends on accepting this condition. They know that the path to career success is strewn with obstacles, and that close allies in one activity may be competitors in another. This is why it seems odd to describe these kinds of actors as always 'unified' in conduct or outlook.

The class as a whole, however, may be described as 'unitary' in the sense that individuals and groups within the broad stratum agree on one thing: that the hierarchical system they have inherited is the best ground upon which to secure their goals and extend their positions. Their aims are nonetheless achieved within particular circumstances, and depend on the use of collective structures in competition with other interest groups in a contested field. So, for example, 'government hierarchies' must 'form networks with non-governmental organisations in order to be able to implement centrally decided policies' (DeLanda, 2006: 34).

In pursuing a particular aim, elements of the bureaucracy have to configure their resources in ways that cannot be repeated in the same form when a new project is undertaken; a fresh venture requires the recombination of existing assets, or even the creation of new ones. Through this process, institutional characteristics are adjusted in the light of circumstance and the whole organisation is reproduced in an altered form. No individual actors, however powerful, can predict the exact outcome of their efforts, because activity sets in motion forces that cannot necessarily be controlled. DeLanda gives the example of a marketplace in which 'decisions to buy and sell' are made on purpose, but the price of goods is arrived at through a more impersonal process (DeLanda, 2006: 36). Prices are 'an unintended, collective consequence of those intentional actions', and then create a situation that imposes itself on the actors (*ibid*).

THE US, ISRAEL AND THE MEDIA

If this insight is applied to the supposed collusion between Israeli and American politicians, it is evident that their intentions were essentially similar: to exercise some control over the news agenda during a period when their interests might not exactly coincide. That there was no open antagonism should not be explained as the triumph of reason, but as one of the outcomes of a long-standing relationship between the two states. The difference between the temporal status of the two 'stories' was that the inauguration of the new President was set in advance, while the end of the military intervention took advantage of the existing US schedule. After all the condemnation of Israeli manipulation and duplicity, one question remains: in what sense could the Democratic administration be said to have connived in the management of the two occasions?

No decision of this nature is sudden; public conduct is based on established patterns of behaviour, yet has to adapt to current circumstance. The degree to which Israeli politicians could feel assured that the new President would be unlikely to object to any continuation of military action would have had some basis in Obama's record on the Middle East. His support for Israel, recorded for example in a book on the activities of pro-Zionist lobbyists in the US (Mearsheimer and Walt, 2008: 4), might suggest that he would say little to discomfit its representatives.

The point is not that the apparent coincidence of the ceasefire and the inauguration points to a purely personal failure on the part of the President, but that it can be read as an example of the commonality of a simple interest: the continuation of a relationship between the two events. The Israeli leadership might indeed have expected to receive unqualified *public* support from the Democrats, but also understood that there would be no point in making this too explicit, since it would not serve their own interests if Obama appeared unable to negotiate some form of restraint in the Middle East.

The primary purpose of the Israeli action had been to weaken Hamas to the point at which it could be brought into an unequal form of negotiation. This, and the termination of hostilities, was the most important service Israel could render to the new US administration. The eventual outcome, therefore, could not be based on some hurried agreement hammered out between the US core executive (at that point, led by Bush/Cheney), the office of the President Elect, and the Israeli leadership. The entire situation was produced by an earlier consensus that allowed many international participants, including the European Union, the US, the UK and many Arab states, to agree on the operational basis for imposing a 'two state' solution on the region, in which the Palestinian people would be given some kind of formal status while remaining in a condition of economic servitude.

In order to pursue this aim, a *public rationale* had to emerge, just as the timely appearance of the concept 'weapons of mass destruction' (see Chapter 2) provided the 'bureaucratic compromise' for the initiation of the Iraq war. It was not necessary to secure the active consent of all sections of the 'international community' for the attack on Gaza to begin, just the existence of a general perception that Israel had to deal with an uncompromising and implacable foe: in this respect, the mediated view of Hamas as essentially a terrorist group went largely uncontested despite the efforts of some diplomats to categorise it as an organisation devoted to a 'single issue'. The militant group had supplied the motive upon which the campaign could be fought. The 'hardliners' in Hamas in particular did not perhaps appreciate their role; for 'moderation' to be viable there has to be a group committed to violence, unreason and the dictatorship of the fundamentalist. This, again, leads to the concept of structural, rather than voluntaristic complicity.

It seemed very difficult for rational critics to make this connection without appearing, as argued above, to give credence to conspiracy theory. Certain representational forms are, however, able to bring the notion of *deep* or *structural* collusion into view. The appearance of a number of cartoons, which of course depend not only on linguistic but also on visual references, seemed able to express the suspicion that the US and Israel shared not just a common perspective, but a commitment to similar forms of deceit. One carried the caption 'Vote Zippy' and portrayed Barack Obama, mouth zipped shut and fingers crossed, turning his back on a scene of destruction, as helicopters and jets poured fire on Gaza. The smoke from the aircraft had scored the words 'vote Tzipi' (the Israeli Foreign Minister's first name) across the sky (Brown, 31 December 2008: 25).

Just over two months after the end of the Gaza incursion, the Obama administration finally moved away from the phrase that

Figure 2 Vote Zippy: Dave Brown's view of Obama's role in the Gaza crisis, 31 December 2008.

had become synonymous with the excesses of US state power. Senior Pentagon staff were told that the administration 'prefers to avoid using the term Global War on Terror ... please pass this on to your speechwriters' (Burkeman, 26 March 2009: 18). The replacement was to be 'overseas contingency operations', a phrase that marked the transition from the rule of the ideologue to that of the bureaucrat.

2
War, Terror and the Real

And I know too this was real war, this wasn't the pretend stuff that happens in films, it was real war, it was real bloodshed and real casualties.

(Tony Blair, Speech to Service Personnel, Iraq, 29 May 2003)

When those in authority replicate the idiomatic expressions associated with ordinary conversation, they do so for a purpose, attempting to align themselves with 'common knowledge' and by implication the *order of experience* from which it grows. Blair's statement, made to soldiers serving in Iraq, plays on the everyday distinction individuals make between real events (which produce material consequences), and narrative references to these same events. Appreciation of the difference between these two conditions (the actual and the figurative) is used by authoritative speakers to demonstrate their grasp of fundamental realities.

In extreme conditions, such as those produced during wars, the *unforgiving nature of the real* becomes a particularly salient theme, especially for those who experience it directly. The dangerous and chaotic nature of this reality is usually, however, the consequence of deliberate policy. As one source of *authorisation* for a war widely acknowledged to be legally and morally questionable, Blair cannot avoid making references to his own role. Nonetheless, the way he portrays himself in relation to other social actors reveals a great deal about the strategic uses of rhetoric.

The speech opens with a standard acknowledgement of his hosts' kindness – 'it is very good of you to have me here today' – which makes it sound as if the troops had some say in the matter (Blair, 29 May 2003). Blair goes on to recognise the controversy generated by the invasion: 'I know there are a lot of disagreements in the country about the wisdom of my decision to order the action' (*ibid*). This assertion understates the case, and restricts the problem to the domestic realm; the exercise of opinion is not seen as a military prerogative. Emphasising his executive role, and without mentioning the UK's subservience to US interests, Blair goes on to assure his listeners that, despite the arguments over the invasion, 'there is absolutely no dispute in Britain about your professionalism and your courage and your dedication' (*ibid*).

This is a fairly typical rhetorical tactic: it seems as though the orator has prepared the ground for a discussion of his or her own actions, but a switch is made to another, closely related topic. The soldiers are told, in effect, that they should not worry about the disputes at home, because they are held in high esteem. As one of the main architects of the particular social/practical reality (see Archer, 2000) the soldiers must face, the real question is how Blair is regarded, but this is not pursued. Instead, he tries to display genuine insights into the nature of warfare, in order to create a 'non-political' act of solidarity with his immediate listeners. This is not, however, the sole purpose of this passage of his speech.

The service personnel form only a minor part of Blair's audience. The larger element of his intended constituency consists of other influential political actors, together with the 'public' in general. Though absent from the scene, they are nonetheless of greater significance. Of course, the electorate did not have an opportunity to vote on the drive to war, so they are invited instead to observe the spectacle of its 'compassionate' management. The speech presents a perfunctory version of events, because it has been staged with public approbation in mind. The soldiers assembled around the prime minister remain silent; they are the mute recipients of effusive praise, designed to underline the fact that they will continue to occupy a position of (professional) subservience.

THE STRATEGY OF CONFUSION: ACTION AND INTENT

In using the term 'real' to acknowledge the validity of front-line experience, Blair also gestures towards the obdurate materiality of the human condition. As a descriptive category, *reality* in such a case refers to the notion of hard facts, appropriate in a speech delivered to combatants. Blair's position stands, therefore, in contrast to the notion of armed conflict as a 'postmodern' event or a series of symbolic gestures,[1] especially where the symbolic itself is regarded as somehow removed from the real. Houen, for example, asks if 'terrorism [is] primarily a matter of discursive and figurative practices' (Houen, 2002: 4), while Scanlan calls terrorism a 'fictional construct' which grows in the public imagination (Scanlan, 2001: 2). If the concept of terrorism has indeed spread throughout collective social consciousness, then the source of its enlargement may be traced back to the conscious circulation of the concept by *governments*, relying upon its mediation through a host of cultural forms, and even on academics who isolate terror and discuss it as if it remains entirely separate from the coercive capacity of the contemporary state.

Other authors, as Chapter 1 noted, focus on the conduit rather than the source, arguing for example that television has become 'weaponised' (Hoskins and O'Loughlin, 2007). The commission of violent attacks on persons, property or institutions by militant groups, states or individuals, is indeed a form of premeditated practical/symbolic action that is both anticipated and recapitulated in narrative form. Yet, while it is true that all concerned, including the perpetrators and victims of violence, may conduct or interpret their behaviour from a 'mediated' perspective, inserting their experience into a wider framework of public narratives, a modified *attitude* to their participation cannot alter the physical consequences – injury or destruction – that may ensue. Instead of identifying the problem as the repeated failure of mediated culture to maintain an objective distance from the terrorist, it might be more productive to consider the 'structural dependence of media organisations on established forms of authority' (Price, 2008: 13). It is the state which sets up the paradigm of the 'terrorist', deciding who should and should not be included in the category.

The exceptional growth of the signifier *terrorism* appears therefore to be the result of its ruthless promotion as a strategic concept, to the extent that its use seems to appear as a reflex action. Headlines declaring that a 'terror plot' has been uncovered, followed a few days later by the revelation that suspects have been released without charge, seem to confirm this perception. This does not mean that the public's understanding of terror is entirely mistaken; people accept the idea that terrorism is an 'activity', usually associated with a definite outcome (acts of violence with physical effects), but that it may also consist of plots which may be foiled by timely intervention. The problem is that the authorities have stretched the category of terrorism to include a wide range of activities that they know are not necessarily related. Correctly perceiving that the work of the terrorist cell requires some *thought and preparation*, they treat the mental phenomena of dissent and ideological conviction as evidence of terrorist activity. For example, it suits the security services to treat any opposition to the economic direction of the state as a form of terrorism – hence the 'fitting up' of direct-action environmentalists as violent subversives. This is not to deny that thought processes are somehow 'insubstantial', or that direct action does not have material effects. However, it seems clear that political conviction becomes suspect, not just because it may produce a violent form of opposition, but because it resists the values of the security state.

Baudrillard articulated a similar theme, characterising the entire realm of terror and conflict as evidence of an 'integral reality' in which war is 'the instrument of a violent acculturation to the world order' (Baudrillard, 2005: 77). In his opinion, 'liberal globalisation' itself has become 'terror based on "law and order"' (Baudrillard, 2003: 32). Wolin takes a similar line when he argues that 'terrorism is both a response to empire and the provocation that allows for empire to cease to be ashamed of its identity' (Wolin, 2008: 70). In responding to and on occasion inventing this provocation, the authorities and their chosen servants in the media have begun to undermine their own arguments about the severity of the terror threat. As indicated above, the public will accept the existence of terror when substantial events are brought to its attention, but it still retains an awareness of the difference between significant incidents (an actual attack or an attack that has been frustrated) and less serious occurrences, even though people may feel that there is 'no smoke without fire'.[2] In order to evaluate the quality of authoritative explanations, it is important therefore to distinguish between the various components (practical, conceptual and social) which make up a terrorist or any other controversial event.

WAR AND TERROR AS PRACTICES

Of course, before 9/11, the degree to which terrorist activity constituted a substantial threat to the western powers was a matter of debate. Laquer for example argued that 'there is a tendency to magnify the importance of terrorism in modern society ... terrorism makes a great noise, but so far it has not been very destructive' (Laquer, 1986, cited in Alexander and Latter, 1990: 1). This remark accords with the perception that many types of human behaviour have qualitative effects, which appear greater than their purely quantitative strength. Knowledge of this fact has always enabled military formations to project coercive force.

When violent acts are said to mobilise a sense of power which is not always matched by actual capability, it is useful to remember that 'impression management' has always been a feature of warfare, based on physical manoeuvres or *feints* on the battlefield, the use of spies and rumour, and so on. Armies employ symbolic *demonstrations* of power (Price, 2008), ruses of various kinds, designed to reduce the psychological confidence of an enemy before a shot is fired. Military intervention is therefore not a pure realm of 'action', somehow counterposed to the verbiage of politicians, because it too intervenes in the symbolic environment in order to achieve its goals.[3]

The actual organisation of warfare requires a degree of physical effort and practical coordination in order to produce symbolic resonance. The construction of a roadside bomb in Afghanistan, for instance, provides a simple example: it is one stage in a sequence of actions that is meant to lead to an explosion. If successful, the purpose of the detonation is to alter the physical structure of its immediate environment and, by virtue of this change, to achieve a military effect (causing death or injury to western troops and a subsequent reduction in morale). The wider symbolic effect is to demonstrate that the authorities do not control the territory they claim to dominate. An attack is thus organised both as a practical military event, and as a social/political phenomenon. If a bomb fails to detonate, then not only its physical but also its representational impact, is nullified.

Combat is a *practice*, made up of various forms of directive and cooperative utterance, of action and movement, and will involve explosions, fire-fights, injuries and deaths which may afterwards be depicted in alternative ways (as victory, defeat, or stalemate). Years later, a battle might even be described as a 'turning point' when placed in an historical narrative. War therefore provides a particularly stark analogy to the 'irrational insistency' of facts (Sherif, 1994: 54), creating an environment in which fatal hazards are deliberately produced. Blair, for example, referred to those soldiers who 'aren't going back home', and offered his 'respect for everything they did and the sacrifice they made' (Blair, 29 May 2003).

War can destroy not only life, but also the assumption that there really is some form of moral order; politicians are forced to 'repair' this apprehension in their rhetorical pronouncements about the worth and significance of sacrifices made in the name of the preferred cause. War is therefore never deemed to be a general social evil, and its negative consequences are supposed to be confined to its effect on individuals. It is certainly true that combat produces individual trauma, a kind of mental affront or shock. Yet in accepting the idea that it is an event that 'shatters people's assumptions' about the character of the world around them (Brewin, 2003: 4), we are led back to the social. This, in turn, supports an argument that those in power are so anxious to resist – that war (however 'necessary') damages the social fabric. Although warfare is represented as a form of conflict in which two sides direct their violence against each other, brutality provides the rationale for the *internal* imposition of discipline.

Acts of violence and forms of bullying contribute to the negative socialisation imposed on soldiers, representing an acclimatisation to the production of lethal force; the internalised resentment and anger of the recruit is directed outwards, so that anyone at whom violence is directed is deemed to be its legitimate recipient. This hostility can sometimes extend to the civilian population, though most of those killed in military operations seem to be casualties of routine practices like bombing, rather than massacres conducted by troops on the ground. Right-wing accounts of combat try to excuse the latter by emphasising the difficulty of distinguishing between civilians and irregular forces. Describing urban warfare in Iraq in 2003, one writer argued that 'Coalition forces will try to limit collateral damage, but it's hard to know who to trust with Iraqi militia dressing like civilians' (Yourish, 7 April 2003: 31).

It is only when overwhelming evidence is produced, or when a particularly powerful symbolic act reveals the true extent of military indoctrination, that civilian deaths are taken seriously. So, for example, the anger that greeted the revelation that Israeli troops had been encouraged to shoot civilians in Gaza was confirmed by the symbolic 'materialisation' of this intent, when it was revealed that a popular T-shirt bought by IDF troops depicted a pregnant Arab woman holding a gun, with the cross-hairs of a target superimposed over her womb. The slogan 'One Shot, Two Kills' provided the key to the whole design (Macintyre, 22 March 2009: 35; Beaumont, 22 March 2009: 37). This does not mean that such behaviour was universal, or that pregnant women were made into a particular target. It does, however, suggest the general currency of a masculinist *proposition* that the best and most cost-effective way to deal with Palestinian resistance is to extinguish both current and future generations of (non)combatants.

WORDS AND ACTIONS

When Dillon argued that 'words could not refer to other words unless they also related to things' (Dillon, 1995: 167),[4] he meant that language is not endlessly self-referential, that one reference does not simply lead *ad infinitum* to another without the production of some timely effect. In Jensen's words, 'no social structure ... could exist without procedures for ending language games' (Jensen, 1995: 11). The point of committing an act, according to this author, is to alter some aspect of that larger (practical) reality upon which social representations are built. In the case of *military procedures*, actions have an autonomous impact over and above the explanations offered by combatants and politicians; if one side has, for example, been weakened militarily, then in the practical realm this may become apparent in the next encounter, reducing its ability to generate *symbolic* as well as practical effects. An actual symbolic advantage may, of course, be gained even when an operation is not a success, but this is usually only temporary: eventually, as the American authorities discovered in Iraq, the weight of competing evidence may undermine an optimistic assessment of events.

There are thus limits to the kinds of account that can be generated. This does not just mean that some descriptions will (however temporarily) provide a more convincing depiction of the phenomenon than others, but that all expression has a referential limit. If someone is killed by a bomb, for example, it is no use claiming that they are still alive, though it might be possible to characterise their death as heroic, or tragic, or a waste, or as revenge for an injustice, depending on the intention of the speaker. The reputation of an individual can, of course, be enhanced through the manner of their death and thus 'live on' in the practices of their community, but the actual person is removed from the realm of embodied agency.

REALISM, RELATIVISM AND THE WORLD

Warfare has been theorised from a number of perspectives. In general, however, realist perspectives on representation have achieved less prominence than constructionist points of view, which have become almost the default position for discussing the relationship between signs and objects. As Mikula argues, 'constructionism is the privileged paradigm in cultural studies, to the extent that its underlying assumptions are by and large taken for granted' (Mikula, 2008: 174). One of the tenets of this position is that 'meaning cannot be explained ... in terms of the "real" world' (*ibid*) while discourse is accorded the power to create events. There is no doubt that the representation of things (the way they are categorised), determines how they are understood, and in this sense discourse does have socially constitutive powers and is as a consequence part of actual existence. Constructionist studies can, therefore, give rise to many insights into how practical action is partly led by the metaphors used to describe phenomena (see Hulsse and Spencer, 2008).

A realist model of representation, however, tries to examine the overall process through which materiality is understood. It attempts to demonstrate that different types of phenomena are *drawn into* the field of discursive reality, becoming the objects of valid social interrogation at the point at which they are classified. Without such a process, objects or incidents in the natural and practical worlds would not assume the status of real (socially useful or relevant) things. If, however, they have not yet been 'discovered', phenomena do not disappear from existence altogether, but remain confined to the natural realm. The constructionist position, at least as expressed by Mattern in her study of 'soft power', begins with a similar line of argument, in the sense that she also thinks the social field provides a vital resource for imagining the real. 'Reality' is in her opinion constituted by 'the broadly accepted facts of the world and the socially expected behaviours that are implied by those facts' (Mattern, 2007: 99). This formula would, however, exclude any thing or event that is not 'broadly accepted'. In addition, Mattern's view of reality is that it is not 'pre-given and objective, but socially constructed through an ongoing collective process' (*ibid*). The notion that the real is not 'pre-given and objective' requires some thought. If Mattern's definition of reality is composed of two conjoined elements ('broadly accepted facts about the world' and 'socially expected behaviours implied by those facts'), then it seems that she does not doubt the existence of a 'world' about which 'facts' are composed. This indicates the existence of an objective referent, something to which the symbolic points, and from which human societies draw their notions of the actual. In this case, 'world' has been in effect substituted for the real, even if this world is largely composed of language and representation.

The idea of 'broadly accepted facts' needs therefore to be treated with some caution; it is clear that even a widespread belief in various phenomena can be misplaced or misdirected. So, for example, the belief that divine authority shapes human life says more about the character of faith than it does about the demonstrable existence of the supernatural. Mattern does not, however, explore the reliability of perception, so that disputes, errors and new developments do not enter her discussion. The realist perspective would also argue that, when the social world does reach a consensus, such as with the 'broadly accepted' notion that lightening bolts are produced by an electrical discharge rather than the anger of Zeus, it does not mean that even *a correct* form of explanation can alter or determine the physical conditions that give rise to stormy weather.

At the level of the social, it might not matter which form of belief is held, but physical circumstances are indeed 'pre-given and objective', not because they carry an independent *meaning* beyond the symbolic, but because they have an independent or phenomenal effect. If Mattern were to describe a *social* or *discursive* reality, then of course her portrayal of a condition 'constructed through an ongoing collective process' would be broadly correct. This act of collective endeavour could not, however, create a set of behaviours that did not *begin by recognising certain objective conditions*. A universal agreement that 'walking', for instance, should be known as 'flying', might be acceptable if widespread agreement could be reached; but no general consensus could support the proposition that individuals must actually leap into the air, and fly instead of walk. In such a case, the natural order would set limits to the practical order, and no amount of sophistry in the discursive realm could alter that.

NOTIONS ABOUT THE WORLD

The second part of Mattern's definition of 'reality' is the existence of 'socially expected behaviours that are implied by facts', where facts are notions about the world that are 'broadly accepted'. This indicates Mattern's awareness of social norms, those conventional behaviours drawn from pre-existing social conditions, forms of conduct that can be, alternatively, exploited or challenged, depending on the goals of the individuals who enter into either competitive or cooperative relations. This is certainly an example of 'social construction', because behaviour is discussed, can become codified, and is thus reproduced across time and space.

This does not, however, reinforce the view that 'expected behaviours' are never 'pre-given and objective'. Behavioural codes are inherited, representing a set of values 'external' to the infants who, while they may eventually interpret such rules in the light of their own collective experience, must nonetheless deal with the circumstances they encounter. The human condition is 'to be born into a social context ... which was not of our making' (Archer, 1995:

72). While it is possible to alter and even revolutionise a public institution, the process must begin with the fact that human subjects are 'involuntaristically situated beings' (Archer, 1995: 200).

Mattern's subsequent argument, that 'actors interpret the world in unique ways', seems to be employed because it offers a category (the 'unique') that is opposed to the 'pre-given'. However, a unique individual interpretation would imply the existence of limitless versions of reality; this would contradict the previous notion of collective effort, so the author describes a process in which a vast catalogue of ideas is whittled down to 'a few socially legitimated interpretations' (Mattern, 2007: 99). It is not clear how the social order carries out this process of selection, but it ends with this handful of notions assuming the status of the 'real truth'.

Mattern decides that because 'communicative processes occur most fundamentally through the medium of language, it follows that "reality" is a *sociolinguistic construct*' (Mattern, 2007: 99). Of course, the term 'reality' is a linguistic reference, one that has been created by human individuals to indicate the entire realm of natural, practical and social experience (Archer, 2000: 162). However, it does not follow that, because communication is primarily sociolinguistic, our appreciation of reality is constructed purely from such representational materials. The constructionist argument as it is expressed by Mattern is essentially that A (a 'reality' of facts about the world and consequent behaviours) is created by B (collective social processes), not by C (pre-given objective conditions). The question is, if B (social process) creates A ('reality'), then what creates B? 'Reality' cannot produce society, according to this schema, because society produces the real; yet reality is *already* social, made up of 'accepted facts' about the world. The world seems to supply the stable, 'pre-given' category-object lying at the heart of this formula.

While representation does offer a 'composure' of reality and thus seems complete (as though there is no other real beyond description), it would be more accurate to say that *one aspect* of reality (the discursive and social) is composed of linguistic/representational practices, while another, the practical and experiential, consists of the impact caused by natural phenomena. This impact can be thought about, interpreted and narrativised in, for example, words or visual art, but it operates as immediate *sensation*. Too much emphasis is placed, perhaps, on the primacy of language and the work of representation.

A 'UNIVERSE OF SIGNS'?

When Žižek, for example, says that 'we are submerged in the universe of signs', this is certainly the case for any cognitive process, which may be used to anticipate and rationalise our visceral encounters with the phenomenal world. However, the 'symbolic framework' that 'structures our perception of reality' (Žižek, 2005: 191), does not determine the character of the physical encounter between the human individual and external phenomena. Archer draws attention to 'the correct belief that conceptualisation is ... indispensable', but also argues that 'this is coupled with the erroneous conviction that concepts have to be linguistic' (Archer, 2000: 125). Although this may stretch the standard view of what we mean by a 'concept', it serves as a reminder that the *conception* of any activity is wider than the symbolic process, while some responses are not even planned in advance: the visualisation of an action and the production of instinctive movement in an emergency offer two relevant examples. Archer also provides a useful distinction between the social concept of self and the 'sense of self' that is 'forged in our environmental relations' (Archer, 2000: 125).

There are, of course, variations on the forms taken by constructionism. Lewis, in his book *Language Wars*, argues that 'the phenomenal world may well exist outside the world of imagining and language', but 'it has no constitutive power of its own since we can only access it through language' (Lewis, 2005: 7). Phenomena may be defined as things or objects which appear to the observer, or which make an impression on the human subject. They make themselves known or felt, by intruding, as it were, into consciousness through the senses. Impressing people through experience *is* the constitutive power of phenomena! These phenomena can be natural and human, since both can have an impact on the individual, but there is an important difference between the two. While human beings can certainly create phenomena, such as impressive buildings or terrorist acts, using their ability to combine materials in the realm of practical activity, natural phenomena, such as earthquakes or a sunrise, are not constructed from representational matter such as speech, writing or images; they can certainly be reported using such forms, and their meanings are assigned to them through representation, but they have their *undesignated* origin in nature.

It may be useful to remember that language, which is related to practical activity as both guide and interpretant, is composed of a) phonology, the sound system of each language group, b) syntax, or the rules of sentence formation, and c) semantics, the system of meaning (Price, 1997: 128). Natural phenomena are provided with but do not *require* any linguistic introduction, as they act through the senses; a natural experience is seen, heard, smelt, felt or tasted. Human awareness of natural things is certainly conveyed through language, but once again, this does not prove that phenomena depend on language for their existence; though *semantically* dependent, they must be physically distinct for the representational act to have something to describe. Such forms of experience demonstrate that access to the world is possible through other processes than the medium of language, even though it may need to be expressed or rationalised in some symbolic form.

It is, nonetheless, this depiction of representational and phenomenal values which leads Lewis to make claims about the power of television. He seeks to emphasise the 'ways in which language facilitates representation' through 'a new global semiosis of mediated and televisualised political violence' (Lewis, 2005: 7). Television, he claims, is the most important medium 'in the global communication of terror and violence' so that 'global terror and political violence' are not only able to take advantage of public media, but are actually 'formed in relation to these new modes of mediated meaning-making' (Lewis, 2005: 7). There are two questions here: first, whether it actually is the case that television alone as an institution – and not its web-based supplements and rivals, which provide the opportunity to 'isolate', create or review events – is the primary driver of the representation of terror; and second, whether it is true that political violence is really created in order to take advantage of established forms of mediation, or whether in fact the perpetrators of such violence attempt, where possible, to control the process of representation (using, for example, alternative genres like the 'jihadist video' to reach specific audiences). While some media coverage might entice the 'terrorist' to produce a *routinely* spectacular act, extended combat within long-running wars as in Afghanistan is less easy to 'package' and thus less amenable to news management by the state, insurgents, or the traditional media.

Despite the divisions between realists and constructionists over the role of mediated terror, both positions have treated the appearance of the 'dominant' reality with scepticism, and both have produced trenchant critiques of formal authority. Again, although the exact character of the real and representation is contested, theoretical approaches must in general address the real as a foundational concept, so that no academic perspective can afford to dispense with the idea itself. The existence of an autonomous reality beyond discourse may be affirmed or rejected, but the act of assertion or denial depends on the mobilisation of reality as a sign. In other words, 'the real' is employed in academic discourse to indicate a number of conditions, and as a concept *against which* other notions, of the *not* or *less* or *more* real, are measured. This can be expressed in the distinction between the *false*, the *copy* and finally what Baudrillard calls the *hyperreal*, a condition in which reality becomes 'over-exposed, pushed to an extreme' and ultimately even 'in flight from itself' (in Levin, 1996: 274).

So, in invoking the notion of reality as a reference against which the *quality* and *range* of representation can be measured, writers cannot help but acknowledge the primacy of (conceptions of) the real. It is notable that authors who make representation their primary focus have to explain their decision. Fiumara, for example, begins her study of the symbolic function by recognising that 'attention is directed away from "objects" ... almost as if ... we were not even considering reality' (Fiumara, 1992: 1). Conversely, work that begins by focusing on the 'real' (whatever its philosophical predilection) seems to proceed without needing to compose an apology.

POLITICAL DISCOURSE AND TIMELINESS

> ... this new world faces a new threat: of disorder and chaos born either of brutal states like Iraq, armed with weapons of mass destruction; or of extreme terrorist groups. Both hate our way of life, our freedom, our democracy.
>
> (Tony Blair, Address to the Nation, 20 March 2003)

As the opening argument of this chapter tried to make clear, rhetorical propositions are generated by the desire of an authority to establish plausible (if not necessarily logical) accounts of the goals it wishes to pursue. In the case given above, the claim that a 'new world' faces a 'new threat' is not supported with evidence, but with another set of assertions; references are made to basic, universally recognised categories (the sovereign state of Iraq), which are linked to generally accepted conditions (its brutal treatment of political and religious opponents), and then to unproven allegations about the nature of Iraqi armaments. The attempt to achieve semantic coherence, however, is slightly offset by the inclusion of terms and statements which more usually appear in North American political discourse, especially the close physical and ideological proximity of its references to *freedom* and *democracy*. This may be attributed to the need to offer consistent exophoric[5] agreement between US and UK policy statements.

George W. Bush, in a joint appearance with Blair in 2003, repeated much of the same propositional content,[6] saying that '[Colin Powell] will make it clear that Saddam is a menace to peace ... and he will also talk about Al-Qaeda links, links that really do portend a danger for America, and for Great Britain, and anybody else who loves freedom' (Bush, Press Conference, 31 January 2003). In tracing the rhetorical techniques found in such material, general reference to discourse or representation promotes a rather abstract approach; it might be better to ask how expressive acts work to make references, categorise events, circulate themes and build propositions. Political rhetoric prepares attitudes, trying to create a kind of psychological *accommodation* in its audience, without requiring it to produce any dynamic response.

RHETORIC AND THE SANCTITY OF APPEARANCE

No technique of persuasion necessarily guarantees success, but then such an outcome is not actually required for executive action. Despite the fact that official depictions of events (even where contested) are automatically accorded pre-eminence in the composition of the 'social narratives'[7] which emerge in news reports, corporate announcements, political literature and public relations, the point of formal *allocution* is to reinforce hierarchical structures through the sanctity of appearance and the rhetorical qualities of utterance. Political interventions depend upon the exercise of 'timeliness' (in Greek, *kairos*). They appear for a purpose at a specific moment and do not even attempt to attain the status of 'the last word'. While some journalists continue to treat the statements of the powerful as matters of record (Price, 2008: 5), the actual function of rhetoric is to provide provisional utterances which can eventually be 'contextualised' and repeated in new forms.

They are not meant to be entirely truthful, but are instead necessary formalities within a system that is *presented* as being democratic. The use of rhetoric is thus functional; there is no intention to establish 'fixed' or final signifiers.[8] Poststructuralist theorising, with its preference for the existence of a 'differential network, a fabric of traces' (Culler, 1985: 84), might perfectly correctly conceptualise such speeches as indeterminate or provisional[9] texts of a 'literary' character, yet, as *discursive events* in a political context, they are *timely* interventions designed for instrumental purposes.[10]

As the intense propaganda campaign on the subject of Iraq demonstrated, the political leadership of the US and the UK did not base the argument for invasion on an effort to establish 'undeniable' evidence, but on general plausibility. As Dillon argues, where there is 'no ground against which the truth of ... interpretations can be measured', then 'defending a position becomes more a matter of stamina than truth or relevance, [or else] a matter of aesthetics' (Dillon, 1995: 167). It is this which helped to frustrate the opponents of the war; reasoned arguments about oil and imperialism seemed pedestrian by comparison with the *bold fictions* offered by the warmongers, and incapable of countering the chaotic network of impulses these compelling stories generated.

In a cultural milieu where the United States plays a coordinating role, and where 'the attractive power of US models of production and culture' are increasingly 'unified in the sphere of consumption' (Anderson, 2002, cited in Panitch and Leys, 2003: 9), the use of the aesthetic appeals mentioned by Dillon are indicative of a broader *cultural* strategy that includes the valorisation of war. In this situation, symbolic resources are drawn from famous examples of historical oratory (such as the inaugural speeches of past presidents and prime ministers), but also from movies, novels, simplified national myths, indeed all of those events 'that make up the ideational/affective realm by which our physical world of material things is interpreted' (Barber, 2003: 81). It is this cultural tradition that has provided orators with a resource for their explanations of events.

DEMOCRACY AND AUTHORITY: ECHOES OF THE PAST

When Winston Churchill, who had become prime minister on 10 May 1940, gave his first speech in that capacity to the House of Commons, on 13 May, he repeated the statement he had already made to the members of his Cabinet, to the effect that he had 'nothing to offer but blood, toil, tears and sweat' (Churchill in MacArthur, 1999 [1940]: 188). The concluding section of the speech, which described the magnitude of the challenge faced in the war against the Axis powers, contained widespread exploitation of the inclusive force offered by the pronoun 'we'. In using this formula, an orator asserts the unity of separate individuals, of assorted groups, or of disparate social forces, through the temporary rhetorical occupation of a common subjective position.

The fact that this orientation is transitory is recognised in the dictionary definition which describes 'we' as 'the collective name' for the speaker 'and all others of the class that context shows him to be representing *for the moment*' (Concise OED, 1964, my emphasis). It is only natural that the exact character of a group will change depending upon circumstance, but political leaders, who make a show of taking on the mantle of 'national' responsibility, are also fully aware of the advantages to be gained from speaking on behalf of others, and habitually shift the compass of their reference in order to reinforce a complex proposition with a more basic reference that seems unassailable. Churchill had, however, prepared the ground for this transition within the course of his address, by detailing the multi-party character of his administration, and making it clear that the war would become 'one of the greatest battles in history', requiring a combined effort to achieve victory (Churchill in MacArthur, 1999 [1940]: 187). On this basis, he went on to argue that 'we have before us an ordeal of the most grievous kind', before employing another oratorical device, the rhetorical question (see Atkinson, 1984). In this procedure, the speaker answers a query, which although attributed to others, has been posed as a way of reinforcing an argument.

Churchill made this apparent in the passage which begins: 'you ask, what is our policy?', answering this with 'I can say, it is to wage war, by sea, land and air, with all our might and all the strength that God can give us' (*ibid*: 188). The moral basis for the whole task is variously identified, both in negative descriptions of the enemy and through the positive attributes accorded to the British cause. So, for example, the opponent is described as 'a monstrous tyranny, never surpassed in the dark, lamentable catalogue of human crime' (*ibid*). This is perhaps an unremarkable description, in the sense that the Nazi regime was generally understood as violent and totalitarian. What is more unusual, from a modern perspective, is the depiction of British values. 'Without victory', Churchill argued, there would be 'no survival for the British Empire, no survival for all that the British Empire has stood for', and ultimately 'no survival for the urge and impulse of the ages, that mankind will move forward towards its goal' (*ibid*).

For Churchill, the progressive qualities of the Empire seemed self-evident, so the precise nature of the goal towards which 'mankind' must strive is left unexplained. In any contemporary piece of mainstream political discourse, a reference to Empire would make little sense, especially as a positive category. There is, of course, no longer any such institution, because the Allied victory, rather than the defeat Churchill feared, ensured the dissolution of the British Empire as a *dominant* transnational political entity. The point is that a modern leader would use references to democracy as the explicit basis for any attempt to rally his or her listeners; it is the 'default' position for any expression of political faith.

On 20 March 2003, Tony Blair made an address to the nation in which he, like his predecessor, announced his determination to overcome a foreign enemy. On this occasion, however, there were certain differences. Saddam Hussein, the dictator Blair and the US President sought to overthrow, had been in no position to oppose British or American allies or interests, since Iraq's military strength was feeble. Hussein did not stand at the head of a formal alliance, as had Hitler, so could not call upon other nation-states to reinforce his position.

The threat he was supposed to represent was the use, at some time in the future, of 'weapons of mass destruction', a capability which many analysts were certain that he did not possess. The other danger he was meant to pose was the possible development of links with terrorist organisations, which might then gain access to the destructive technologies Iraq was supposed to be hiding. Blair argued that his opponents, the 'brutal states' and terrorists he described, 'hate our way of life, our freedom, our democracy'. He also appeared to echo some aspects of Churchillian rhetoric, announcing that 'British servicemen and women are engaged from air, land and sea' (Blair, 20 March 2003).

However, whereas Churchill had spoken at length of the unity amongst various political and military forces, in an attempt to make the 'nation' as a whole fall into line, Blair could not describe a similar situation because public opposition to the war was too much in evidence. Instead, he acknowledged that 'this course of action has produced deep divisions of opinion in our country', then went on to suggest an emotional unity through the assertion that 'the British people will now be united in sending our armed forces our thoughts and prayers' (*ibid*).

Thus, the controversy was to be subsumed within an immaterial expression of national empathy, though patriotic atheists would presumably have to be content with the production of sentimental thoughts alone. The struggle in this case is not, however, for survival, but is to be a struggle against 'disorder and chaos' (*ibid*). A reference to the effects that could be created by the weapons Iraq was alleged to have developed offers the most revealing outline of Blair's value system. He identifies the 'carnage they could inflict to *our economies, our security, to world peace*' (*ibid*, my emphasis). Carnage, however, refers to mass bloodshed, the massacre or slaughter of many human beings. Economies cannot suffer carnage, nor can abstract notions like security, nor a 'world peace' that exists as a platitude and not a real condition.

The purpose of this analysis is not simply to suggest that the democracy Blair envisions is bogus, or that he is 'insincere'; rather, the point is to take the category of democracy seriously, and ask how such a society manages to be exceptionally capable in the use of propaganda, determined in its repression of dissent, and highly skilled in the production of military force. It is interesting that the democratic nations are the ones taking pre-emptive military action, and that they are able to shatter the structure of the 'brutal' states that are meant to be so dangerous. In other words, the purpose here is to examine the use and value of those terms which are taken for granted in conventional political discourse. Political positions are legitimated by the fact that the political figure is a 'representative' of a group of voters, so that speakers need only to flourish these democratic credentials in order to speak 'on behalf' of others.

MEDIA, REFERENTIAL POWER AND REALISM

In contrast to the duplicitous and aestheticised representation of war, some types of public expression use plain-speaking as a political ploy. New Labour's John Reid, for example, in line with his strategic antipathy to squeamish euphemisms like 'collateral damage' and his preference for a more explicit form of utterance, told the world to prepare for 'unavoidable civilian deaths' during the Iraq war (Ramesh, 2003: 290). In fact, the first confirmed fatality in Baghdad was a Jordanian taxi driver, killed by an American missile supposedly intended for Saddam Hussein (*ibid*: 57).[11]

Some of the fabrications constructed to make the case for war depended on the simple movement between reference to a world of phenomena and propositions about what those phenomena meant. Where the reference to reality itself seems insecure, the propositions built on this shaky foundation are less likely to be believed. The reference to Iraqi weaponry presented to the United Nations by Colin Powell on 5 February 2003 fell into this category.[12] Weapons inspectors were said to have laughed at the content of the televised presentation,[13] while Powell himself is rumoured to have despaired over the quality of the information he was supposed to use, asking in a less than gentlemanly fashion what he was supposed to do with this 'bullshit'.

This kind of material may have an impact in so far as it is based on an accepted *function* of language and symbolisation – that is, its ability to indicate qualities, phenomena or things in general other than the actual symbol itself. The *purpose* of symbolic content is of course to 'point *away*' from itself. As Collier writes, language 'is a pointer' and to study it 'without reference to what it points to' is to make a fundamental error (Collier, 1998: 48). So it is perfectly reasonable to believe in the existence of trucks, biological agents and storage tanks, the first stage in Powell's *plausible assertion* that they may under certain conditions be brought into a particular form of use. The referential force of Powell's words depends, however, on their ability to produce a form of recognition and acceptance – to gain, in effect, symbolic currency.

The supposed power of political utterances is circumscribed by what it is possible to say. Political speeches are, for example, never *pure* statements of intent, because no set of precepts remains unaffected by alternative currents of thought, and very rarely will any political group give voice to the exact character of its beliefs. The analyst must therefore always consider the distinction between belief (itself rhetorical, in Billig's [1991] conception), and whatever *position* is presented in public. The effectiveness of public communication depends on the degree to which all parties concerned have access to other forms of social power (see the Introduction), including the ability to reproduce an agenda that stands a chance of being carried out. In a democracy, there are supposed to be established procedures for ensuring that the wishes of the people are at least considered; the problem however lies with the way in which democracy is conceived.

WAR, DEMOCRACY AND PUBLIC CULTURE

The *institutional* referent of democracy draws attention to a formal political process, but is also dependent upon the ideal of social equality which the term inevitably brings to mind. In other words, the symbolic resonance of *democracy* lends legitimacy to the practical organisation of those human societies that wish to distinguish themselves from tyrannies, oligarchies, absolute monarchies and one-party states. Therefore, the exact form of the democratic process is supposed not to matter, provided some form of popular sanction (usually based on universal suffrage) operates at some stage in the composition of the social order. So, for example, proportional representation and 'first past the post' are both regarded, at least technically, as democratic processes.

In a similar way, constitutional monarchy is usually regarded as perfectly compatible with electoral democracy. The wide range of forms it assumes may attest to the 'strength' of bourgeois democracy in general, but also reveals the difficulty of describing (quite apart from *establishing*) a system truly representative of the popular will. This problem applies to all periods in which democracy has been the preferred form of social organisation. Meanwhile, the rhetorical utterances of the powerful seek to conflate the ideal and pragmatic aspects of the concept in order to avoid challenges from those who think that political democracy has become increasingly limited.[14]

The debate about the political character of contemporary states seems to begin from a simple distinction between democracies, or those nations 'making progress towards democracy', and dictatorships. The latter, countries ruled by single parties or tyrants, are often referred to as 'regimes'. Equally, some ruling groups that appear to deserve severe approbation seem to escape from censure and remain within the realm of 'government'. The point here, however, is that the term *regime* is used to suggest a less than legitimate form of rule, and draws attention to the systemic and functional character of power. However, the fact that the word provides an insight into the operative structure of political rule as *a general practice* makes it easy to apply to any authority that has been constituted through some 'undemocratic' mechanism or special intervention, legal or otherwise.

This explains the readiness of politicians to identify 'evil regimes' and 'undemocratic regimes', in order to assign the negative connotations of governance to subordinate nations. Yet, the continued existence within mainstream democracies of structures that do not require popular sanction, including factions, cabals and permanent officials, points to the fact that authority prevails because it is *organised* power, remote perhaps from its subjects, but brought into uncomfortable proximity by the regulation and *disruption* of any act that might, through accident or design, trespass on the ground of its dominance.

A 'democratic regime', just as easily as a despotic one, can apply this force at arm's length. No particular law or close supervision is needed for repressive action to take place. For example, the use of police in any confrontation with the public will provide the grounds upon which officers can make innovations in the application of the law. All that is required is the declaration that a certain situation has arisen (disturbance of the peace, riot, terrorist incident) and the authorities can follow operational procedure. When individual officers apply this modus operandi, they have in effect fulfilled their obligations and cannot be held accountable for the 'systemic' failures that might occur during the pursuit of larger ('democratic') goals.

Furthermore, the purpose of parallel structures (hierarchical relationships between forces that operate beyond popular control) is to produce the vicious acts that political leaders do not want laid at their door. An executive does not necessarily, unless in time of war, intend to carry out a *specific* outrage; the whole system is set up to produce a general effect upon a particular ground, to apply force where it can produce exemplary results. State violence is never usually presented as illegal or illicit, but is described (depending on which side of the artificial debate is preferred) as either *justified* or *excessive*. If an operation goes wrong (or succeeds in too obvious a way), it is not supposed to be the fault of the political executive – which sets the wider social conditions for activity and may not even learn the details of an incident until it is over – but of the commanders 'on the ground'.

Where responsibility has become too diffuse and confused (owing perhaps to a national emergency), then the advantage of bureaucratic structure is that individual liability disappears (though, curiously, collective accountability is often avoided as well). The narrative of the 'betrayed' operative or agent, who after applying the required violence is then hung out to dry by superior officers, reveals a great deal about the mentality of subordinate power (see Chapter 5).

DEMOCRACY AND THE MARKET

In the neo-liberal social order, democracy, 'reform' and marketisation have been inseparable within political speech, while references to 'market reforms' were used almost to *guarantee* the growth of democracy and freedom.[15] The shift in the neo-liberal order towards 'service' economies encouraged the notion that a 'post-productive' society had arrived, in which the notion of *flexibility* (together with the idea of doing 'more with less') achieved wide circulation in the public realm. This conception emerged in the speeches of politicians and policy-makers (Fairclough, 2000: 63), within the self-help doctrines of the international business community, and as part of the received wisdom of 'globalised' corporate networks.[16]

Overall, flexibility was presented as advantageous to the employee, but the consequences of having nothing but a positive outlook and a set of 'soft skills', with no recourse to structures like left-wing political parties and unions, provided little defence against the onset of recession: without the cohesive force offered by class solidarity, the 'masses' have only numerical superiority.

Writing during the rise of fascism, Simone Weil observed that the submission of 'the greater number to the smaller' seemed to be the 'fundamental characteristic of nearly every form of social organisation' (Weil, 1988: 140). This statement prepared the ground for further reflection, on why the power of 'an infinitesimal minority' could be exercised over vast multitudes of apparently quiescent individuals. Weil's conclusion was that 'number ... is a weakness' (*ibid*: 143).

If the majority in any society are in most circumstances politically ineffective, it is worth observing that there are a host of elements which may limit the practical capacity of 'the people' to act in mutual solidarity, quite besides the coercive dominance of a ruling group. In all historical periods, these include the distribution of citizenship,[17] the scope of any political 'franchise', the ways in which certain activities are policed, and how rights of participation are exercised. The differences between citizens and outsiders, and between grades of citizenship, are powerful factors in the maintenance of the social order. As Brubaker says, 'citizenship is a powerful instrument of social closure', guarding against the easy assimilation of outsiders (cited in Pierson, 1996: 130). Although Weil pointed to the difficulty of establishing cohesion among the oppressed, she did acknowledge the fact that, in certain periods (she cited the Spanish revolution of 1936), the masses have acted as one, forcing the powerful to know what it is 'to feel alone and defenceless' (Weil, 1988: 143).

DEMOCRACY AND FASCISM

In his discussion of western policy on Iraq, the peace activist and author Milan Rai describes 'the restoration of leading fascists to power', and the 'attempted re-nazification of Iraq' (Rai, 2003: xix). Here, as in many academic and popular accounts of the invasion and occupation, political terms that originated in the 1930s and 1940s are reintroduced to describe contemporary actors and events. Such an approach may not be entirely counterproductive, because nationalist movements have traditionally provided one of the main sources of fascist growth. The value of the designation 'fascist' depends, however, on its accuracy and the ability to draw productive lessons between the past and present.

Wolin, in his dissection of US power, makes just such an attempt to draw historical comparisons, noting that in 'definitional or conceptual' terms, 'a true democracy and a dictatorship are mutually exclusive', yet it seems nonetheless possible for 'a form of totalitarianism, different from the classical one, to evolve from a putatively "strong democracy" instead of a "failed" one' (Wolin, 2008: 55). Wolin's depiction is of an 'inverted totalitarianism' which is only in part 'a state-centred phenomenon', and which represents the '*political* coming of age of corporate power and the *political* demobilisation of the citizenry' (*ibid*: x).

The historian Mazower also offers an argument about the survival of fascist beliefs, noting that former Nazis and fascists took up roles in centres of post-war European power, including police forces, intelligence services and industrial organisations. Although the regimes did not survive, the goals of the Right were to some degree fulfilled under democratic arrangements. The most significant element of Mazower's thesis, however, concerns not the post-war reconfiguration of fascist values, but the real character of the distaste shown by the democracies *towards the Nazis during the war*. This, he argues, was based on the shock of discovering that what the 'imperial powers did abroad', the Nazis were doing in Europe (Mazower, 2008: 577). 'The Nazis', writes Mazower, 'shared that imperial desire but did something with it that was unprecedented and shocking to the European mind ... they tried to build their empire in Europe itself' (*ibid*: xxxix).

Rai, for his part, provides no definition of fascism, and merely attaches the label to the Iraqi regime and security state. He is right to note that after the invasion the coalition appointed senior Ba'athists to positions of power (Rai, 2003: 111), and equally accurate in his critique of the US intention to 'decapitate' the Iraqi regime (*ibid*: 106). The conclusion he draws from this, however, is that the employment of Ba'ath officials and police was 'rather as if Britain and the United States had said in the final stages of the Second World War that the problem was Adolf Hitler and his inner circle ... but that the Nazi Party could continue to rule' (*ibid*: 107).

This comparison makes a number of assumptions, besides the initial assertion that there is a convergence between the political character of fascism and the Ba'ath regime. The first new conjecture is that, in offering Hussein an escape route, the British and American authorities implicitly confirmed that they wanted the Iraqi power structure to remain intact. It seems, however, even from Rai's own evidence, that rather than attempting to perpetuate Ba'athist rule, the US and UK only intended to use members of the Ba'ath party as bureaucrats in the service of coalition interests; western lack of principle in using senior figures and criminal elements from the state does not prove that the real strategy was to maintain Ba'athist power. There is no doubt that many individuals escaped justice, but the old state structure was irrevocably broken.

In attempting to sustain the comparison with the post-war policies of the western Allies in 1945, Rai provides examples of individual Nazis who were appointed as police officers. He argues that 'denazification' programmes were 'shallow and ineffective' and 'reversed within a few years of the liberation of Auschwitz' (Rai, 2003: 191). Once again, however, the inadequacy of denazification as a process of political decontamination does not prove that the Nazi party was still in de facto control of the nation. The actual practice pursued by the US and UK was to make an example of the Nazi leadership, to allow the return to civilian life of less prominent (but often no less guilty) functionaries, and to employ intelligence officers and scientists in their new drive against the Soviet Union. This was a corrupt process, designed not just to 'cherry pick' individual Nazis, but to learn from the organisational principles embraced by fascism; it did not, however, constitute an attempt to keep the Nazi party as such in power. The totalitarian regimes of the 1930s and 1940s had provided an instructive example, the main lesson of which was that the fascist impulse was best concentrated in the elite formations of the state, so that it would not contaminate the separate, specialised function of electoral democracy, nor pose a threat to bureaucratic rule: in effect, it involved the creation of a fascist enclave without the need for public hysteria or shows of loyalty.

In conclusion, it seems clear that Rai unintentionally weakens the force of his suggestion that the coalition policy on Iraq was so extraordinarily perverse that it paralleled the maintenance of National Socialist dominance in Germany. The point depends on the notion that a Nazi restoration would have been outrageous, and that the actual case was different. At this juncture in his argument, Rai makes the point that denazification was carried out against 'all the institutions of power in Germany' (Rai, 2003: 107). In a much later passage, he presents what he then calls 'shallow denazification' as evidence of an 'historical precedent' for similar practices in Iraq (*ibid*: 191). If the US and UK had indeed followed this precedent, the model they copied was not the revival of a fascist system, but rather the strategic use of defeated enemies – ultra-right nationalists who could be retained as useful assets in the new configuration of 'imperial' power. As Mazower says, 'just when the Germans started talking about the Monroe doctrine, the Americans were looking far beyond it and starting to imagine themselves as a world military power' (Mazower, 2008: 579).

3
Media and the Reproduction of Meaning

Rice: Iraq trained al-Qaeda in chemical weapons
President Bush's national security adviser ... said Saddam Hussein
has sheltered al-Qaeda terrorists in Baghdad and helped train some
in chemical weapons development – information she said has been
gleaned from captives in the ongoing war on terrorism.
(CNN online, 26 September 2002)

This short excerpt from a news report, taken from CNN's online
service, offers a fairly straightforward reproduction of one US
executive statement, made during the early development of the 'war
on terror'. The story is attributed to an authoritative informant
(Condoleezza Rice), but the simple techniques of association and
negative identification (the rhetorical hallmarks of manipulative
speech) are re-circulated in the simplest form. Positive terms like
'sheltered' are linked with categories that carry a negative charge
– in this case, 'al-Qaeda terrorists'.

The excerpt seems to reflect the propositional order of the original
utterance, in which the endophoric[1] structure of the sentence links
two supposed enemies of America – Saddam Hussein and 'al-Qaeda
terrorists'. The piece concludes with a reference to 'captives' taken in
this 'ongoing' and seemingly interminable conflict, and states that the
information was 'gleaned' from these individuals. The word *gleaned*
seems innocuous, but the methods of interrogation used by the US
military would eventually become a news story in their own right.

Two types of attribution are used within the CNN piece. The
first is the reference to Rice as spokesperson ('President Bush's
national security adviser'), while the second concentrates on the
social actors who are supposed to have collaborated in the project
to develop chemical weapons. In effect, the narrative works by
associating known (real) entities and individuals (Rice, Hussein,
al-Qaeda) with statements and activities (saying, sheltering, training,

developing chemical weapons). CNN cites Rice (who is the 'input source' [Bell, 1991: 57]), but does so *with reference to her role* as a US official; it is not, therefore, presented as a private opinion. The second use of attribution merely repeats Rice's assertion that Hussein was responsible for a series of undesirable activities. As a consequence, the reader is presented with a scenario composed of actual phenomena combined with plausible, yet ultimately fictional, conceptions. In other words, no autonomous perspective is created and, once again, we encounter the use of *truth-claims in a story-world* (see Price, 2007).

The question is, if this kind of report is really meant to be a serious account of events, should 'mediation' here be understood as no more than the formal transmission of information (Edles, 2002: 56) rather than a critical process? Dependence on authoritative utterances exists because journalists assume that the speaker is able to initiate events as well as describe them. In addition, as Bell notes, 'journalists love the performatives of politics ... where something happens through someone saying it' (Bell, 1991: 207). Therefore, when an individual with 'the requisite authority' makes an announcement, 'the *saying itself constitutes an indisputable fact*' (*ibid*, my emphasis). In this sense at least, the principle of basing reports on 'the facts' has been observed.

This does not mean that there is no discussion of the source. As the CNN piece proceeds it notes that 'the comments made by Condoleezza Rice were the strongest and most specific to date' on the 'White House's accusations linking al-Qaeda and Iraq' (CNN, 26 September 2002). However, this additional material does not really qualify as a critical comment, despite the provisional nature of the term *accusations*. Reliance on established sources of information (see Altschull, 1995) means that the basic terms used by those in authority always provide the initial impetus for discussion. During times of crisis, or national emergency, news journalists seem particularly receptive to the categories established by authoritative sources. In the initial phase of the assault on Iraq, for example, a number of terms ('weapons of mass destruction', 'regime change', 'shock and awe', etc.), supplied the *referential alibis*[2] which provided the basis for news reports in the US and UK.

REPEAT AFTER ME: IRAQ HAS WMD

Within the repertoire of practices available to political leaders, one technique is therefore the simple production of an overwhelming *number* of preferred references, in order that these become the standard categories or markers for debate. So, in presenting a public case for war in 2002 and 2003, both US and UK political executives emphasised the notion that the Hussein regime possessed 'weapons of mass destruction'. The existence of such munitions as a verifiable category is of course not in doubt: Britain and America, for example, have this capability, certainly with regard to nuclear weaponry. It was the *attribution* of the ownership of WMD to the Iraqi state that provided the simple pre-condition for a series of references to the dangers of such weapons – before the onset of hostilities they could be presented as grounds for military action, and during the fighting as a threat which revealed the truly reprehensible character of the enemy.[3] Challenged about WMD in an ITV interview (when it seemed clear that they would never be found), G.W. Bush retreated further from established standards of proof when he argued that 'he [Saddam Hussein] had weapons' (*Breakfast with Frost*, ITV, 16 November 2003). Since it was indeed the case that the Iraqi dictator possessed some munitions, Bush argued triumphantly that Hussein had 'to disarm something' (*ibid*). The US president ended by diluting his argument to the thinnest consistency, departing from the third person to utter a remark which made no sense, even if Saddam Hussein had suddenly materialised in the room: looking at the interviewer, Bush voiced a dramatic command to 'dismantle your programmes' (*ibid*).

So, even at this stage, authoritative sources were able to refer to an *established category* as though it had not only an actual referent in a material universe of solid objects, but also a physical location within a rogue state. The primary goal of US policy appeared to be the promotion of the concept of war as an appropriate response to an intolerable fact (an enemy's possession of WMD), while eventually adjusting other descriptive categories to take account of a perceived divergence between the (extra-discursive) reality of 'failure' in Iraq, and a (discursive) rhetoric of reconstruction and democratic attainment. When it emerged that the US government had offered a financial reward for discovering the weapons, one writer remarked that the Americans seemed to be running 'a competition with a prize for those who locate a reason for the war' (Žižek, 2004: 181).

Just as the flexible category 'weapons of mass destruction' lost – if it was ever intended to possess – explanatory force once its 'real-world' nuclear, chemical and biological referents proved elusive, so US rhetoricians had to alter and eventually abandon the referential value of various terms (terror, war, democracy, freedom) in order to defend a more fundamental notion. This was the idea that the safety or physical survival of American citizens depends upon an interventionist foreign policy: the basic notion was, if 'we' don't fight our enemies on their own turf, they will come here. In other words, if an implacable enemy is left alone he/she will take advantage of western vulnerability. This, in turn, disguised an equally doubtful proposition: that such interventionism would help to secure the geo-political status of the US as the world's unrivalled military 'superpower'.

STRUCTURAL SUBSERVIENCE AND HIERARCHICAL DIFFUSION

The existence of hierarchical *diffusion*, of agenda-setting from the top down, is present throughout all the communicative structures of contemporary organisations and is a feature of modern neo-liberal and state-collectivist societies alike. Irrespective of precise conditions, meaning appears to flow 'from existing institutions ... to the mass media, not vice versa' (Jensen, 1995: 61). This situation is the consequence of established relationships of power, played out within the institutional spaces that various actors and organisations occupy.[4]

The structural subservience of media to the state has reinforced the idea that they constitute 'a system for communicating messages and symbols to the general populace' (Chomsky and Herman, 1988: 166). This position is justified in positing a linear process of communication, from source to audience via media. There are two problems here, however: first, that web-based content is proving difficult to regulate and therefore is not necessarily subjugated in the same way as older forms; and second, that this model of power uses the hierarchical transmission of content as evidence that certain values are being promoted, ideas that will 'integrate' people into the institutional structures of the social order (Chomsky and Herman, 1988: 166). Such theories may, at first sight, appear to offer only a crude account of the general reproduction of power in society. Yet, if 'media are called upon to play multiple roles', it is at 'moments of crisis that the dimension of these roles takes on its full meaning' (Raboy and Dagenais, 1992: 120). In other words, the transmission thesis can be tested not only as a general proposition, but as a *system* that comes into its own during periods of 'emergency' (manufactured or otherwise).

In the midst of confusion and uncertainty, TV reports in particular often rely on official depictions (both visual and linguistic) of military action. During the first reports of a missile attack on Baghdad (represented as a strike against the person of Saddam Hussein himself), news organisations had to acknowledge that their previous expectations (of, for example, 'a devastating two-day shock and awe' [ITV news, 8.54 a.m., 19 March 2003]), were in need of revision. Dependent on the descriptive language used by one powerful faction within the US state, reporters discovered that a new representation of the opening salvoes had appeared. The phrase 'a target of opportunity' began to emerge; the question was to what degree this represented an 'official' change and how it might signify a departure from previously established plans.

On 20 March 2003, the studio presenter in ITV's newsroom sought clarification from Neil Connery, the correspondent in the Iraqi capital. Over a rather static live shot of an early morning in Baghdad, the presenter remarked that this is 'clearly not at the moment a city under attack'. Connery confirmed this perception, adding that:

> This isn't playing out how we all thought it would (.) eerm (.) the (.) the talk of shock and awe (.) eerm (.) we all expected to (.) to get underway straight from the beginning (.) eerm (.) of course these are very early stages as I look out from my hotel balcony now I can see a couple of taxis going along the road it's very (.) very quiet here (.) yesterday this city was effectively like a ghost town John... (ITV News, 4.21 a.m., 20 March 2003)

The footage from the capital was used as a form of *visual evidence* to verify the perception that the city was not under the kind of attack outlined in advance by the American military. There is a vital distinction here between the term 'shock and awe' and the journalist's more cautious reference to 'the *talk* of shock and awe', indicating a basic feature of language use. There is always a process of readjustment when descriptive categories do not match other forms of symbolic evidence (pictures of the scene, testimony of 'witnesses', reports from the military, etc.). Once the original expectation had been undermined, two alternative perceptions were possible: first, that the adjustment was justified as an attempt to take account of a new state of affairs; second, that all descriptions previously offered by those in authority were either flawed or intentionally misleading.

In the news broadcast outlined above, the journalist and the presenter attempted to draw out possible meanings based on uncertain evidence. A short excerpt of videotape was interspersed with this 'relay of words and looks' between the two inhabitants of what Morse calls an 'intradiscursive space', a privileged location in which anchors, reporters and commentators speak amongst themselves and are also able to address implied viewers (Morse, 1985: 6). In further, more developed bulletins, reports of the attack on Baghdad were supplemented with official material:

> This is the cruise missile attack (.) a Pentagon video I'm told now (1) this was how the attack began at quarter to three in the morning our time I should point out that erm this film we've put on a loop (.) just to keep showing it (.) it's a very short shot (.) this is the missile (.) we're repeating the shot of it being fired (.) while we're looking at it I'd like to bring in Adrian Britten our correspondent in Washington. (ITV News, 4.21 a.m., 20 March 2003)

The journalist is careful to explain that the film shown was 'on a loop', because the visual effect seemed to be of multiple launches where in fact there was only one; this demonstrates an attachment to *technical accuracy*, while the larger question of truth causes greater difficulty within the course of the bulletin. The reporter in America was then introduced to confirm recent developments, and was questioned by the journalist in Britain:

> Are you able to (.) to eer back up what we've eer read on the wires here in London that eer unidentified officials eer in America *have* confirmed that eer this attack was not the opening of the massive rain of cruise missiles and bombs eer that we were expecting to launch this campaign (.) that it *was* a limited attack?

> Yes certainly unidentified officials are saying that there was (.) what they're putting *a target of opportunity* and this was very recent intelligence information.

The viewer was left with a strange kind of certainty: that there has been *a confirmation that this attack should be interpreted in a certain way*, and that the source of this confirmation cannot be identified or called to account. This tendency has always existed in news reporting and emerges from the need to appear authoritative while at the same time providing a point of identification for audiences. This dual requirement can be embodied in individual news anchors or presenters, but must also be reflected in visual and linguistic codes. McQuire, referring to cinema, argues that it offers the viewer 'axes of identification and structures of coherence' (McQuire, 1998: 65). News attempts to provide a similar sense of orientation for its audience, offering a spatial and political location from which to understand the discourses presented. With so many examples available, it is hardly surprising that the propagandistic and rhetorical character of political discourse produced during the 'war on terror', together with its recapitulation in news stories,[5] continues to form the basis for an important strand of academic enquiry (Lazuka, 2006).

THE POWER OF TERMINOLOGY

In most academic analyses, the relationship between the political executive and media operatives provides an important focus for understanding how a public agenda is created. So, for example, in paying attention to the concept of war as the 'decisive expression' in articulating a public response to the 9/11 attacks, Montgomery draws attention to 'the interface between journalism and significant public figures' (Montgomery, 2005: 239). The reference to 'significant public figures' shows that this is not an attempt to nominate the ruling political alliance as a cohesive class, though it does suggest the hierarchical character of the association between leaders and mediators.

Montgomery's central argument, however, is that 'war' *as a term* re-organised the 'discursive fields' mapped out in response to 9/11, leading the entire debate in 'a fateful direction' (Montgomery, 2005: 239). There is no doubt that a very determined repetition of key terms and phrases was initiated by an executive authority and taken up by media organisations. While it may be true that 'other expressions' could have provided what Montgomery calls 'competing currencies of description', and that '*war* quickly came to dominate public discourse', it is doubtful that the term itself came 'ultimately thereby to dominate events' (*ibid*).

In the sense used by Montgomery, an event is presumably a phenomenon that has a practical character, one that can be described through some form of symbolic interpretation – the alternative 'currencies of description' he mentions. If events do have some formal independence from language (and especially from the propagandistic declarations made by executive power), then the question is to what degree they can be 'determined' by symbolic intervention.

A strict interpretation of this position would lead to the conclusion that an actual war could be started as a result of language use alone, or at least, as Montgomery puts it, that 'rhetoric paved the way to a literal war' (Montgomery, 2005: 239).

This might suggest not only that an agenda can achieve dominance through cumulative circulation ('discursive amplification', in Montgomery's words), but that such discourses were the primary cause for the material initiation of war. Too much emphasis, perhaps, is placed on *public* communication, when it should be clear that the mobilisation of armed force through military orders, an institutional practice that is not reproduced in public, would be the decisive factor in making war a practical reality.

The view that a 'rhetoric of terror' (the *public* depiction of a particular condition) has been used as 'a tool in the management ... of state hegemony' (Lewis, 2005: 23) provides another example of the belief that rhetoric is central to the reproduction of social effect. While bourgeois politicians retain the right to initiate action (e.g., pass laws or announce policies) and, as argued above, to provide forms of *explanation* for the decisions they have made, the power of public language is nonetheless limited. No linguistic category can retain a uniform ability to dominate a perceptual field (see the Conclusion). The *withdrawal* signalled within the British establishment, from their previous commitment to the term 'war on terror', shows an awareness of this problem.

REDUNDANT AND PROVISIONAL EXPLANATION

In the opening phases of the war on Iraq, the Pentagon represented its initial bombardment of Baghdad as designed to produce 'shock and awe', a demonstration of air power intended to convince the Hussein regime that it faced 'overwhelming force'. Yet, as we have seen, once the attack was underway, reports began to indicate that the air campaign was less than devastating. As a result, the notion of a 'precision strike' started to circulate. Similarly, in describing the aftermath of the invasion of Iraq, Bennis notes that 'President Bush exulted that the administration had "found the weapons of mass destruction"' and that this 'triumphant claim quickly took over headlines across the country and around the world' (Bennis, 2007: 208). Prados draws attention to a theme that arose quickly after the September 11th attacks but has been little used since; this was the supposed resemblance between the destruction of the Twin

Towers and the Japanese assault on Pearl Harbor in 1941 (Prados, 2004: 325).

The difference between these two examples of categorical utterance (on WMD and Pearl Harbor) is easy to identify. In the first case, the term used had, initially at least, an apparently stronger connection with material-symbolic reality, in the sense that such destructive weapons certainly do exist and WMD remained a flexible category composed of multiple elements (Price, 2007). The second example was an attempted comparison between two acts, designed to transfer the moral outrage associated with the earlier to the later event and, by implication, to reanimate an established theme (Barker, 1989). This theme is the moral superiority ascribed to the Allied powers in the Second World War. The notion that the US government had known about the Pearl Harbor strike in advance, and the uncomfortable parallel this suggested with the conspiracy theories surrounding the 9/11 attacks, may however have made the authorities reluctant to pursue the comparison.

For those in positions of *executive* authority the struggle over the depiction of events is intimately connected to the maintenance of a dominant political stance. This does not mean that formal utterances ensure successful reception, or that all official sources speak with the same voice; uncertain effects and divergence in opinion are inevitable in a system composed of competing centres of authority (see the Introduction). It is worth noting, however, that collaboration between state and private agencies has been another notable feature of the narrative composition of the 'war on terror'.[6]

An early report described how the US government used scriptwriters and producers in an attempt to imagine the circumstances under which the 'terror wars' might be fought. A joint discussion group at the University of Southern California, for example, used the expertise of film-makers (including the screenwriter of *Die Hard*) to offer the military assistance with tactical planning, including 'understanding plot and character ... [and] advice on "scenario training"' (Lister, 10 October 2001).[7] The production of a scenario is, as I argued in the Introduction, an increasingly salient feature of the security state.[8]

The attempt to give life to a particular interpretation of events is not helped, however, by the inability of factions within government to agree on how major trends should be described. Chapter 1 gives an example of the argument over the Iraq 'surge', but conflicting labels were also applied to the internecine conflict in Iraq before the surge took place, when the category 'civil war' began to appear in the media. Leading elements in the US administration were reluctant to admit that the 'coalition' had lost control of the country, while others regarded this admission as an essential step towards implementing a new policy.

This was not, therefore, simply some quibble over the technical accuracy of the term, because a great deal of economic and political investment was at stake. President Bush, speaking in a radio address in September 2006, argued that 'our commanders and diplomats on the ground believe that Iraq has not descended into a civil war', despite the publication the day before of a Pentagon report which noted that 'death squads and terrorists are locked in mutually reinforcing cycles of sectarian strife' and discussed the possibility of civil war in Iraq (Harris, 3 September 2006).

The designation of the conflict as a 'civil war' may, of course, have proved premature, but the fact that the US executive recognised this description as a challenge, demonstrates the degree to which referential language use[9] can run counter to the interests of ruling alliances. This 'mutation' of linguistic categories (Semin and Fiedler, 1992) can, however, be presented by political leaders as a process of natural adjustment, in which descriptive language, tested in everyday use, reflects changed perceptions or circumstances. According to this model of representation, the alteration of terms is explained as a necessary adjustment, in which description has to 'catch up' with a reality that would otherwise begin to slip away from accurate assessment.

THE MEDIA AND *STRUCTURAL COMPLICITY*

For their part, media forms have been accused of being 'implicated in the political activities of the terrorist organisation' (Lewis, 2005: 25). This position is the mirror image of the long-standing observation that the western media have taken on, or at least unintentionally reproduce, the ideological functions of the state (Gerbner, 1992: 96). Whereas the state's interventions are usually thought to assume the form of manipulative language, the terrorist agenda is assumed to be spread by emotive images. In fact, both these forces are able to use either form. The British state, for example, was able to mobilise an armed 'demonstration' at Heathrow in 2003 (Price, 2008), and the Islamist cause has been promoted through simple terms like 'jihad', which everyone across the globe has come to (mis)understand.

The whole media-terror scenario, in which the goals of the insurgent are passed on through news reports, seems to depend on accepting the notion that some form of sense-impression (fear, wonder, even fascination) is inevitably reproduced by the mediated account of a terrorist event. This is not to deny the oft-repeated observation that the western news media seemed to dwell endlessly on the collapse of the World Trade Center, but rather to argue that emotional response is too readily associated with the symbolic 'victory' of the insurgent. Too often, the attack on the Twin Towers is used as the paradigm, which has given the impression that the terrorist enemy is considerably more powerful than it is.

When Blondheim and Liebes argue that the 'instigators of the disaster' (the terrorists who carry out an attack) 'may well have the modus operandi of journalists in mind' (Blondheim and Liebes, 2003: 187), such an awareness must also apply to the other side in the conflict. The 'terrorist' group promotes its activities as a legitimate form of resistance (directed against military and civilian targets, in the belief that both sustain their enemies), while the western state tries to reinforce the proposition that the threat faced (by the public and the soldiers fighting 'on behalf' of the people), is primarily terroristic. It is this – a shared awareness of the media's significance in circulating rival perspectives – which ensures that the 'media are built into the design of any political event, war, or terror attack' (Hoskins and O'Loughlin, 2007: 3).

Arguing, however, that the media may have entered into an 'inadvertent covenant with terror' (Blondheim and Liebes, 2003: 187), excludes the role of the representational/coercive apparatus of the state. The implication seems to be that an unofficial complicity has developed between media and terror-networks, and that this, rather than the compact with executive authority, is of most significance. Blondheim and Liebes are not alone in this belief. Two other authors entertain the 'possibility that "journalists do terrorists'" work' (Hoskins and O'Loughlin, 2007: 16). Both sets of commentators seem to present the terrorist threat as a symbolic force and television/media as the handmaidens of terror. The difference lies in the emphasis placed on structure (see below). Hoskins and O'Loughlin believe that, since 'terrorism is ... a communicative act', it must follow that 'television becomes weaponised' (*ibid*). It does not seem clear how this weapon operates, who its targets might be, or whether psychological or symbolic ammunition alone will have sufficient effect. The point is that terrorism is not simply 'communicative' but also physically destructive; it is practical as well as representational.

Blondheim and Liebes are also clearly dissatisfied with the conduct of the media, arguing that television (presumably as an institution) should conduct 'a careful review ... of its ethics and standards' in order to 'diminish the incentives for the ruthless to engage in violence in order to reap the fruits of media coverage' (Blondheim and Liebes, 2003: 196). The 'ruthless' here are the terrorists, not any other armed collective. Hoskins and O'Loughlin weigh in by calling for 'proportionate, substantiated, and contextualised reporting' (Hoskins and O'Loughlin, 2007: 16) and end their study by noting that 'understanding how viewers respond' to the media environment is a 'critical issue' (ibid: 192). They regard an appreciation of the audience as important because it requires 'an interdisciplinarity from academics and their critical engagement with policy practitioners attempting to "order" the War on Terror' (ibid). In other words, the viewer is simply the object of expert attention, the point of which is not to discover or help to articulate any independent voice, but rather to enable the media analyst to make an impression on those who really wield influence. There is no indication, in this excerpt at least, that the prosecution of the 'war on terror' has produced any negative consequences for the public.

The position taken by these essentially conformist critics stands in marked contrast to the radical perspective current in the earlier phase of critical media analysis, when 'professional newsmaking' was regarded as 'not so much like an accidental congruence with dominant values but more like open complicity with the state' (Goulden et al., 1982: 72). The essential question is how forms of collusion in general (between media, state, insurgent and citizen) should be conceived. What, for example, does it mean to claim that 'television ... [enters into a] triangular covenant with the stagers [of terror] and the public' (Blondheim and Liebes, 2003: 196)? The assertion that media forms 'had no choice but to play the game set up for them by the likes of bin Laden' (ibid) might also acknowledge the fact that bin Laden learned the rules of the game in an arena organised by the Americans. Blondheim and Liebes argue that the media promote the terrorist message because they are obliged to observe three forms of constraint: i) 'technological capabilities', which means that the transmission of live material is so highly valued it bypasses editorial control; ii) 'economic pressures', that force each channel to try to outdo their competitors; and iii), their own 'professional ethos', which makes 'comprehensive surveillance of the environment' an obligation (*ibid*: 187).

The negative outcome of these constraints, in the opinion of these authors, is 'anxiety and vulnerability' (*ibid*). Leaving aside the questionable notion that the routine transmission of the terror narrative leads always to genuine fear, the idea of an unintentional 'covenant' between media and terror can be extended into a more developed theory of *structural complicity*. Rather than argue that the media are to blame for spreading terror, it might be better to ask which goals are shared by media organisations, the state and the insurgency – if we accept for the moment that these aims are played out within the complex arena known as 'media space' (Couldry and McCarthy, 2004).

The universal aspirations of each of these three centres of influence are to maintain a viable structure, to secure forms of attention, to propagate core values and to reduce the influence of (rather than necessarily to destroy) any competitor inhabiting the same field of operation. So, when a particular media channel tries to be 'first with the news' this may lead its executives to reproduce a significant event simply in order to maintain the company's profile. Armed combatants, meanwhile, may attempt to force their narrative or event into pole position, but not without trying to ensure that the moral alibi chosen for their behaviour is understood; if an armed group is involved in an act that seems to undermine the logic of its position, then the incident must be repudiated or justified, or made the subject of an enquiry. These relationships between structures do not mean that every aspect of their association is necessarily of the same kind. So, for example, it should not suggest that, where one form of interest coincides with another, the reason is simply some failure in moral discrimination.

OPPOSITIONAL MEDIA? THE CASE OF CHANNEL 4

When the political values of a media organisation appear to lie outside the mainstream, yet its practical development remains firmly tied to existing institutional structures, its survival as a forum for alternative views is not guaranteed. At its inception, Channel 4 presented a genuine opportunity for the production of a consistent critical perspective. Yet some critics believed from the beginning that the only worthwhile test of its independence was to ask if it could mount a serious opposition to the state itself. 'Given its much vaunted innovative and mould-breaking specifications', one group of academics asked, 'is the Channel any use for naturalising, not state but oppositional/alternative popular consciousness, and can it discipline that state?' (Goulden et al., 1982: 72).

Naturalisation, as it is used by these authors, is the process of making certain values the unquestioned norm within an institution or social order; yet the whole idea that the hierarchical structures and practices associated with television news could have created an alternative consciousness may itself have confused the existence of an unconventional discursive perspective with the ability to generate alternative centres of power. Unless the recipients of this discourse could build their own autonomous organisations, or at least space within the institutions they already occupied, the struggle to make the state accountable would remain a near impossible task. Yet Goulden and her co-authors realised perhaps that it was exactly the stark contrast between their critique and the actual character of the new institution that would provide an assessment of its future role.

'Unconventional' systems of representation need to break their dependence on authoritative sources, and in this case the organisation had no political or economic autonomy. The prospect of a fresh approach, based on a progressive remit, might therefore have misled some early enthusiasts, who did not perhaps recognise the ways in which the goal of cultural diversity would be associated with the aims of entrepreneurial capital. While the left focused on the relationship between Channel 4 and established authority, an ostensibly 'progressive' form of capital-interest, in alliance with government functionaries and media managers, pursued a commercial objective, and did so within a formally regulated environment.

Once the influence of a coherent leftism had dissipated, the spirit of innovation associated with Channel 4 mutated into a less exalted form of endeavour – the pursuit of novelty. One symptom of this tendency was the production of spectacle, the culmination of which was Endemol's manipulative psycho-drama *Big Brother*. Nonetheless, it appears that the Channel's principle of critical scepticism did survive within the news format, partly because an in-depth, hour-long bulletin had been established as a principle (Hobson, 2008: 103). The institutional structure that supported this venture suggested, however, a preference for established forms of production. Initial misgivings about the decision to commission ITN as the body that supplied news for Channel 4 were based on Independent Television's time-honoured and supposedly conformist practices. In his critique of this development, published in 1982,

Lambert drew attention to the ways in which ITN had been endorsed by powerful ruling interests. He notes that 'the question of who would supply Channel 4 with its news service was a virtual *fait accompli*', achieved through a series of manoeuvres carried out by the IBA and its Conservative allies such as William Whitelaw (Lambert, 1982: 135).

Roger Graef, a Channel 4 board member, believed that 'we were under instruction to work with ITN from the IBA and even to a certain extent from Parliament', and spoke of 'State political reasons' (Graef refers to both parliament and the executive) for the preference shown to Independent Television (cited in Hobson, 2008: 104). The point of this intervention was to secure the production of 'mainstream' journalism. Despite this inevitable limitation, Channel 4 news has managed to reinforce the interrogative tradition represented in other forms by, for example, the BBC's *Today* programme. The Channel's chief correspondents, including Jon Snow, Alex Thomson, Samira Ahmed and Krishnan Guru-Murthy, have made a number of notable attacks, if not on the 'state' itself, then on government representatives, employing the interview form to challenge official alibis. In addition, the tenor of reports has offered a much more distinctive position than the corporate consciousness displayed in mainstream BBC news, yet they do not represent a complete departure from the institutional techniques evident in the BBC *Today* radio programme, or BBC 2's *Newsnight*. Nonetheless, the radical potential of a group of journalists organised within the paradigm of an investigative frame can produce some remarkable results. Take, for instance, Alex Thomson's opening remarks in a report on the US attack on the 'insurgent stronghold' of Fallujah, in 2004. They offer a radical perspective, drawing attention to Thomson's belief that there was a serious deficiency in the entire process of mediation: 'the world is watching a one-sided fight *and a one-sided view of it*. No pictures today from the insurgent side of the battle of Fallujah' (Channel 4 News, 9 November 2004). The delivery of such a statement would be almost unimaginable on many other news channels, because there would be no sense that an 'enemy' needed any form of representation.

9/11: TRANSCRIPT OF CHANNEL 4'S COVERAGE

Despite its ability to offer an alternative agenda, there is evidence that, depending on the magnitude of the event under scrutiny, Channel 4 shares an essential attribute of any news organisation:

the need to make sense of material which may, at least initially, be difficult to analyse. In such cases, the existing values of the social order will be mobilised, and brought into an expressive conjunction with the temperament of the journalist. This was the case on the morning of the 9/11 attacks. The transcript below is taken from Channel 4's news broadcast of 11 September 2001, covering the brief period of time between the collapse of the first and second towers of the World Trade Center.

There are a number of features that attest to the great impact of the occasion. The first element to note is that the vast majority of the broadcast is spent in visual contemplation of the consequences of the attacks which are, for the most part, shown live. Where the Channel uses recorded material, this is drawn to the attention of the viewer, so that he or she is aware of the transition between the representation of 'real time' and the move to sources designed to give context to the assault. Both the physical and political magnitude of the event are given detailed coverage, and are 'voiced' separately, almost as though they represent rival viewpoints; the newscaster Jon Snow, the science correspondent Julian Rush, and Channel 4's foreign correspondent, Gaby Rado, all make a contribution.

These three male commentators speak among themselves, *without the intercession of the political class*. The shock and disorientation of the attack seems to have dislocated the ability of the executive to dominate the procedures which lead to the composition of 'coherent' meaning. The speakers are designated as Jon Snow (JS), the news anchor, Julian Rush (JR) and Gaby Rado (GR). The excerpt begins with the Channel 4 logo shown in the top left of the screen, with an inset of a burning tower in New York. Julian Rush is shown in the studio, though he appears initially in a smaller inset at the bottom right of the screen. As the report progresses, whenever there is a cut away from live or recorded footage, all three contributors are shown in conversation. (Material is transcribed by the author.)

JR: It would have *ripped* right through that building and clearly (.) erm shook its eer f- to the foundations it (.) damaged the structure beyond (.) eer eer a point where it could stay up and (.) as we saw a few moments ago (.) it it collapsed in that eer extraordinarily (.) dramatic way (.) erm scattering debris all over the streets [Rush voiceover as full screen given to scene in New York] below (.) smoke everywhere (.) erm if there were casualties from the people inside the building (.) casualties from the eer eer passengers on the plane (.) there would then have been *further*

maybe hundreds of casualties (.) of the people below in the streets
the rescue workers the people trying to um get up to fight the fires
the (.) people being evacuated from the buildings around ...
JS: [voiceover] Julian Rush let let me just bring in eer Gaby Rado
here our [studio shot of Snow, Rush and Rado, shot from behind
Rush and Rado] foreign affairs correspondent now Gaby (.) eer
the the State Department is now saying that the State Department
is now being evacuated eer owing to an incident which suggests
something has happened there too (.) *this* has been (1) the the
level of coordination *defies* surely anything we know about [shot
of Rado nodding] any known terrorist group ...
GR: Absolutely extraordinary (.) and the only thing it (.) very
vaguely reminds me of ...
JS: car bomb at the State Department I'm just seeing from the
wires here [return to shot of Snow, Rado and Rush]
GR: really =
JS: car bomb =
JR: so
GR: yeah
JS: three planes (.) a car bomb coordinated attack over a space
of (.) an hour and a quarter ...

As usual in any news organisation, authoritative sources (in
this case the US State Department) are cited in order to provide
a starting-point for further discussion, yet this only provides
information that the State Department itself is being evacuated.
During the crisis itself, formal centres of authority appeared to
have no clear conception of the overall meaning of the incident and
seemed in many cases to *disappear* from the mediated realm. The
discourse produced by Rush, in his role as science correspondent,
is characterised not by a political re-conception of what the attack
might signify, but instead by a *practical* or technical assessment of
how the physical structure was destroyed, together with speculation
about the number of casualties. Snow introduces the expertise of
the Foreign Affairs editor to provide this missing political analysis,
though again it is free from the rhetorical miasma that pervades the
airwaves whenever a politician begins to speak. At the point at which
Snow announces (erroneously) that a car bomb has exploded, Gaby
Rado speculates on the origin of the attack, before the group as a
whole take up this point in discussion. It is worth noting that, even
at this early stage, Rado raises the idea that al-Qaeda is responsible
for the attack.

GR: [shot of burning tower] I suppose the very first suspicion has got to (.) has got to be on the the Osama bin Laden *led* eer group of eer of terrorist organisations erm [close up on top of burning tower]
JS: But there is a claim from the Palestinians
GR: There is a yes from the Democratic Front for the Liberation of Palestine ...

At this point, a discussion follows, in which the DFLP claim is regarded as only a weak possibility, before Jon Snow changes the topic and focus, and uses another staple of the news organisation – reference to eye-witness reports. Ordinary individuals are usually quite low in the formal hierarchy of sources but, in any significant case like the 9/11 attacks, the public offers an essential insight into 'actuality':

JS: Let's eer eer now just break away for a moment from these live pictures of the World Trade Center still ablaze the one lone tower left the other has already collapsed (.) let us now turn then to some reaction from eye-witnesses in New York itself ...

Here, Snow clearly *prepares* the audience and *liaises* with his editors in order to introduce a pre-recorded US TV report, featuring an eyewitness speaker, who describes his attempts to assist the victims: he is shown in streets covered with clouds of thick white dust from the fallen tower. Suddenly, Snow draws his viewers' attention back to the present and the immediate:

JS: -s now from the world c- the World Trade Center the second tower is collapsing [live shots of tower collapsing and scene from street level] (.) eer this (.) smoke is now all that is left (.) of the (1) *extraordinary* and fine and gorgeous beautiful sumptuous buildings that were the World Trade Center (.) they have gone (.) both towers destroyed (.) in a terrorist attack (.) launched by air (.) by hijacked planes one of which a major passenger (.) passenger airliner hijacked from Boston the other an apparently smaller (.) plane (.) which hit the second tower eighteen minutes later (.) all this nine o'clock Washington time two o'clock (.) London time (.) a pall of smoke is all that's left (.) of (.) one of the greatest trading centres in the world (.) the World Trade Center (.) one hundred and ten stories eer an *absolute* world landmark (.) in an age of new building this would be regarded as one of the seven wonders of the world the (.) World Trade Center and it is no more for (.) more than a decade it has defined the skyline of downtown New York (.) it has (.) marked etched upon the world's consciousness the (.) financial power of (.) New York (.) of the United States and (.) the global reach (.) of this extraordinary society and this is a *devastating* assault upon its very soul (5) let us now return to those (.) eer shots of the f- the *main* tower (.) the last remaining tower (.) this is in slow motion you will see *this* eer great (.) totem of financial power (.) collapsing before our eyes *this* is the most *wou::nding* possible assault on the American psyche (.) and it's something that will fill the rest of (.) civilised mankind (.) with a great foreboding that we are launched upon a terrible era in international politics (.) no longer the great world wars of (.) times gone by but the representation and here you see the consequence of terrorist attack ...

This extraordinary passage is marked by Snow's highly aestheticised account of the appearance of the Twin Towers ('*extraordinary* and fine and gorgeous beautiful sumptuous buildings'), which creates a contrast between their previous condition and the state to which they have been reduced. This perspective runs alongside the provision of 'essential' information (time of impact, number of planes, etc.), which both fulfils the need to observe basic journalistic responsibility to provide hard facts, and acts as a tonal counterpoint to the flights of descriptive eloquence. In the days that followed, the emphasis on the World Trade Center's visual magnificence was repeated, and in some cases acquired a sexual or romantic overtone.[10] Snow continues to concentrate on the architectural impact of the buildings, observing that 'in an age of new building this would be regarded as one of the seven wonders of the world'.

He moves from a description of the Towers' iconic appearance to discuss the commercial power they represented. The World Trade Center had 'defined the skyline of downtown New York' but had also 'etched upon the world's consciousness the financial power of ... the United States and the global reach of this extraordinary society'. The attack, as Snow describes it, was 'a *devastating* assault upon its very soul' and 'the most *wou::nding* possible assault on the American psyche'. The ability of the electronic media to recapitulate the event is brought to the fore, as the journalist confirms that 'this is in slow motion' and tells the observer that 'you will see *this* eer great totem of financial power collapsing before our eyes'.

In the course of the report, it is clear that the images of the attack and the commentaries that accompany it do not, certainly at this stage, amount to the circulation of a terrorist manifesto, in the sense proposed by Blondheim and Liebes, or by Hoskins and O'Loughlin: yet, if the media are complicit in the event, it is as shocked observers, in awe of an act that is powerful not only because of its scale, but because they have to search for an explanation that is not offered by its perpetrators. Rush's contribution, which is made as the slow-motion scene is repeated, is again more technical than Snow's because Rush must fulfil his role as scientific commentator, drawing attention to the way in which the structure collapses because of the 'tremendous heat of the fire':

> JR: What you're seeing there John is the (.) top section of the (.) tower collapsing down (1) and almost taking with it (.) the tower below (1) that first that was the tower that was hit first (.) it was hit (.) *fairly* near the top it looks like it was hit some (.) ninety stories up of the hundred and ten *hundred and twenty* stories of the (.) the tower but (.) the fire had obviously burnt its way through the structure (1) the concrete and the steel erm finally eer succumbed to the tremendous heat of the (.) fire that was raging inside over (.) ten floors inside the tower ...

This practical, level-headed analysis of the physical character of the event, is addressed to Snow, though it is clearly enacted within a performative space that serves the *communal* rubric of explanation, a form of reappraisal or 'talking through' that offers a *public* account of technical matters which, in the absence of a political/ moral narrative, assumes greater importance in the production of understanding. It stands in contrast to Snow's response, which starts as soon as Rush finishes speaking, and begins to address some of the themes that are later replicated in press reports, including those references to popular culture and film which were to become so familiar. The journalists themselves are positioned by circumstance as (under-informed) spectators, and in this respect share some of the limited perspectives of the viewers. The difference is that they have access to official sources that are able to provide certain types of information, which is then relayed to the audience:

> JS: Nobody has ever (.) *dared* do this even in fictional celluloid (.) this is eer New York as no-one ever ever ever even *feared* to see it (.) this is eer (.) a truly devastating assault on an absolutely

humungous scale it is the (.) gravest single terrorist assault
anywhere in the history of (.) of mankind
JR: There there's a scene from the f- ground I think as the (.)
the second tower comes down (.) you see the (.) firemen the (.)
running for their lives away from the falling debris ...

The point at which Snow declares that 'Nobody has ever *dared* do
this even in fictional celluloid' testifies to the conceptual magnitude
of the attack, and provides one of the earliest 'everyday' references
to the relationship between the terrorist mentality and the dominant
'imaginary' of violent dissolution. While cinematic forms had not
anticipated the full extent of the destruction, they had circulated a
scenario of terror in which the 'terrorist action' could be understood.
Snow reinforces the *standard* definition of terrorism as a type of
activity produced by 'non-state' actors, when he appraises this attack
as 'the gravest single terrorist assault anywhere in the history of
mankind': in the heat of the moment, the sense that this event might
be compared to, for example, the effects of officially sanctioned
saturation bombing, never appears on the agenda.

CHANNEL 4 AND THE IRAQ WAR

The interaction between journalists described above may have
contained some surprising elements, in the sense that particular
emphasis is placed on the aesthetic qualities of the buildings, and on
a series of technical assessments: the expectation might have been
that the larger part of the exchange would have been devoted to the
question of casualties. Nonetheless, this was not controversial at
the time, because images of deaths were unavailable, and because
the bulletin was clearly a collaborative effort designed to provide
the viewer with the larger context in which the attack should be
understood. In the traditional news interview, however, when there is
no 'emergency' to describe, a journalist can return to the interrogative
role, supposedly assumed on behalf of an absent public.
  Like any institutional event, the news interview represents a
concentration of physical, economic and intellectual resources; its
format is well known to those taking part and those who form the
audience, and includes the 'external' social and political position of
participants, and the setting in which the event occurs. The televised
interview exemplifies the 'multidimensional' character of the media,
at once 'resolutely material', and at the same time seemingly removed
from the 'material plane of existence' (Couldry and McCarthy,

2004: 2), through its appearance as a de-spatialised spectacle. While the formal setting governs content and conduct, so that departures from the broad agenda are immediately recognisable, it cannot account for all the nuances of meaning found in each momentary utterance, intonation or physical behaviour.

Heritage notes that the individual roles assumed in everyday conversation may shift during the course of an exchange, while the positions taken in news interviews are determined by 'pre-established ... institutional identities' (Heritage, 1985: 99). These institutional identities depend, in turn, on the various forms of subjectivity that are inculcated by the wider culture as a whole. The provision of airtime to interviewees represents what Heritage calls an 'antecedent decision', taken in the belief that the individual concerned has 'some personal experience ... or opinion that is newsworthy' (*ibid*: 99). The 'decision' is antecedent because it acts as an established principle, one that predates the speech event, and should be understood as part of the structural architecture that informs the exchange.

INTERVIEWS: TACTICAL DISCOURSES

The formal interview is thus usually conducted as a series of questions, put by the journalist or presenter to a politician, ostensibly as a vital part of the interrogative mode of the democratic order. The interviewer is not therefore meant to introduce his or her own preoccupations, or reproduce the agenda of a news organisation. Such immoderate behaviours are seized upon by the political class, on the grounds that politicians are more truly representative of the public will than journalists, since the latter have not been elected to office. The politician may also attempt to justify his or her position through reference to the integrity of a particular outlook or ideology, and might try to represent the interlocutor (the journalist putting the questions) as unreasonably interested in sensationalism. One example occurred during a live interview with Adam Ingram, Home Office Minister, broadcast on Channel 4 News, at 7.20 p.m. on 27 March 2003.

The context of this exchange was the statement made by Prime Minister Blair, earlier the same day, that two British soldiers, killed in Iraq on 23 March 2003, had in fact been executed by the Iraqi military. Footage of the bodies of these two men had been shown on al-Jazeera television news, which had caused British and American spokespersons to condemn both the nature of the report, and the execution that was thought to have taken place:

> JS: well now the armed forces minister Adam Ingram is at Westminster eer Minister the eer alleged ac- eer assassination or execution of these eer British (.) soldiers erm (.) what do you know about it? ...

In this case, Snow's introduction is rather laboured, characterised by some hesitation and mistakes, such as the moment where, thinking ahead, he appears to combine 'assassination' and 'execution' in the aborted word beginning 'ac'. The question 'what do you know about it?' looks like a simple request for further information, but also constitutes a challenge for Ingram to give an account of the controversy itself. Asking an individual what they know about an incident may produce, however, a rather perfunctory response, because it can be taken as a request to provide one's personal knowledge, which may be presented as limited or non-existent. Ingram's tactic is to represent the heart of the problem, not as linked to Blair's obsession with soundbites, but as the consequence of inappropriate behaviour by the media in general:

> AI: well what I'm going to say to you John is is very simply this that eer (.) it's easy to dress this up as some sort of drama (.) but it's really trauma to the families who have lost their loved ones and and (.) I don't think we should eer probe ov- probe into this too too greatly eer on the news media we have a very sensitive job eer to handle in dealing with those service families (.) and remembering that tha- we we still have tens of thousands of troops out there (.) ah the point made by the Prime Minister is one which I hope (.) is is taken on board and that is (.) the depravity *of* Saddam Hussein's regime (.) it's to his own people it's to his own soldiers (.) ah and it's to our prisoners of war ah and to those eer that that the- capture and and treat them in an appalling way [=

Ingram makes it clear that he will respond to the initial ploy on his own terms, using a preparatory formula that appears to prefigure content, but in fact sets out the *conditions* for his reply ('well what I'm going to say to you John is very simply this'). Such a tactic sets limits to what will be said and also marks time, giving the speaker an opportunity to compose the answer. Ingram then attempts to avoid the specific issue of Blair's remark by shifting the moral tenor of the event, trying to substitute one topic (the propagandistic quality inherent in the term 'execution'), with another (the role of the media or journalists in turning the occasion into a 'drama'). It is this which Snow regards as a distraction, as he tries to bring the discussion back to the point:

JS: [but is ob- it is
AI: = that's why that's why we're *in* Iraq (.) because of the nature of that regime
JS: but it is obviously important to know whether they are flouting eer Geneva conventions and simply executing prisoners of war (.) or whether (.) they have simply been the eer eer the very tragic and ghastly victims of battle
AI: I don't think there's any question at all that they've flouted eer the Geneva conventions and the way in which they have they have been maltreating eer eer prisoners of war the way in which (.) that has been graphically shown on on some channels and exploited for propaganda purposes
JS: (inaudible) the pictures are absolutely ghastly but it's impossible to tell from the pictures that we've seen (.) what happened how do you know what happened?
AI: Well we have to assess this in in terms of best intelligence but I I've made my point here John and and I am *not* going to go down this road of (.) giving you great drama in in this (.) I'm more concerned more about those families and I would hope you are as well

PAXMAN STEPS UP

That evening, Ingram was interviewed about the same subject on the BBC *Newsnight* programme. His interlocutor was Jeremy Paxman. The excerpt below gives an insight into what is undoubtedly a more combative approach, an aggressive style quite alien to Channel 4's Snow, and one that has become the hallmark of journalists like Paxman. Few women working in news environments have adopted this belligerent method, and there appears to be some truth in the perception that the production of such talk can be explained as the appearance of 'social-psychological' determinants such as 'culture, gender and class membership' (Titscher et al., 2000: 155).

The question of institutional structure and the degree of autonomy it allows, addressed at the beginning of this chapter, is particularly relevant when discussing the interactions between reporters and their guests. The social-psychological dimension is, after all, the product not just of life experience in an abstract sense, but of individuals' ability to ignore, 'overcome' or deploy their embodied subjectivity (based on class, ethnicity and gender) as they progress on a career path through various organisations. Although Channel 4 may have allowed a more radical approach to the news in general, the *method* of interviewing adopted by Paxman has certain advantages within the hierarchical and largely male *structure* of television news. It depends on many of the same techniques used by Snow and his colleagues, and must rely on good background research, but this is probably less important than the implacable determination of the interviewer and, in effect, his 'masculine' belligerence. The transcript which follows does not include the first response made to Paxman by the minister:

JP: well we're joined now by the armed forces minister Adam Ingram (.) do you accept that confusion has undermined the credibility of the coalition

[Ingram's reply]

JP: (exhales) can you help us with another question on this (.) question of language (.) why did the prime minister talk about British soldiers being (.) *executed* today

AI: because that eer was the the view he adopted on the basis of the information [

JP: [does he have *evidence* =

AI: [we::ll

JP: [= that they were executed =

AI: [well I've I've

JP: [= it's a very strong term to use [=

AI: (nodding) [yes I I OK yeah

JP: [= and a powerful term an important term

AI: I think it is a powerful term and I've done a number of interviews today on this and (.) what comes immediately to *my* mind is the *families* who are grieving because of the loss of their loved ones (.) and what we're having here is some *great* analysis on on the *minutiae* of language when the *families* [

JP: [= the Prime Minister *chose* to use that term

AI: [of course he did of course he did

JP: he *justified* that term President Bush *backed* him up saying he knew what had *happened* and the term was legitimate (.) now that was a deliberate choice of language (.) *Why?*

AI: Because what it was it was also put in context and what was the context (.) that this is a regime that brutalises its own people whose (.) which is prepared to terrorise its own soldiers to fight

JP: nobody argues about any of that

AI: ah we:ll

JP: but this is a *specific* comment made by the Prime Minister in the context of the deaths of two British servicemen (.) *does* he have evidence to substantiate it

AI: I think the Prime Minister made it very clear today and eer that that eer is is is backed up by those by by the the intelligence and by the by the photographs we've seen of all this (.) plus the knowledge of that particular regime (.) it is capable of anything
[

JP: [of course it's capable of anything =[

AI: [= It's why we're there (.) well it's why we're there [

JP: [= I'm not asking about anything I'm asking about this *specific* case

AI: well I I =]

JP: [= we know this for a fact

AI: what I'm saying to you is I'm conscious of families tonight (.) that are grieving and many many thousands of families (.) proud families =[

JP: [nobody

AI: [= but worried families as well

JP: nobody denies the distress of the families concerned =

AI: [= right so so let

JP: but the use of language was the Prime Minister's =

AI: but *why?* (.) Jeremy I've I've got to say to you that that at the at the centre of all of this and in the field we try and establish *facts* (.) we try then to

JP: precisely

AI: we would then try to impart the truth (.) you're the you're part of the mechanism for that ah and ah cynicism and and constant (.) criticism

JP: I assure you there's no cynicism

AI: and the way and the way in which imbalance comes into all of this does not help the overall objective (.) of what we're trying to achieve

JP: Minister (.) thank you

Throughout this excerpt, Paxman attempts to establish Ingram's position on a controversial issue. Responding to Paxman's first question, the minister does not provide an actual defence of the 'execution' thesis; instead, he constructs a 'positional' rationalisation for Blair's stance, describing it as 'the view he adopted on the basis of the information'. In this altered version of events, the view was *taken on* rather than *produced by* Blair, a tactic designed to reduce his responsibility for the original utterance.

Challenged to give a coherent account of the incident, Ingram, under greater pressure than he was in the Channel 4 studio, tries to use the same technique (references to the grief of the dead soldiers' relatives) as a defensive strategy: 'what comes immediately to *my* mind is the *families*'. He follows this up with the accusation that the interviewer is displaying a cynical attitude, in an attempt to tap into existing perceptions of journalistic excess. In this interview, the government representative cannot sustain his earlier position for two reasons: first, because the story has undergone a significant development since the earlier exchange with Snow, and second because Jeremy Paxman did not allow him to obscure the central issue – that there was at the time of the interview no firm evidence that the British troops had been executed.[11] Eventually, in 2006, a coroner found that the two soldiers had been captured and 'unlawfully killed' by Iraqi intelligence officers, after they had been ambushed in the hostile town of Zubayr, near Basra (Judd and Sengupta, *Independent*, 3 October 2006).

4
Surveillance, Authority and Linguistic Categories

> De Menezes was an innocent man who was not acting suspiciously
> and did not run from the police ... police wrongly identified him
> as a possible suicide bomber.
>
> (ITV News, 10.30 p.m., 16 August 2005)

SURVEILLANCE AND THE REPRESENTATION OF ORDER

The power of the state to 'define, classify, segregate, separate and
select' (Bauman, 2004: 21) is achieved through practices associated
with, and generated by, acts of surveillance. The term 'surveillance'
might suggest uninterrupted, close observation, undertaken by
expert analysts for the purposes of maintaining an authoritarian
or paternalistic form of public security. This is certainly evoked by
much of the publicity surrounding the use of CCTV in particular
(Goold, 2004: 11),[1] but the reality of the condition is the exercise
of social control as a *principle*, irrespective of how technically adept
or administratively thorough the process itself may be.[2] Surveillance
in general is thus not simply a deterrent but a means of 'producing
knowledge of populations that is useful for administrating them'
(Goold, 2004: 4). This viewpoint places less importance on the
determining power of technology, and thus offers a contrast to
Ellul's perspective, which emphasises an 'orientation towards
"means" rather than "ends"' (cited in Lyon, 2007: 52).

This is not to say that the actual employment of CCTV, as one
element within a larger domain of supervision and intelligence
gathering, is not widespread and intrusive, and partly driven by
new developments in technological capability; nor that the general
availability of cameras and the possibility of web-based dissemination
does not provide a form of 'counter-surveillance' that may oppose
the practices of the security state. The argument made in this chapter
is that, while the growth of CCTV helps to provide the authorities
with 'a wealth of information about suspect populations' (Goold,

2004: 3), its reputation as an *effective* technique of control depends not only on its concrete or literal uses[3] (such as the monitoring of public space), but on the way it is promoted within a variety of public discourses.

In other words, CCTV has come to stand for or represent surveillance in general, and awareness of authoritarian control is created by a number of cultural practices which themselves emphasise visual observation and other types of monitoring. Forms of intervention include government announcements and publicity campaigns, television commercials and dramas, movies and news reports, all of which may produce layers of meaning related to, but often quite distinct from everyday encounters with the technology itself. In addition, the use of both recorded and live CCTV as a form of entertainment, helps to make the 'mediated voyeurism' of human activity a mainstream and increasingly uncontroversial experience for many viewers (Calvert, 2004: 91).[4] Of course, individual genres and texts are unlikely to produce identical messages; the point is not the similarity of their content, but the range of allusions (linguistic and/or visual) made to the pervasive existence of electronic observation.

Advertising, for example, reproduces a number of points of view relating to the existence of surveillance; these can range from ironic postures within scenarios that posit total scrutiny,[5] to narratives in which technology in general appears as a social benefit,[6] often associated with the practices of corporate social responsibility.[7] The conventions reproduced by the state, in comparison, are framed more in the terms of traditional social control, and include warnings to system-abusers and reminders of existing regulation.[8]

JOURNALISM AND SURVEILLANCE

One concern of this chapter is the role of journalism, in the sense that television news and the press 'play a central role in "representing order"' (Coleman, 2004: 219). Order here is understood not only as a moral condition, but as 'a procedural form and social hierarchy' that is both 'symbolically and visually persuasive' (Ericson et al., cited in Coleman, *ibid*). This is indeed a symbolic conception of order underpinned, in Coleman's opinion, by 'powerful and idealised visions for urban public space that have been developing under a rightward political shift' (*ibid*: 3).

The strong resemblance between those discourses devoted to the creation and maintenance of social stability has led theorists like Ericson to draw analogies between the production of news and the legal process. The usefulness of this approach lies in its understanding of the similarities between the exercise of power within commercial and state sectors. In fundamental terms, this is based on the determination of 'both state and class' to 'extract resources from the populace' (Gill, 2003: 13). Equally, the aim of commercial and governmental centres might also be described as an attempt to secure allegiance from the people, within a context in which responsibility for the 'management of risk' is moved away from the national state to 'local governments, community partnerships, and non-governmental agencies' (Garland, cited in Goold, 2004: 4).

Regarding both law and news as 'disciplinary and normalizing discourses', Ericson and his collaborators argue that they are essentially concerned with '*policing* ... as a mechanism for the moral health and improvement of the population' (Ericson et al., 1991: 7). Electronic surveillance, a form of policing framed[9] within a moral discourse, provides the visual code from which both practices are able to draw illustrative material. Reference to a 'moral' quality here is of course concerned with distinctions between right and wrong, but should also be interpreted as indicating the existence of a *normative* standard.[10] This chapter argues that media outlets often reproduce, especially at times of 'crisis', the simple techniques of negative identification generated by coercive authority. Furthermore, their use of images taken from electronic surveillance is presented as an integral component of news reports, documentaries and other forms of public discourse. The effect is the normalisation of a technique, while lending an air of veracity and drama to the convoluted issues of state and individual security.

This is not meant to suggest that the moral principles endorsed by public institutions are always necessarily hypocritical or oppressive, but rather that they represent an established state of affairs that individuals encounter without the opportunity to exercise active consent. Equally, as Pierson indicates, the 'aspiration to lawful government' should not be confused with an actual desire on the part of executive powers to 'extend democracy' (Pierson, 1996: 20). The institutional conception of democracy is, of course, at odds with the ideal that the term brings to mind. Contemporary democracy relies less on participation or partnership than on a populace 'delegating' its sovereignty 'by means of a political system of representation' (Escolar, 2003: 29).

On the individual level, however, it is through the pursuit of norms of behaviour, achieved within hierarchal relationships and reinforced by the myth of social continuity (shared histories, national values, gendered behaviours, etc.) that individuals are encouraged to monitor their own behaviour and identity. The conventional social order functions, therefore, through a form of self-assessment and self-adjustment in response to external stimuli. This becomes, in effect, a constant process of comparison between individual values, attitudes and beliefs, and external standards. 'Internal' modes of scrutiny are therefore partly composed by the external types of observation circulated within mass media forms. This externalisation includes the narrative dramatisation of situations, particularly in film, where individual subjects are shown to be under observation and the audience is given 'privileged' access to the process of tracking and recording (see Chapter 5). The viewer is thus placed within the ideological perspective of surveillance, and temporarily 'empowered' as a voyeur, while in everyday life being the unqualified victim of the entire process.

STATE POWER AND NORMATIVE STANDARDS

Gill regards the primary function of the state as the management of 'political affairs' (Gill, 2003: 3).[11] Yet, as Poulantzas notes, the state 'exhibits a peculiar material framework' that cannot be reduced to 'mere political domination' (Poulantzas, 1978a: 14).[12] In other words, there are a number of state functions that cannot be reduced to the exercise of formal political authority, such as social security (*ibid*: 13). Frankel, in attempting to clarify the special quality of state institutions, describes them as 'all those non-privately owned and non-voluntary public institutions' whether 'administrative, legal, military, educational [or] cultural' (Frankel, 1983: ix). Among the functions displayed by these organisations is the *bureaucratic* management of individual subjectivities (see Chapter 5), which represents a manifestation of class and patriarchal power revealed through the right to identify and classify the recipients of support or punishment as 'clients' or consumers. Surveillance is therefore not simply state-sponsored regulation, but is framed both as authoritarian 'care' and a mode of personal 'facilitation' within a consumer environment. In Gill's words, this suggests the existence of 'administrative capacity and coercive potential' (Gill,

2003: 15).[13] Yet, all legitimate forms of power also provide their subordinates with 'moral grounds for cooperation and obedience' (Beetham, 1991: 26).[14] Public recognition of an institution's legitimacy is thus based partly on the fact that those individuals who exercise power on behalf of an authority will seek consent 'from at least the most important of their subordinates' (Beetham, 1991: 3).[15] In everyday circumstances, however, the maintenance of the relationship between 'leaders' and the subaltern relies upon established conduits of communication.

Within the workplace and institutional life, these can be entirely internal, involving for example written edicts, work reviews, personal 'audits', verbal instructions, face-to-face discussions and management meetings. With regard to the wider social order, messages assume a number of generic forms, but in all cases they seek to establish some meaningful contact with an audience; they do so through an appropriate type of address, where address is as an attempt to animate some aspect of a recipient's subjectivity (Price, 2007: 1).

While the media do not function simply as mouthpieces for executive power, and they may, for instance, help to initiate limited forms of political action, where they do reproduce the priorities and values of dominant powers it is often through the most basic mode of intervention – the repetition of existing patterns of representation (see Chapter 2). The simplest form of this tendency is the duplication of key terms and those essentially moral classifications used for conducting routine business (Ericson et al., 1991, 8). These categories may not always coincide with those produced by executive power, and are often questioned (see Montgomery, 2005), but they do, especially in times of crisis, provide an essential framework from which subsequent reports are composed.

One example is the habitual activity of state agencies and spokespersons in sorting the population into various subjective domains, including ethnic and other divisions. Escolar describes the pre-history of this process as the 'slow build-up of a monopoly of legitimate coercion, the concentration of tax-collecting and the bureaucratic centralisation of public administration' (Escolar, 2003: 29). The whole process depends on the use of linguistic categories, definitions that are subsequently employed in order to animate larger moral associations; these include for example the association of categories like ethnicity with belief, behaviour and appearance.

SOCIAL CATEGORIES AND NEWS JOURNALISM

If it is true, in Lyon's words, that 'the people themselves are not really "seen"' in the network of practices that constitute surveillance, but instead 'yield data' (Lyon, 2007: 1), it is nonetheless the case that those individuals actually recorded on camera are fitted into pre-existing categories, *mis/identified* according to the classificatory systems employed by the state. Once individuals have been characterised in a certain way, often based on the close association of social groups with particular roles, they are then *displayed* within the narrative discourses of various news formats. This is especially the case within those processes (primarily legal) that provide a 'public interest' rationale for the generation of reports, together with ready-made binary structures such as good and evil, for journalists to reproduce.

As Ericson explains, 'the very act of classification, including disputes about misclassification, involves questions of right and wrong' (Ericson et al., 1991: 7). It is this rather blunt and mechanical process that was supposed to have produced the case of 'mistaken identity'[16] that led to the death of Jean Charles de Menezes, who was killed by armed police at Stockwell tube station in 2005. A preliminary question is therefore how exactly such conceptions, based on 'appearances', are framed, and how they are aligned with pre-existing social categories. One notable example was produced within press coverage of the failed bomb conspiracy of July 2005, during which the *Daily Express* re-animated an established theme based on the supposed conjunction between two 'negative' categories, *terrorist activity* and the process of *seeking asylum*. This produced the headline 'THEY WERE ALL SPONGING ASYLUM SEEKERS' (*Daily Express*, 27 July 2005: 1). In this instance, the established resonance of the term within the right-wing press (see Bailey and Harindranath, 2005: 274) is made explicit with the addition of the adjective 'sponging'. Certain newspapers, and not only the *Express*, had, over a period of many years, tried to turn a 'neutral' activity (seeking asylum) into a form of cynical opportunism. This established theme (Barker, 1989) was then used to provoke hostility to refugees by associating them with the would-be terrorists.

Productive analysis does not, however, depend solely on identifying the conjunction of negative identification (popularly associated with the creation of *stereotypes*)[17] and the appearance of inaccurate or oversimplified news reports. There is also the more fundamental issue of categorisation as a linguistic and social process. Categorisation is a procedure in which 'objects, events or living things' are sorted into 'a series of classes or groups' (Price, 1996: 182). It is this practice that may account for the existence of established and seemingly natural ways of describing phenomena, and which carries with it significant implications for the study of public meaning.

The point here is that each human generation inherits an order of representation that, despite inevitable mutations in language use, presents individuals with a mode of linguistic exchange that is not of their making.[18] Effective exchange within a social order depends on established agreement on the meaning of terms and references. Yet these conventional systems produce contradictions based not only on traditional interpretations of meaning, but also on the human tendency to confuse different sorts of classification. So, to take a simple but instructive example, *natural kind, human artefact* and *social* categories are often mixed up (Semin and Fiedler, 1992: 11), with the consequence that things produced by human agency are represented as a natural state of affairs.[19] Another problem lies in the existence of *mutually exclusive categories*, powerful conceptions that 'dominate the psychological field' in a way that inhibits multiple classification (Semin and Fiedler, 1992: 29). In its strongest form, this amounts to a denial that a person, event or thing can occupy more than one subject-position. So, for instance, when the value of two contrasting categories is at odds, such as those of *doctor* and *thief*, then even children as old as eight tend to claim that an individual cannot belong to both categories (see Price, 1996: 195). This sort of process was apparent in the mediated descriptions of the Stockwell shooting.

'MISCLASSIFICATION': AN EXCUSE

The circulation of the images of four men associated with attempts to set off explosions in London on 21 July 2005, based on CCTV images released by the Metropolitan police the following day, appeared in a number of media forms. National news reports followed the established practice of circulating these surveillance pictures, making them a centrepiece of their reports and thus aligning themselves with the state's public appeal.

During 'a catastrophic failure of the surveillance operation' (ITN News, 16 August 2008), none of the officers involved in tracking de Menezes could be certain he was one of the wanted men. This early confusion, which turned into misinformation during the initial police news conference,[20] was combined with the journalistic practice of presenting public issues as simple binary oppositions, and helped to limit the wider moral and political implications of the incident. As the story unfolded, the conjunction of an initial 'misclassification', followed by the codification of moral qualities and the eventual exercise of 'mutual exclusion' (see above), provided an excuse for the actions of the police. As a leaked report from the Independent Police Complaints Commission testified, the 'description' of de Menezes and, more arbitrarily, his 'demeanour', were assessed, leading to the conviction that 'he matched the identity of one of the suspects wanted for terrorist offences' (confidential police report, cited on ITN News, 10.30 p.m., 16 August 2008).

Over a period of weeks, the process of 'mutually exclusive' categorisation, described above, could be traced in news reports. When de Menezes was found to be 'innocent', he became a 'Brazilian electrician' who was 'another victim of the terrorists' (Comment, *Daily Mail*, 25 July 2005). In turn, the polarisation of guilt and innocence provided a framework in which it was possible for news journalists to hedge their bets. There was considerable movement between these two, mutually contradictory positions. Guilt was linked not to the possibility of 'terrorist' activity, but to any evidence of deviant or negligent behaviour. Dubious information spread by news media included pieces about a supposedly invalid visa, and the groundless accusation that de Menezes had been responsible for a sexual assault (later disproved through DNA testing).[21] The function of this simple opposition between good and evil behaviour was not only to cast doubt on the status of the victim, but to reinforce the notion that a would-be bomber could be condemned to death in a country in which there is no legal provision for such a penalty. Such constraints were deemed irrelevant in the case of the 'split second decision'.[22]

Two years after de Menezes met his death, the Independent Police Complaints Commission's review of the shooting prompted news coverage that not only questioned the procedure that caused the incident, but also maintained the previous discourse of guilt and innocence. Avoiding the assignation of either condition to the police officers responsible for the killing, news outlets reproduced the error of mutual exclusion. In explaining the blunder made by the police, the process of categorisation was revealed; 'in fact, the dead man was Jean Charles de Menezes, *an entirely innocent Brazilian electrician*' (ITN News, 2 August 2007). Later in the same report, a caption added to a graphic showing the development of events on 22 July read: 'Victim confirmed as Brazilian and not a terrorist' (*ibid*).

The effect of this distinction was to remove any suggestion of guilt from de Menezes, but to leave intact the larger proposition that an individual labelled a 'terrorist' is automatically culpable for any action taken against their person. The shooting of a man by Federal Air Marshals in the US is a case in point. Reporting the actions of his officers, Jim Bauer told reporters that the dead man had 'remained non-compliant with their instructions', and that 'his actions had caused the FAMs to fire shots and in fact he is deceased' (BBC News, 8.07 a.m., 18 July 2007). It is almost as though he had pulled the trigger himself.

The corollary to all such events is, however, the fact that the 'guilty' (those from whom the authorities expect an attack that has not yet taken place), *or* the 'innocent' (those who appear in external terms at least to have no malicious intent, or who cannot be forced into a misdemeanour), *or* the 'indeterminate' (that class of individuals whose activities turn out to be ineffective) can be used as the subject for the exercise of lethal force. It can all be rationalised at a later date. In Britain, the publicity surrounding the use of a 'shoot to kill' policy associated with Operation Kratos (the designation for a number of anti-terror procedures), obscured the fact that it was no more than the formalisation and extension of a power that armed police officers already possessed. The fact that the Stockwell shooting was passed off as an 'accident' reinforces the argument that it is exactly 'the circulation of closed-circuit images under "incontestable" circumstances' which is at fault, because it reinforces the 'wider and largely unreflective reproduction of public surveillance *as a principle*' (Price, 2009a). According to Lyon, the practice is part of a larger development – the growth of 'pre-emptive surveillance and "categorical suspicion"' (Lyon, 2003: 168).

MEDIATED INTIMACY AND 'UNINTENTIONAL' EAVESDROPPING: THE G8 SUMMIT

Mr Blair was widely criticised by MPs and media commentators for being 'supine' when his private conversation with President Bush at the St Petersburg G8 Summit two weeks ago was recorded by a live microphone.

(*Guardian Unlimited*, 27 July 2006)

Bush: Yo Blair (.) how are you doing
Blair: I'm just =
Bush: You're leaving =

Blair: No no no (.) not yet (.) on this trade thingy [indistinct]
Bush: Yeah I told that to the man
Blair: Are you planning to say that here or not
Bush: If you want me to

Press and television news is not the only place that social actors are made visible and their actions replayed, because audiences now inhabit an environment of mediated and *dramatised* intimacy in which the 'reality/surveillance' format has been given great impetus by game shows, documentaries, dramas and celebrity 'snooping' in general. News discourses will inevitably be re-conceptualised when events pass across the semi-permeable barriers of popular culture. In turn, the significance of real events in a narrative context will find a new expression within the fictionalised genres of entertainment.

This does not mean that popular forms such as news and drama are inevitably reactionary, merely that incidents are handled in both cases thematically, generating forms of explanation which follow a narrative imperative rather than the simple journalistic objective of establishing the truth. These stories are based, in turn, on relatively straightforward but inflexible categories (terrorist, innocent, asylum seeker) already established in the lexicon of descriptions available to both the authoritative sources responsible for animating them and the journalists who, especially in times of emergency, follow their lead.

Unlike the population as a whole, 'elite' state actors are supposed to be observed within a controlled environment; yet the fact that they are presented within a mediated context that contains other famous individuals has led to the assumption that there are few situations in which they deserve privacy. The significance of the informal exchange that took place between President Bush and Prime Minister Blair on 17 July 2006 was that their conversation – on the crisis in Lebanon – was never intended for public consumption and was in effect overheard. It was widely circulated by the world's media and used to reanimate an established theme: the well-worn thesis concerning the apparent subordination of British national interests to those of the United States. The perceived existence of an essential imbalance in the respective status of the US and the UK, supposedly exemplified in the relationship between the two leaders, had already appeared in a variety of popular mediated discourses, with Blair represented as George Bush's obedient pet dog.[23] In order to appreciate the particular significance of this event, certain aspects of its character need to be addressed. In the first instance, it can most obviously be studied as a conversation, a spontaneous, yet rational activity having a strategic dimension (Nofsinger, 1991). The excerpts presented here (see above and below) certainly display qualities associated with everyday speech, including hesitation, self-correction and interruption, and could not be confused with the heightened rhetorical condition which prepared texts try to attain (Atkinson, 1984). It is not, however, a paradigmatic instance of 'broadcast talk' (Scannell, 1991: 1).

At first sight, this statement may seem contradictory, in the sense that the kind of speech heard on radio and television obeys the norms 'not of public forms of talk, but ... those of ordinary, informal conversation' (Scannell, 1991: 3). The key to its meaning as an event, however, lies not simply in its generic or normative character as 'conversation' but in the fact that it was not intended as a deliberate *performance*. I take performance to be the production of unscripted talk, but talk that is nonetheless *consciously shaped* for an 'overhearing audience'[24] (Heritage, 1985), and which thus attempts to maintain thematic coherence. The Bush and Blair exchange follows the norms required during face-to-face conversation (see Grice, 1989) and, rather than the production of 'self-conscious' speech, represents a private review in which the participants reorient themselves to the conception of future tasks.

As 'revealed' by news media, however, the conversation assumes the form of an unexpected insight, one which carries the power of factual utterance. As Sheriff so compellingly argued, truth as a *factual* or obdurate condition may be recognised because 'it makes no profession of any kind, has no intention, does not stand for anything else' (Sheriff, 1994: 51). The conversation's lack of intentionality, in the public, 'propagandistic' or ideological sense, seems to guarantee its authenticity as an unscripted exchange. However, the participants' assumption that they are obeying only 'private' norms (see the discussion of Grice, below) has another, related, effect: it means that there is no pressure to meet *standards of public expression*. These standards would include an adherence to formal or appropriate language, but also to the expectations created by a context in which politicians are required to give an account of their activities. In other words, despite their apparently 'redundant' and rhetorical nature, and the fact that they can be used to provide alibis or excuses for actions, such announcements remain part of a circumscribed democratic discourse.

The question of truth, and of the 'ideal' condition of truthfulness that is meant to determine speech, is relevant here. For truth to operate as a meaningful category, it must be recognised as a standard practice in both public and private circumstances. Grice, presenting his 'supermaxim' for sincere exchange, offers this statement for consideration: 'try to make your contribution one that is true' (Grice, 1989: 27). He reinforced this idea with two further demands: 'do not say what you believe to be false', and 'do not say that for which you lack adequate evidence' (Grice, 1989: 27). Bach and Harnish, following Grice, emphasise the preconditions needed in order for speech to produce *intelligible* pronouncements: these are the avoidance of ambiguity, obscurity and unnecessary length, and an adherence to *orderliness* of expression (Bach and Harnish, 1979: 64).

Habermas, in a formula that runs parallel to the conversational 'maxims' produced by Grice, theorised the norms operating behind any conversation. He suggested the existence of four 'validity claims', against which participants could estimate the reliability of information provided and, as a consequence, the trustworthiness of each speaker. These conditions for interaction are as follows: that what is said is comprehensible, that it is true, that it is right, and that it is a sincere (*wahrhaftig*) expression of the speaker's belief[25] (Habermas, 1991, cited in Outhwaite, 1994: 40).

In order to be understood, therefore, authors or speakers must offer clarity of expression (comprehensibility); in order to be trusted, they must also demonstrate truthfulness, sincerity and consistent reliability (correctness). Unfortunately, because many politicians seem to operate under different rules of engagement, the fearless *parrhesia* described by Foucault – in which a speaker makes a bold and courageous assertion, offering a 'complete and exact account' of his/her sincere belief, in order to create 'an exact coincidence between belief and truth' (Foucault, 2001: 14) – is rarely witnessed in public settings.

THE 'GAFFE' AS NEWS STORY

One explanation for the interest excited by the conversation is clearly the sense that the 'public' had inadvertently gained access to a confidential exchange in which slang, subterfuge and bad language stood in stark contrast to the formal exercise of diplomatic speech. Edward Lucas, a correspondent for the *Economist* writing in the *Daily Mail*, argued that 'the familiarity and laziness of their discourse jars hideously when set in the context of the summit. For these are not two dullards with some piece of GCSE coursework to be plagiarised. These are our leaders...' (Lucas, 19 July 2006: 14).

The comparison between 'dullards' and 'our leaders' reveals the kind of discourse that extends from stricter forms of political analysis to other established themes, in this case the identification of a wider social malaise based on conventional right-wing attitudes to class. Atkinson, in a more rational vein, remarks upon the 'natural habitats' of politicians, distinguishing between their behaviour in public and their conduct in places so private that 'an outside observer would never be allowed anywhere near' (Atkinson, 1984: 7). Yet, since Atkinson made these comments, cultural practices have undergone a significant alteration. Audiences now inhabit an environment of mediated and *dramatised* intimacy, with ready access to forms of recorded surveillance. In these circumstances, the everyday expression of 'informal' personality has become an established genre.[26]

The controversy over the Bush–Blair conversation resembles the news activity generated by the political 'gaffe', a category of blunder that reveals social ineptitude or some fundamental ignorance at odds with the status of the individual concerned.[27] CNN, for example, focused on the single expletive uttered by Bush, reminiscent of a previous outburst when during the 2000 election campaign he called a *New York Times* reporter a 'major league asshole' (Boehlert, 19 October 2004). There are problems however in placing this event in the general category of the gaffe, a type of error or outburst of limited duration. Such instances might include President Bush's reference to 'illegal non-combatants' during an attempt to define the status of prisoners held at Guantanamo Bay, although there was some speculation that it was an attempt to avoid legal responsibility through the production of shifts in category.[28] A more definite example of descriptive error occurred when John Prescott, the then British deputy Prime Minister, referred in a radio interview to the danger posed by 'massive weapons of destruction' (BBC Radio 4, 24 November 2004). Despite its grammatical integrity, this failed to conform to the established designation 'weapons of mass destruction' and therefore made a doubtful proposition even more risible. Rather than file the famous 'Yo Blair!' exchange under this heading, it might be more useful to consider the question of intention and structure.

INTENTION, STRUCTURE AND INFORMALITY

Agency, defined in social theory as 'the socioculturally mediated capacity to act' (Ahearn, 2001: 112) and as 'embodied practices in the world' (Archer, 2000: 7), is usually attributed to human beings. From the *Guardian Unlimited* report cited above, the truly active agent in the event appears to be a live microphone; the media seem reluctant to assume responsibility for the recording. Yet an essential issue is how the transposition of communicative purpose from *the participants* to *the media*, reveals the structural constitution of a *broadcast* rather than simply a *speech* event. In certain cases, media framing of the exchange reflected an intention to make all aspects of the conversation fit a pre-existing discourse of subordination. So, for instance, the political editor of the *Daily Express* characterised Blair's remarks about a gift given to Bush as 'a fawning joke' (Hall, 18 July 2006: 2).

There was certainly substantial evidence of an imbalance in power. Goffman's account of an earlier instance of presidential informality provides a useful comparison. Describing an incident in which President Nixon passed comments about the appearance of a female news reporter and asked her to perform a pirouette, Goffman identified it not only as 'a moment in gender politics' (Goffman, 1981: 125) but also used it to illustrate points about the nature of footing. Goffman developed these observations by noting that 'whenever two acquainted individuals meet for business ... a period of small talk may well initiate and terminate the transaction' and would 'probably invoke matters felt to bear on the "overall" relation of the participants' (*ibid*). Admittedly, Bush does not follow Nixon's practice in its entirety; he does not ask the British Prime Minister to give him a twirl, but his initial greeting 'Yo Blair!' does accord with two aspects of his particular idiolect; first, the masculinist joshing he favoured, and second his habitual form of greeting to subordinates. In his study of the president's early days in office, the speechwriter Donald Frum noted that: 'Normally, Bush addressed his writers by their last names, British boarding school fashion ... [we] were summoned into the Oval Office for a get-acquainted chat on a mid-February afternoon at four o'clock ... he gave me a sceptical once-over and replied, "Welcome, Frum"' (Frum, 2003: 25–6).

Frum provides another insight when he describes Bush's tendency to make unguarded assessments of other political leaders. Frum draws attention to the fact that 'this tightly controlled man' would regularly 'let fall in the course of the conversation at least one jaw-droppingly candid remark', not only 'a brutally frank assessment of some foreign leader' but more significantly 'an expression of doubt about some program to which he was publicly committed' (Frum,

2003: 28). Here, the gulf between an avowed position and actual belief seems to be exemplified.

One explanation for the unabashed informality of Bush's 'Yo Blair!' greeting attributes the entire mode of behaviour to the president's early experiences as a member of a college fraternity. In the third volume of his study of the administration's internal planning for the Iraq war and the insurgency which followed, Woodward noted that 'Bush still enjoyed frat-boy pranks', recounting a story which demonstrates how this interest could sometimes threaten to produce inappropriate outcomes. Bush and his advisor Karl Rove apparently 'shared an array of fart jokes'; on one occasion, the president placed a remote-control toy under Rove's chair, intending to set off the 'farting sound' it produced during a senior staff meeting scheduled for 7 July 2005. When, however, Bush 'learned about the terrorist bombs in the London subways and buses' on that morning, 'the prank was postponed' (B. Woodward, 2006: 402).

Another instance of the reproduction of unthinking informality occurred in early July 2003 when, responding to a question about the rising US casualty rate in Iraq and the apparent unwillingness of allies to provide sufficient military support, Bush declared that those who believed America to be weak were making a mistake. In order to emphasise this point he said 'bring 'em on, we got the force necessary to deal with the security situation' (Bush, 7 February 2003). The statement 'bring 'em on' was cited as evidence of Bush's tendency to bluster and of his cavalier attitude to the realities of warfare.

ALIGNMENT, IDEOLOGY AND SPEECH

In the case of the G8 incident, Bush and Blair assumed that they were operating within a private bubble, allowing the reproduction of exactly the kind of 'frank assessment' that provided the press with confirmation of previous suspicions about the imbalance in their relationship. The degree of affiliation within the exchange is clearly apparent, as the informality that caused so much offence to observers helped to maintain the bond between the two leaders. Nofsinger's study of *alignment* is useful in this respect. He cites Stokes and Hewitt's definition of this conversational strategy as 'largely verbal efforts to restore or assure meaningful interaction in the face of problematic situations' (Stokes and Hewitt, 1976, cited in Nofsinger, 1991: 111–12). Here, 'problematic situations' may well represent the breakdown of mutual understanding but, considering the inevitably social character of speech, can also refer to a field of external realities which, in everyday exchange as much as in political discourse, represents the pressing intrusion of factors beyond individual control.

An *ideological* reading of alignment would acknowledge not simply the apprehension of a 'wider world' (a material challenge which speakers must acknowledge and attempt to manage during exchange), but also the activities of the subordinate as they attempt to 'move closer' to the demands and perspectives of the dominant. This must be done without necessarily sacrificing the appearance of independent capability, through which their own peers in *national* political discourse will assess their efforts. In this way, it is possible to understand Blair's offer of mediation as a tactic that would play well to his own national agenda, while establishing his 'backstage' usefulness to the American leadership. The problem was the unintended revelation of this manoeuvre:

> Blair: I don't know what you guys have talked about (.) but as I say I am perfectly happy to try and see what the lie of the land is (.) but you need that done quickly because otherwise it will spiral
> Bush: I think Condi is going to go pretty soon
> Blair: Right well that's (.) that's (.) that's all that matters (.) But if you (.) you see it will take some time to get that together.
> Bush: Yeah, yeah
> Blair: But at least it gives people (.)
> Bush: It's a process, I agree
> Blair: At which you and and [
> Bush: [I told her your offer to (.) =
> Blair: = Well (.) it's only if I mean (.) you know. If she's got a (.) or if she needs the ground prepared as it were (.) Because obviously if she goes out she's got to succeed (.) as it were (.) whereas I can go out and just talk

The speech-act theory associated with Austin (1975), Searle (1969) and Labov (1972) is essentially concerned to interrogate forms of utterance in the belief that they represent communicative 'acts';[29] what speakers say is an attempt to produce effects in a hearer or in a group of listeners. In the work of Grice and Habermas, however, we encounter an additional quality – a sense of the normative conditions that underpin the classification of speech activity. The question is the degree to which it might be helpful to regard the passage above as a traditional speech event, since the incident has to be understood in its larger context as a phenomenon 'produced' by mediation.

There are certainly simple models of conversation that might be appropriate for understanding the basic mechanics of the Bush/Blair interaction. Coulthard, for example, outlined a series of typical paired exchanges, including 'question/answer', 'challenge/response' and 'invitation and acceptance' (Coulthard, 1985: 7). Similarly, Searle's hypothesis that 'speaking a language is performing speech acts ... such as making statements, giving commands, asking questions, making promises, and so on' (Searle, 1969: 16) seems equally helpful. The more complex issues pertaining to behavioural norms and motivation – such as *intention*, *role* and the attribution of *agency* within private conversations – are, however, more difficult to analyse.[30]

In the passage above, Blair revealed that he was not in fact fully conversant with the content exchanged within the primary in-group represented by Bush and his closest aides; he admits that 'I don't know what you guys have talked about'. He then introduces a qualifier that also acts as a reminder of an existing offer: 'but as I say I am perfectly happy to try and see what the lie of the land is'. This move is not entirely unconditional, as Blair emphasises the need for a rapid decision. He presents this as a challenge, yet one that is meant to be persuasive: 'but you need that done quickly because otherwise it will spiral'.

Although the British press is ostensibly unfamiliar with the principles of discourse analysis, most commentators realised that Bush's response, 'I think Condi is going to go pretty soon', represented a rebuff. Bush achieved this end by producing an 'indirect' speech act which employed a certain 'strategic ambiguity' (Bavelas et al., 1990: 21). In response, Blair's agreement was simply provisional, before he reintroduced the notion of urgency; 'that's all that matters' is followed by the return of this theme ('it will take some time to get that together'). Blair revealed himself to be subordinate, in the sense that he sought permission for his diplomatic efforts from another leader; it is this inequality of power that seemed to exemplify a larger, national subservience.

The kind of moves analysed above do not seem to match traditional notions of an appropriate 'language of government' (Fairclough, 2000: 11). The 'fawning' of Blair also indicates an attempt to establish and maintain *political alignment* between the dependent position of a less influential state and the power it seeks to exploit or emulate. So, for example, in the rhetorical maelstrom which followed the 9/11 attacks, a British journalist reported that some of Blair's aides were 'particularly pleased' that the US president had used the notion of 'patient justice'. Blair had been especially keen on the term 'justice', which eventually began to 'feature regularly in Washington' (Grice, 22 September 2001).

THE MEDIA RESPONSE: POLEMIC AND RHETORIC

What stuck in the maw of many political commentators was not the wisdom or otherwise of a 'belligerent' party attempting to make inappropriate diplomatic efforts, but the belief that Blair was merely trying to curry favour by offering himself as a factotum. The *Guardian*, for example, described the passage cited above as 'the most embarrassing part of the exchange for Tony Blair', and argued that 'he sounds less like the head of a sovereign government than a Bush official, waiting for the boss's green light – which he does not give' (Freedland, 18 July 2006: 3). The writer concludes that 'another servant of the president, Condoleezza Rice, is going instead' (*ibid*). Lucas, in the *Daily Mail*, decided that the offer represented 'a damning indictment of Britain's weakness, of the contempt in which we hold ourselves, and of our readiness to prance to the tunes of others' (Lucas, 19 July 2006: 14), while the *Mail*'s leader comment was that 'begging for permission' to be a 'messenger boy' was 'demeaning and degrading for Britain' (19 July 2006).

It is clear then that the British news media made a 'polemical' use of the exchange, by framing it within established discourses and by employing it, in whole or part, as a metaphor for US dominance. The *Guardian*'s verdict on Blair's offer of intercession was typical – 'a terrible admission of Britain's place in the scheme of things' (Freedland, 18 July 2006: 3). The act of mediation itself may thus be seen as an ideological phenomenon, certainly in the sense that the media presented the exchange in an openly polemical context; in essence, Right or Left, this followed the theme of national subservience in which 'we' as British subjects had been aligned with (and in some accounts shamed by) the unseemly behaviour of 'our' leader. Take, for example, the summation offered by ITN's political editor, Tom Bradby, on 17 July 2006, as he stood (significantly) outside 10 Downing Street:

Well there you have a very cool in command very casual (.) George Bush (.) Tony Blair very keen to make a difference (.) eer (.) by going to Syria (.) eer (.) George Bush (.) not quite dismissive but certainly a bit offhand about it (.) 'yeah (.) that's (.) eer (.) that's a matter for Condoleezza Rice really' and I think people are kind of reading a lot into that (.) maybe we should just get used to the fact that it's inevitable (.) America is the world's superpower and we aren't (.) and maybe we just need to realise that but certainly people are reading a lot into it[31]

News media assumed therefore a *rhetorical* position, in which use of the 'inclusive we' (Atkinson, 1984) elides the distinction between different subject-positions. As a consequence, senior journalists and political editors, who are relatively close to the executive procedures they describe, speak on behalf of a wider community that receives but does not shape news content. This assimilation of subjectivities into a unitary outlook is part of a system of representation identified by Schlesinger, in which there remains an enduring connection between 'modes of social communication and national political spaces', a link which remains 'fundamental for conceptions of collective identity' (Schlesinger, 2000: 100).

This form of utterance, in which established themes are animated in the service of a consistent perspective, represents an attempt to recompose a 'national' discourse through a standard perspective. This proposition may be glossed as 'Britain has lost the leadership it once exercised' and becomes *ideological*[32] in particular ways once other statements are attached to it. In other words, the 'trunk' of the description (usually deemed inescapably 'true' or at least uncontroversial) may produce a variety of branches. Van Dijk's observation, though not identical, reinforces the view that individual statements and a more developed position are semantically generative; he argues that statements appear to suggest a coherent position, just as a fixed position on an issue generates associated statements (van Dijk, 1998).

This is not to say that such an outcome is inevitable; the identification of national dependence may act as a prelude to a call for a break with US foreign policy and the pursuit of a moral course entirely at variance with traditional notions of national interest. If, however, the argument is merely that a British leader should not play second fiddle to an American, then the outcome may simply accord with the requirements of formal political democracy – to judge the quality of leadership by its ability to represent a 'national' interest, a notion that may, at best, be used to argue for greater or lesser degrees of 'independence'. Where there is over-investment in the concept of leadership, and it is perceived to be weak, then the political process itself remains stalled or, as one commentator described in the British case, 'in limbo, as everyone waits for Blair to step down' (BBC World News, 4.35 a.m., 19 November 2006).

FROM CONVERSATION TO IDEOLOGY?

One issue requiring further comment is exactly this assertion, which often characterises journalistic accounts, that the 'chief political executive' is the most important factor in the maintenance of national status. This kind of association emerges from rhetorical techniques that offer the listener a subject-position based upon a set of assumptions about a particular 'national' trajectory. There is also, however, a more useful critical purpose in examining the links between 'everyday' utterance and rhetorical technique. Within academic enquiry, the analysis of everyday categories might allow for the closer integration of conversation analysis and critical discourse analysis.

This may seem a tall order, but in fact there seem to be many aspects of these methods that share basic assumptions. So, for example, in their debate over the respective merits of these approaches, Schegloff and Billig both adhere to wider contextual principles that go beyond the vernacular utterance and its descriptive analysis, and bear upon the unequal distribution of power within the social order (see Billig, 1999: 543–82). While the argument over methodological precision versus ideological significance continues, it may be worth examining those approaches which suggest that speech acts always represent attempts to secure material advantage. The essence of the question here is that conversation represents an act of communication for a purpose, and as such constitutes the pursuit of particular goals, however ordinary or limited in scale such aims may seem in comparison to mediated events. I noted above Nofsinger's observation that conversation is 'a rational activity having a strategic dimension' (Nofsinger, 1991: 6–7); Wrong takes another step towards a more trenchant assessment of power and utterance when he argues that 'people exercise mutual influence and control over one another's conduct in all social interactions; in fact, that is what we mean by social interaction' (Wrong, 1979: 62).

The usefulness of this observation for the present enquiry lies in its location of power in apparently ordinary, uninflected exchange; the principle must therefore be that power exists within interaction in all its guises, rather than being confined to a more specialised use of discourse alone, in for example what Fairclough calls 'unequal encounters' (Fairclough, 1989: 44). My objection here is not to the notion of inequality (so easily identified in the Bush–Blair exchange), but rather to any hint that there may be situations where power is *not* an issue. This also bears on the question of agency; while practitioners in the field of conversation analysis are right to note that one should assume that participants are 'active, knowledgeable agents, rather than simply the bearers of extrinsic, constraining structures' (Hutchby and Wooffitt, 1998: 5–6), this also perhaps underestimates the power of structure. Individuals 'bear' structures, but structures determine the extent and force of individual agency. One can be an agent of history, of an organisation, of a more powerful individual, but not it seems of oneself. Ahearn examines this notion by drawing attention to the fact that 'we know that the most salient person in a linguistic interaction is the speaker' (Ahearn, 2001: 123) partly because the first person pronoun places the speaker in the position of agent. A speaker will therefore make narrative constructions in which they act upon others, rather than admitting that they are acted upon (*ibid*).

Although Ahearn is right to point out that there are differences between grammatical and social categories of agency, under current conditions the social and communicative power of actors is limited by the persistence of objective conditions, linguistic and social, which are not of their making. As Benton contends, it is necessary 'to distinguish between those activities which are really exercises of [the individual's] own intrinsic powers', and those activities which are 'exercises of powers that reside in social structures, but operate through the activities of human agents' (Benton, cited in Archer et al., 1998: 305).

Archer, with a bias towards the effects of structure, argues that '*pre-existing* properties *impinge* upon contemporary actors', in many cases 'implying no compliance, complicity or consent from the latter' (Archer et al., 1998: 370). When Cerny describes structures as 'the pattern of constraints and opportunities for action' (Cerny, 1990: 4), he provides a simple but accurate depiction of any formal, bureaucratic organisation. These constraints and opportunities do not merely represent the wishes of some abstract 'authority', but are '*material practices*' embracing the 'customs and lifestyles of the agents' that inhabit state structures (Poulantzas, 1978a: 28).

Individuals who join state organisations are not the unthinking drones of an apparatus, but embark on a 'career path' in which their progress is *sanctioned* by various rules and practices. As a noun, '*sanction*' is one of those terms that simultaneously indicates two apparently opposed conditions, in this case either a reward or a penalty. As a transitive verb, to *sanction* something means in essence to authorise, to direct activities or control individuals through incentive or punishment. The point here is that such an action depends on the existence of a simple distinction between two forms of subordinate behaviour – obedience and disobedience.

This observation must be extended to take account of the larger context in which the Bush–Blair exchange took place – namely, the restless *projection* of state authority beyond geographical boundaries, in which traditional distinctions between domestic and 'foreign' policy become less tenable (Brenner et al., 2003: 2). Individuals deemed a threat to a new 'coalition' of states have their basic rights annulled by 'occupying powers' or find themselves assigned the status of non-persons in spaces which escape the rule of international law (Sands, 2005: 145).

THE MYTH OF PERSONAL AGENCY

A private discussion between significant political actors achieved notoriety because of its transference to a mediated public realm; it was not composed or directed within the formal institutional structures of broadcast media, but reproduced after the fact. In other words, it appeared as 'natural talk' within an institutional system which can treat this as the stuff of broadcast news, but which also makes a considerable investment, through established generic forms, in notions of an accessible, popular yet clearly staged 'reality'. As a consequence, it did not display the communicative intentionality associated with 'directive' address (see Price, 2007). Directive address is a species of formal, ordered or scripted utterance, associated with public rhetoric (Atkinson, 1984) and dependent upon continuous speech directed from an authoritative source to an assembly which either accepts, or is in no position to challenge, the prevailing conditions set by the dominant power. In the Bush/Blair case, the very dependence of journalists on authoritative sources produced an unexpected inversion of the usual process, in which powerful agents deliver formal orations, which then receive critical mediation *after the fact*.

The incident could have been employed by news media as a way of introducing discussions about the informal operation of secret power, but the preferred discourse seemed to emphasise a critical assessment of the 'special relationship' and an associated narrative of national decline. One salient aspect of the mediated event was the apparently superficial treatment of a crisis described in *official* statements, whatever their perspective, as urgent and serious. It is the appearance of informality and disrespectful utterance, therefore, which seems to reinforce a view of Blair as weak and subservient.

This is not to say that the comparison between the two individuals does not relate to the respective position of their nations, because the existence of this exchange cannot be disputed. Rather, it is the limitation imposed on the scope of debate by an adherence to the paradigm of 'personal' agency. The weakness of an analysis based on agency would be perhaps more clearly demonstrated if the British political system were to produce an individual capable of defying US interests; under such conditions it might become clear that British subservience is a structural matter, not an issue that depends on individual influence or choice.

5
Film, Bureaucracy and the Gendered Protagonist

Towards the end of the movie *Platoon* (dir. Stone, 1986), after the final battle in which many of the main characters have been killed, an armoured personnel carrier emerges from the jungle and passes through the carnage of the previous night's battle. This vehicle flies a swastika banner, and a human skull swings from the barrel of its mounted gun. The American troops who accompany it are clearly marked as experienced and ruthless; they begin to collect trophies, including ears taken from the corpses of North Vietnamese soldiers. This kind of activity, together with the Nazi flag, is clearly meant to refer to an 'authentic' set of practices, and to represent the creation of an *esprit de corps* through brutal and deviant behaviour. The scene as a whole forms one part of the *coda* that ends the film, in which an ethical conflict between US soldiers has been identified as the real focus of the struggle.

In *Platoon*, American guilt over Vietnam is explored through a division between good and evil, represented by two figures, Sergeant Elias and Staff Sergeant Barnes. Barnes is the instigator of various crimes, but retains influence because he is perfectly suited to the extreme environment in which the troops are forced to operate. At one point, he explains himself by saying 'I *am* reality', before presenting his pragmatic worldview: 'there's the way it ought to be, and there's the way it is'. This represents an attempt to assign a whole range of incidents – the murder and rape of civilians, the destruction of a village and the killing of a fellow soldier – to the realm of practical necessity.

The Nazi pennant, though it provokes no comment or analysis within the film, seems to fit into the paradigm of a 'necessary evil' already established during the narrative. The appropriation of the swastika by the Americans is presumably intended to increase internal cohesion within an 'elite' formation, and to inspire fear in the enemy. The display of an ideologically irretrievable sign may therefore be interpreted as the director's way of emphasising the pitiless tenacity of a group of US combatants (some of whom are from ethnic minorities) and to express the particularly vicious character of the Vietnam war. The swastika competes with other emblems displayed in the movie: peace symbols, crucifixes, the Confederate battle flag, totemic objects, good luck charms and so on.

The one emblem that is never shown is the Stars and Stripes. If the American national flag had appeared at the end of the narrative, instead of the Nazi banner, how would the brutality of the scavengers and trophy-hunters have been interpreted? The swastika is, of course, a symbol so loaded with violence that it is impossible to rehabilitate or dishonour, while the appearance within narrative fiction of the Stars and Stripes is used to generate certain types of emotional resonance (see below). Although war memoirs and movies may contain references to deviant subcultural formations, in most official war narratives there is little overt acknowledgement of the irregular procedures that help to motivate combatants. The patriotic notion of service is celebrated, together with an emphasis on the interpersonal solidarity created by military action, but the existence of irregular behaviour 'on the ground' is often dismissed as an isolated, or unusual, form of excess.

CONFLICT AND SYMBOLIC RESOURCE

If the process of representation constitutes an *action* that emerges from, and in turn reproduces, the material/symbolic character of military life, then all forms of discourse, whether or not they are intended for public consumption, may contribute to the general cultural milieu in which violence is interpreted. The point is that the appearance of 'deviant' symbols and practices within cinema reflects a real condition: the existence of a rank-and-file perspective on the use of coercion, often quietly sanctioned or even explicitly encouraged. The use of imagery, such as the pregnant Palestinian woman on the IDF T-shirt mentioned in Chapter 2, and the appearance of objects like skulls and other trophies on military vehicles, illustrates a simple point – that official symbols (regimental colours, badges, uniforms) do not seem to offer an adequate means of expression for the martial temperament; something more visceral and offensive seems to be necessary, when a war of aggression is being fought.

In addition, some elements of military culture seem to encourage the deliberate use of personal humiliation – first to exert discipline over recruits, and then later to intimidate external enemies. The control of prisoners and other victims of imperial or mercenary force is a case in point. For example, in 2003, at the Abu Ghraib prison, morale amongst male detainees was degraded by the threat of rape, while inmates of both sexes were assaulted. Iraqi prisoners were also videotaped and photographed 'in various sexually explicit positions' (Simons, 2008: 71). The Taguba Report, written by a senior US official, contained witness statements from American soldiers, including the testimony of Military Police officer Harman. Referring to the incident in which 'a detainee was placed on a box with wires attached to his fingers, toes, and penis', she explained that her job 'was to keep detainees awake' so that they would be more likely to talk to Military Intelligence (Greenberg and Dratel, 2008: 418). Deviant behaviour, therefore, is not only about the creation of an environment that allows great freedom in the production of force, but is also officially sanctioned and used to achieve practical outcomes.

'ACT HAPPY FOR YOUR FREEDOM': THE STARS AND STRIPES

At the end of the 1991 Gulf War, the writer Anthony Swofford (then serving in the Marine Corps), noted the suspicious appearance of American flags amongst the poor families which greeted the US military on the outskirts of Kuwait. Either, he reasoned, these people had been given the flags and told to 'act happy for your freedom' or they had them 'stowed ... in their kitchen cupboards, waiting for this glorious day' (Swofford, 2003: 241). The *internal* reconstitution of democracy within the US, on the other hand, seems to have required a much more intimate identification of the citizen not only with state, but also with corporate power. Early propaganda in the 'war on terror' turned very much on the notion of renewed confidence, and required expressions of faith in business, in the nation's identity, and in the continued resonance of symbols like the Stars and Stripes. In 2004, the US Joint Chiefs of Staff argued that their mission would require 'the full integration of all instruments of national power', the cooperation of allies, and 'the support of the American people' (Hughes, 2007: 4).

The terrain of US politics and culture has, however, always been crowded with references to loyalty, martial valour and the honour associated with military leadership. During the 2004 Presidential Election, for example, it seemed to one observer as though 'Bush and Kerry are standing mainly for the office of commander in chief' (Garton-Ash, 5 August 2004). Indeed, the whole tenor of Kerry's speech in Boston may serve as a useful motif for the more respectable composition of civil-military patriotism. Kerry introduced himself with a salute, indicating that he was 'reporting for duty', and went on to recall how in Vietnam 'Old Glory' had flown 'from the gun turret right behind my head' (*ibid*). The flag 'was shot through and through and tattered, but it never ceased to wave in the wind' (*ibid*). In this narrative, objectified American values come under attack but remain inviolate. In addition, Kerry had emphasised his own proximity both to the national symbol and to extreme danger.

In America, the flag is the common denominator used to validate public display, while a demonstration of patriotism remains the essential prerequisite for any political event that is meant to be taken seriously. So, for example, the huge display of US flags that brought the 2004 Democratic convention to a close, was described as part of an attempt to mount 'a full-scale invasion of Republican emotional terrain' (Goldenburg, 2 August 2004). Delegates were also issued with placards, while 'the handmade protest signs of earlier years were banished, ostensibly for security' (*ibid*). The entire event, according to one commentator, 'was directed like a Hollywood movie' (Garton-Ash, 5 August 2004).

Barber suggests that, considered as an 'imperial' power, the 'coordinating' role of the United States on the world stage is based partially upon convincing images and discourses, on what he calls 'the actual words and pictures ... that make up the ideational/affective realm by which our physical world of material things is interpreted, controlled, and directed' (Barber, 2003: 81). Yet the 'internal' US system of representation, in which the country presents itself to its citizens, is based on symbols and signs that are supposed to bind together many disparate social groups. Bellah speaks of an 'American civil religion, a national body of meanings, texts, practices, holidays, and images consecrated as holy, [acting] as the secular identity of the United States' (Bellah, cited in Jusdanis, 2001: 161).

The reproduction of *historical* references is, however, fraught with difficulty, because the mediation of these 'signifiers' by Hollywood has to address both a national and an international audience. In certain cases, of course, the production of meaning can satisfy both constituencies, while in others there is no prospect of creating a shared perspective. So, for instance, a British audience might respond quite warmly to the image of a 'racially inclusive'

American emblem, held aloft by the noble warriors depicted in the Civil War drama *Glory* (dir. Zwick, 1989), because it is set in opposition to Confederate racism and intransigence. A similar attempt to generate British empathy with the American cause in the implausible Revolution melodrama *The Patriot* (dir. Gibson, 2000) may, conversely, fail to impress because His Majesty's redcoats are cast as the villains of the piece.

The successful transposition of 'American' values through the universally recognised image of the flag depends therefore on a number of factors, including the cultural predispositions of the audience, the subject matter, and the era in which the material is set. While the American Civil War is often presented as a simple struggle for emancipation, Vietnam, perceived as an imperial or post-colonial war, cannot mobilise *moral* references and is thus forced to generate more restricted propositions, concerning, for example, 'betrayal, comradeship and individual sacrifice' (Price, 2005: 87). If, however, war remains an important theme, which continues to define a significant part of the American psyche, then the surplus capacity for making war may be matched by the 'cultural' appetite for the fictional re-presentation of combat.

The Second World War in particular operates as a primary 'category' for the reproduction of positive meanings associated with war, and provides greater opportunities for the narrative exposition of patriotic values. The billowing flag that appears in the opening sequence of *Saving Private Ryan* (dir. Spielberg, 1998), with its translucent fabric and colours washed-out against the sun, presents a nostalgic and sombre interlude before the slaughter on Omaha Beach. Flying above the orderly rows of graves, the emblem signifies mourning and collective sacrifice, a position reinforced in the conclusion to the movie.

In general, the determination to remember the Second World War as a 'good' war, and those who served in it as the 'great generation', has provided a frame of reference – a model of noble military endeavour – which politicians have attempted to transfer to later conflicts. So, for example, the moral war is defensive, and waged in response to an attack on American soil. Early media responses to the 9/11 attack, for example, compared it to Pearl Harbor. Another requirement – the creation of a visible battlefield overseas – was met in 2001 when the Republican administration and its Democratic allies followed the material logic of a nation-state at war in supporting an attack on Afghanistan in October of that year, and maintaining a 'home front' by introducing laws and practices organised under the category of 'homeland security'. The unavoidable problem to be faced, however, is the sense that the present might not match, and may even contradict, the positive spin put on the past. Where contemporary political authority begins to appear weak or corrupt, new forms of narrative are used to recalibrate the public response, in a move designed to rescue the 'core values' of the US polity from the real, 'deviant' events that seem to threaten its moral standing.

THE FAILURES OF 'REAL WORLD' AUTHORITY

The 9/11 Commission noted that the institutions 'charged with protecting [US] borders, civil aviation and national security' had failed to appreciate the gravity of the threat posed to the United States by a 'sophisticated, patient, disciplined and lethal' enemy (9/11 Commission Report, 2004: xvi). This censure of official agencies may suggest a powerful bipartisan assault on the incompetence of the US security apparatus, but the extent of the critique is limited by the Commission's remit, which was to investigate the 'facts and circumstances' of the September 11th attacks (ibid: xv). The final Report, therefore, did not attempt to 'assign individual blame' but to provide 'the fullest possible account' of the events (ibid: xvi). The ultimate goal, it claimed, was to help prevent another such attack happening on American soil.

The Commission's explicit refusal to determine individual responsibility was entirely appropriate to the role it had been assigned (and presumably also useful in securing the cooperation of witnesses). Another clear advantage in using *structure* (rather than individual activity) as the preferred frame of reference was that it met the need to appear objective. Within the narrative of the Report, however, the formal concentration on systemic problems conflicts with the inevitable appearance of active, culpable human agents. In its assessment of political manoeuvring in the post-9/11 world, for example, the Report clearly implicates individuals. Paul Wolfowitz in particular appears as an early enthusiast for military action against Iraq (9/11 Report, 2004: 352). Initially resisted by some within the Bush administration, this immodest proposal eventually hardened into formal policy.

Despite its declared limitations, the Commission's work provides a revealing insight into the internal mechanisms of state bureaucracy and the role of individual actors in attempting to mobilise resources: it is packed with incidents that reveal the inability of senior officials to make the chain of command effective, to overcome communication breakdowns, and thus to gain an accurate picture of the perils they faced. A salutary example of procedural failure may be found in the confusion surrounding the decision, made on 11 September itself, to shoot down civilian aircraft should they fail to 'divert' from a suspicious course (9/11 Report, 2004: 40). Based on a telephone conversation with President Bush, Vice President Cheney had authorised fighter planes to engage the hijacked passenger jet United 93, unaware that it had already crashed in Pennsylvania. However, the order to 'take out' rogue aircraft was not, according to the Commission, passed to the first set of fighter pilots circling New York and Washington – who were told to 'ID type and tail' – but was communicated to a second group which was scrambled from Andrews Airforce Base (*ibid*: 44). The Report's authors, commenting on this state of disorder, noted that officials 'struggled ... to improvise a homeland defense against an unprecedented challenge' (*ibid*: 45).

Calls for the punishment of public servants, however, lay beyond the powers of the Commission. Together with the reluctance of the Bush administration to accept its own mistakes, this meant there was little visible evidence at the time of the Report's appearance, in July 2004, of any significant protagonist having to pay the price for several very grave shortcomings. The eventual indictment in October 2005 of Cheney's chief of staff, I. Lewis 'Scooter' Libby, on perjury charges related to the administration's decision to leak the name of a CIA official (B. Woodward, 2006: 419; McClellan, 2008: 305), did little to contradict this perception. What remained, therefore, was a sense of general disorder and confusion both during the 9/11 attacks, and in the years that followed. The belief that serious deficiencies existed within the US system of government included a negative assessment of its executive leadership, linked to the increasingly poor reputation of the president.

The Commission's refusal to apportion blame might have had a beneficial effect, in the sense that it prevented an unnecessary diversion from the more urgent study of systemic problems; but the fact that no one was called to account (especially during the Iraq debacle) risked encouraging the rather abstract conviction that 'government' in general was at fault. The plethora of conspiracy theories which followed 9/11 attest to this sense of disaffection with the political system. When, for example, the PR company Ogilvy ran an exercise called 'Topoff' for the Department of Homeland Security, in which it tried to prepare senior officials for the possibility of a fresh terrorist assault on US infrastructure, it encountered 'a number of serious challenges', particularly the fact that 'some members of the target audience were suspicious of possible government involvement in 9/11' (see www.ogilvypr.com).

Besides the growth of political scepticism and disengagement, the public registration of dissent can make itself evident in more formal ways, such as demonstrations, petitions and campaigns of civil disobedience (see Chapter 6). However, citizens can only secure what Dahlgren calls 'consumer choice in the rotation of elites' (Dahlgren, 1995: 3) when an electoral opportunity presents itself. The most significant defeat of neo-conservative dominance in America had to wait for the Congressional, Senate and Presidential elections of 2008. Rather than a complete revolution in political values, the Democratic resurgence in these elections may represent a degree of exhaustion with one form of authoritarian culture: it is the cultural frame that supplies much of the 'knowledge' that individuals bring to the political realm, and it is this force that must now be examined.

NARRATIVE, BUREAUCRACY AND PUBLIC VALUES

Although specific allusions are indeed made to the operational exercise of social control within the police or espionage genre, and television series like *CSI* devote time to a glamorised version of investigative procedure, the representation of institutional forces within the 'story world' (Branigan, 1993: 33) is chiefly undertaken when the condition can be sensationalised. So, for example, a number of genres (like the courtroom drama) will present heightened but superficial dramatisations of bureaucratic procedure. In such cases, an analysis of structure is usually limited to a background sketch upon which heroic identity can be projected. Although real police activity may be described as largely procedural, cinematic narratives show life in the office as a jumping-off point for interrogations, confrontations with authority, rapid departures for crime-scenes and contests with other agencies over the meaning of the law.

The purpose of this discussion is not, however, to describe the judicial, executive and legislative arms of state power, but rather to provide some background for the *fictional re-presentation* of specialist agencies devoted to the suppression of criminality and (through a process of association) *political dissent*. The aim is therefore to ask which aspects of the relationship between authority figures and their subjects, and between *operatives* and *bureaucrats*, are emphasised when they are translated into a fictional *scenario*; I assume, in other words, that the actual affiliation between social actors is re-presented as a form of entertainment.

The tendency of police, espionage, war and paramilitary genres is to celebrate decisive, often violent, 'masculine' action, but this is mediated through a struggle between bureaucracy and 'individual agency'. Although this type of material might suggest the pursuit of a clear narrative agenda (such as unambiguous support for executive action) the issue is more complicated. The ideological trajectory of any narrative that portrays coercive force ('unitary'[1] or otherwise), cannot inhibit the autonomous development of qualities generated within individual scenes.[2] In plain terms we could say that, even where a clear agenda exists, no movie or TV programme can impose an overall discipline on its component parts, which follow a direction dictated by their own status as 'events'.

Based on this observation, it is possible to distinguish between the goal of *narrative coherence* and the challenge of producing *episodic cohesion*.[3] In effect, this point of view offers broad support for Buxton's observation that no ideological project can survive an act of configuration intact (1980); the implication is that the demands of narrative exposition tend to reduce the coherence of any overarching social or political principle. At the same time, the tendency for individual scenes to exert a disruptive rather than a centripetal force, does not mean that they are 'value-free'; even where they offer socially progressive references, they may still reveal a dependence on established narrative techniques. So, for instance, adherence to the protagonist's perspective based on the time-honoured use of an individual as 'hero' or 'heroine', can ensure that actions carried out in pursuit of his or her aims are inevitably justified. Narrative action in realist texts is, therefore, 'rationalised' at every level.

Acceptance of the text's (often inconsistent) position is not, however, inevitable; all *implicit and/or formal explanations*[4] offered for the evolution of fictional events and episodes can be judged against their own contextual references, and examined in comparison with other types of discursive and experiential evidence. So, for example, the animation of references and themes designed to create *resonance*[5] in an audience may succeed in providing access to the 'story-world', but may also militate against attempts to compose a consistent perspective or 'worldview', since all projects are forced to draw upon a wide range of references and positions simply in order to make sense.

Intimately related to this point is the ability of the viewer to nominate extra-textual experiences in response to cinematic cues, which may furnish a counter-narrative or supplement to the material consumed.[6] It is anyway inevitable that the political orientation of the material considered here, dealing as it does with legitimation and power, will vary within the same text and will be interpreted in different ways within established generic constraints. Excerpts from film and television drama are used therefore to identify the mobilisation of social values in the *uncertain service* of narrative propositions. The texts chosen for this study produce 'arguments' which could, in logical, moral or narrative terms, be regarded as inconsistent. Yet the repetition of certain notions, such as the moral worth of heroic individuality, may explain the apparent movement between a variety of positions, including approval for authoritarian methods, distrust of state and corporate power, and investment in myths of personal agency. In actuality, much of the public expression of dissidence appears in a political form (see Chapter 6), but it is this that must be criminalised as the state accepts the full implications of its self-definition as a security regime.

The Marxist writer Goran Therborn noted that the state's impulse to discipline individuals (the *suppression of energies*, described in his work as *subjection*), contradicts another requirement – the need to promote an autonomous capability amongst a workforce, known as *qualification* (Therborn, 1980). According to this dialectical opposition, the effects of a contradiction between subjection and qualification are 'opposition and revolt or underperformance and withdrawal' (*ibid*: 17). This was a description of working-class experience in capitalist society, but it can be applied to any form of servitude within formal organisations.

In narrative forms, however, class distinction often undergoes a process of *ex-nomination*; class disappears as a frame of reference, and is replaced by moral categories which distinguish between groups on the basis of their behaviour within 'economic circumstances'. However, as argued above, mainstream texts cannot rely entirely on the assumption that viewers will align themselves with the physical, narrative and ideological 'positions' offered through the composition or framing of a particular scene. Audiences are offered easier 'points of entry' into narratives, based on the representation of familiar events and everyday experiences. These produce the essential background references which enable more dramatic events to appear convincing.

Work activities are one example of this duplication of the everyday. Information processing, for instance, is a central activity in contemporary bureaucracies, and characterises the working lives of many viewers, yet this feature is made more glamorous by being set within an unfeasibly efficient and advanced technological frame. Indeed, the technical resources of cinema and television display, replicate and exaggerate the precision of information retrieval, by presenting *surveillance* as a purposeful activity devoted to rational (if sinister) ends, carried out by competent professionals. Once again, individual experience of surveillance forms part of the 'knowledge-base' which audiences bring to fiction; indeed, the routine surveillance of citizens has been cited as evidence of the authoritarian control exercised within the social order (Bogard, 1996: 34; Lyon, 2003: 15; Gibb, 2005: 34).

The criminalisation of political activity does not, however, appear as an explicit, coherent theme within the military or police drama, largely because such actions are seen from the viewpoint of the authorities themselves. The preference for authoritarian perspectives and the repression of the 'political', therefore provokes the appearance of some rather perverse notions. The character-function 'criminal', for example, provides a clearly marked contrast to the hero-protagonist, but *in the assignation of motive*, rather than in his or her *application of (violent) method*, which is often identical. The 'dissident' or political role, meanwhile, is often transposed to the central character, a highly-trained operative forced into an *unintended rebellion* (see discussion of *The Bourne Identity*, below). Within the hierarchy of command, the protagonist is often a field agent whose role ensures close proximity to action but which also allows for the possibility of a struggle with desk-bound authority.

It is these kinds of tactic that provide the wider social context for the production of contemporary fictions; to remain relevant and maintain audience attention (to be *contemporary*), narratives must deal with changes in the techniques and purposes that characterise state coercion. So, for example, the re-orientation of police and military organisations towards the 'long war' must be recognised and re-presented within film and television.

Although certain texts are regarded as more 'progressive' than others, all dramas of authoritarian/bureaucratic life share a basic set of references and the replication of familiar scenarios. The viewer is presented with the fetishistic display of totemic objects that testify to the durable character of coercive institutions; guns, badges and uniforms secure access to private spaces in the name of the law. These items 'dress' characters and sets and provide reassurance of collective identity. On occasion, their 'evidential' quality is undermined by the deliberate theatricality of movies which allow the viewer to look 'behind the scenes' leading, perhaps, to the suggestion of direct access to the untidy props and mechanisms of the film set itself.

There is a scene in *Spartan* (dir. Mamet, 2003), for example, in which the protagonist is pretending to be an escaped criminal, in order to intercept two prisoners on their way to jail. He is in fact a member of an elite military unit and, having released the captives from police custody, intends to use one of the men to lead him to his real quarry – the daughter of the US president, who has been abducted by a gang of traffickers. Leaving the two convicts outside a diner, he enters to receive information from a large team of (silent) fellow operatives, who have assembled to add convincing detail to his story. This includes splashes of fake blood added to the front of his shirt, to back up the assumption that he has killed the occupants of the diner. All this is done to deceive the two men outside, yet to the viewer it looks exactly like a mute version of the backstage confusion found in a theatre.

DEVIANT MASCULINITY AND VIGILANTE ACTION

In recent years, the perception that the cinematic text dramatises the individual career-path of the male hero, while the TV series is more concerned with the depiction of moral collectives, has had to alter in the face of hybrid forms which have reordered the moral and temporal appearance of the realist text. Series like *24* seem at first sight to mark a departure from standard practices. They may in fact represent an extension of long-established conventions, adapted to a discursive context in which it is the *open enunciation* of the torture-scenario that marks a decline in 'our ethical and political standards' (Žižek, 9 February 2006). Even this 'departure' from moral principles is not as traumatic as Žižek thinks, since there is a simple calculation at work. The unashamed presentation of brutality in film and television has always been acceptable where the actions are given context. Contemporary references to counter-terrorist operations suggest that the viewer is given privileged access to some hidden struggle, a secret conflict which lies behind the rhetorical assertion made by politicians that there really is/was an active and urgent 'war on terror'.

As long as the police and spy thriller posits a social order in which the law is used to protect the guilty,[7] then extraordinary or vigilante action is shown to be necessary. This does not mean that viewers will necessarily accept this as a principle *to be applied in real-world situations*; rather that they are offered a viewpoint in the text commensurate with the needs of the protagonist. It is nonetheless true that, where 'non-fictional' forms can reproduce the techniques of narrative, then individual readers/spectators are often placed 'as moral participants in the "dilemma" faced by armed officers' (see Price, 2009a). The Stockwell tube shooting of 22 July 2005 is a case in point.

Once again, it is important to note the fictional antecedents of the apparently exceptional conditions presented in recent dramas. The precursor of Jack Bauer in *24* is the hyper-masculine Vic Mackey of *The Shield*, and Harry Callaghan from the movie *Dirty Harry*. An important difference, however, is the enlargement of the police function to concentrate on a markedly *political* intervention, in which 'special forces' and para-military units (*The Shield*'s 'strike team' is an example) are shown *pre-empting* highly deviant and sometimes 'terrorist' activity. This observation must be extended to take account of the restless *projection* of state authority beyond geographical boundaries, in which traditional distinctions between domestic and 'foreign' policy become less tenable (Brenner et al., 2003: 2). Individuals deemed to be a threat to a new 'coalition' of states have their basic rights annulled by 'occupying powers', or find themselves assigned the status of non-persons in spaces which escape the rule of international law (Sands, 2005: 145).

The question here is the degree to which audiences find ways of accepting, at least within the period of exposition, some of the narrative propositions which are offered within film and television. One theory which attempts to analyse this process is that of *identification*. Campbell identifies two distinct forms of identification in film: first, an 'imaginary hysterical' process; and second, 'a more creative, social dreaming' through which experience can be reconstructed (Campbell, 2005: 4).

Although an acute consciousness of manufactured vigilance against 'terrorism' provides part of the discursive context for appreciating the material discussed above, the point is that neither category here represents the 'first stage' of audience identification. A simpler route is offered through the display of *everyday encounters* which express fundamental experiences; these include the protagonist meeting other people, braving the elements, travelling through landscapes and forming relationships. This, the obdurate reality of life, provides the *experiential* referent for audience entry into the 'story-world'.

Responses to the ubiquitous appearance of hierarchical power within political life could be based upon a variety of attitudes, yet some currents seem to predominate within cinematic representation. Individualism and anti-federal sentiment, useful in feigning a vehement objection to the exercise of authority, seems for example to be animated with greater conviction, than the more complex but tentative liberal analysis of power. While *Lions for Lambs* (dir. Redford, 2007), for example, presents a convincing study of right-wing Republican intransigence, its attempt to offer a counter-narrative produces a tortuous account of alternative values, an uneasy dramatisation of sincere but misguided patriotic sacrifice and middle-class liberal principle. The transposition of either 'proto-political' traits or more developed opinions to film does not of course generate an exact correspondence between models of the real and fictional representation, nor does it necessarily produce a successful address to an audience.

Public understanding of political events is, however, already reproduced in a fabular structure, and new occurrences are marked by expectations created from established narratives found in a multitude of sources, including press and TV reportage. Consequently, there exists a great deal of recycled thematic material which moves across generic forms, most of it based on conventional interpretations of the social order. Powerful institutions, responsible for the dissemination and reproduction of meaning, make reference to the various arrangements that make up our perception of reality. The discursive realm, in which narrative circulates, draws from events and activities produced within all three spheres of human experience: the natural, practical and social worlds (Archer, 2000). Cinema is capable of presenting a convincing amalgam of these spheres of existence, but in so doing can confuse the ontological character of events, creating mythical/discursive material out of practical exigencies such as the prosecution of a war.

When the police, war and espionage genres are examined, it seems that the cinematic critique of state power emerges as an attack on fragmented parts of the structure: corrupt officials, 'parallel' or illicit authority, factional conspiracy and, most commonly of all, 'rule-bound' bureaucracy. In other words, the state must receive due prominence in the narrative, but an over-emphasis on the importance or even usefulness of structure would diminish the celebration of individual agency. The hero/heroine is shown overcoming established constraints through force of will, yet these restrictions are, in fact, structural procedures which would in actual circumstances *encourage* rather than disable the legitimate production of effects.

Aligning the protagonist (from the Greek, 'first actor') with officialdom is, however, anathema to narratives which are driven by the desire to highlight heroic agency; the attainment of results must therefore be shown to be made 'against the grain'. This 'anti-bureaucratic' perspective strives to demonstrate and validate the heroic agency of the professional specialist, an individual trained within, but often abandoned by, the coercive apparatus of national security agencies and/or the military. *Human agency* is thus re-cast in fictional form as the attempt by a charismatic individual both to maintain personal integrity and to escape the restrictions of an overbearing and often anonymous structure. As the power of individuals is clearly limited by the attribution of certain capabilities to masculine and feminine characters, the performance of gendered identity and its imagined relation to the exercise of authority is a central aspect of narrative composition.

Authority, generally understood as the 'right' of an established power to expect or enforce compliance, does not necessarily refer to the production of commands and obedience, but rather indicates an individual or group associated with the origins of a policy or enterprise (Watt, 1982: 11). In sum, the effectiveness of this form of influence should be distinguished from the operative character of power, because it resides in a general acknowledgement of eminence or distinction. Different forms of authority – coercive, moral or normative (Etzioni, 1961) – can be used in the accomplishment of tasks, and are also made apparent within the structure of film. It is, however, the distribution of such qualities to different types of individual (righteous coercion to the protagonist, normative conformity to the bureaucrat) that actually reveals the values espoused within each narrative.

REFERENCES TO THE REAL

The simple assignation of character traits and behaviour to individuals is, however, insufficient to determine the political trajectory of narrative forms. So, for example, tales that maintain a distinction between the pathological aggression of the villain and the morally justified violence of the protagonist must demonstrate these attributes through an event which confirms their relative positions. This is often an initiating act in which a criminal or terrorist offence is committed. In the case of *The Kingdom* (dir. Berg, 2007), this is a bomb attack on US civilians living in Saudi Arabia, which kills over a hundred people. The event is therefore intended to create resonance in an audience that might interpret this attack in the light of other supposedly unprovoked assaults on US interests. The particular nastiness of the scenario is apparent in its representation of the slaughter of innocent people of all ages, while they are engaged in playing a baseball game.

This event, the plausibility of which is reinforced through the typical use of TV reports to suggest an authentic social reality separate from the narrative, is received with shock by the authorities in the US. The response of American officials is, however, constrained by diplomatic considerations. Frustrated by a State Department edict preventing the immediate deployment of the FBI at the Saudi crime-scene, the hero of the movie, Ronald Fleury, declares 'I'm gonna get us access'. He then confronts the Attorney General, a character called Gideon Young, in a meeting which sets out the difference between the complacent bureaucrat and the man of action. In attempting to persuade Young to send his team of investigators to Saudi Arabia, Fleury refers to a number of actual locations that contextualise his argument, including Yemen and Iraq. In this way, the necessity for action becomes a material principle, a notion that offers a logical transference from the fictional environment to a wider social universe of political meaning.

One important reason for the use of extensive reference to the external world is the simple need to achieve currency or, in other words, to confirm the social relevance of a tale. A closely related requirement is the 'heritage of realism' (Leishman and Mason, 2003: 2), which fulfils a perceived demand for authenticity. Where violent action is portrayed, for example, the current requirement (set out in the *Bourne* trilogy and taken up by the *Bond* franchise) is for accurate reproductions of hardware and a convincing presentation of martial skills. Productions call on the talents of a host of physical trainers, ex-special forces personnel, weapons handlers and other experts. Actors, tasked with mimicking the established conception of the skilled field operative, speak of their devotion to real-life exercises as they prepare for their roles. Matt Damon, star of the *Bourne* films, described in an interview of 2002 how he strove for realism in his characterisation of the agent: 'Say ... I picked up the gun and it looked like I didn't even know what I was doing, the audience would pick up on it. So I had to spend hour after hour loading and shooting pistols' (Morris, 2002).

The desire for authenticity is attributed here to the demands of the audience. Mamet, describing his production of the script for *Spartan* (2003), tells how his perusal of the book *Inside Delta Force* by Eric Haney (2002) led to his use of the author as a technical advisor for the film. In this case, the 'war on terror' is not made into an explicit frame of reference, as it is in *The Kingdom*, but is based instead on another related theme, the trafficking of women by foreign criminals. The state mobilises its most effective operatives in order to rescue the President's daughter, abducted by gangsters who do not realise the identity of their victim.

'Real world' references once again underpin the general proposition of the movie. Disillusion with formal authority, referred to in the material on 9/11 (see above) is represented by a deep and pervasive cynicism, applied to a host of representative characters (a college professor, an inept agent, the President himself) who are corrupted by their sexual weaknesses. It is the emphasis on this particular theme that distinguishes Mamet's overall position from the perspective taken in *The Kingdom*, which is predicated more firmly on the simple representation of violent retribution, meted out by a 'rainbow' coalition of determined agents.

'YOU'RE ENTITLED TO SHIT': GENDERED BEHAVIOUR AND IDENTITY

Mamet's reproduction of the heterosexist utterances of a military elite is not assigned to the stoical protagonist, who stays aloof from such casual expressions of disdain. While a corrupt internal faction attempts to protect their immoral Commander in Chief from scrutiny (even to the extent of planning to kill his daughter), the principal agent, Scott, delves beneath the surface to establish the truth and retrieve the kidnapped woman. His superficial purity enables him to act against subordinated social groups (criminals, students, traffickers, brothel keepers) who possess the information he needs. In this, it is possible to discern the application of extreme measures associated with the US prosecution of the 'war on terror', but the explicit message seems to be the necessity of acting beyond the bureaucratic confines of the law.

In one particularly telling scene the hero, played by Val Kilmer, is shown first threatening to kill and then nearly choking a woman called Nadya Tellich. Since it has been established that this hero does not reproduce the sexist utterances and behaviours of his colleagues, the action is presented not as deviant but as no more than the necessary application of force in the service of a higher justice. The departure from legality is clearly signalled in the conversation that precedes this event, when another agent confronts Tellich. Tellich, a Serb working in the US on a green card, runs an escort service (in effect a brothel), and thus provides a crude means of proving the unscrupulous character of those who evoke the law in order to frustrate the progress of an urgent investigation:

> Nadya Tellich: I'm entitled to my lawyer.
> Agent: You're entitled to shit. You're entitled to tell me what you know.

BEYOND EXPOSITION

While such discussions of power, agency and ideology, applied to the realm of film and television narrative, suggest the deployment of various forms of textual and cultural analysis (semiological, psychoanalytic and genre-based approaches have provided major paradigms) it is also important to recognise the distinctive quality of film and TV texts, one that moves beyond their role as a means of exposition. Movies and television programmes are effective where they offer a convincing visual and auditory experience, one that reproduces aspects of human sociability, speech and gesture, allowing audiences to interpret quite subtle behavioural signals. These 'naturalistic' aspects of the repertoire of film and television may express or contradict the explicit meanings presented within single narratives but, irrespective of such tendencies, help to confirm the viewer's sense of access to an intimate social universe.

Crossley, writing from a sociological perspective, draws attention to bodily 'techniques' which are 'oriented to social situations' and which may therefore be classified as a form of 'social action' (Crossley, 1995: 135). The on-screen appearance of such *performances* is of course planned (scripted) in advance, but can only be given life through the process of direction in which real individuals reproduce the types of activity which audiences can accept as legitimate, including intonation, gesture and facial expression. So, for example, scripted utterance in film parodies everyday exchange, revealing an awareness of the 'design' of conversational strategies, in which apparently minor interactions achieve important tasks. In film, unlike in examples of real exchange, these tasks are not always chiefly practical (designed to advance a real project or desire), but primarily narrative and explanatory. Yet, to be convincing, they must be more than didactic; they must be represented by persons and 'clothed' in behaviour. When this is achieved, the audience may be 'subtly insinuated' into the text's 'action and internal social relationships' (Horton and Wohl, 1956, cited in Tolson, 2006: 14). The reproduction of a naturalistic environment, including the imitation of natural speech and everyday conduct, may however create conflict with larger narrative purposes. Representations of the ordinary world suggest only commonplace activity, while the purpose of the thriller or war movie is precisely to represent traumatic intrusions into this settled activity.

THE BOURNE IDENTITY

The Bourne Identity (dir. Liman, 2002) is based on the first novel from a three-part trilogy, and has its origins in Cold War politics. Nonetheless, the film represents a contemporary study of the security state and its internal factions. The central character, Jason Bourne, is an American agent conditioned to become an assassin, brainwashed under a secret programme called Treadstone. Having lost his memory, he tries to discover the truth about the inner workings of the CIA. He is assisted by a woman called Marie Kreutz, whom he has paid to help him escape from his enemies. When Bourne discovers that he has a flat in Paris, the two fugitives travel there to gather information – Bourne because he has no recollection of his own personal history, and Kreutz because she needs to assess Bourne's character and social status.

As the scene develops, the naturalistic exchange between the two characters, who seem to be on the verge of starting a relationship, is not developed in its own right, and the larger narrative trajectory intrudes as Bourne discovers that he is under threat. The tension focuses, at this point, on his anticipation of an attack. As a choreographed fight sequence begins, the brief glimpse the audience has had of Kreutz as *protagonist* disappears. In shock after the struggle between Bourne and his assailant, she becomes incapable of action and speech and must rely on Bourne's dynamic and 'automatic' reversion to the skilled production of agency.

AGENCY AND 'INNOCENCE'

In many films and TV series, the values and behaviour of the protagonist are called into question by other characters. Ostensibly, the point of such contested exchanges is to 'test' the quality and accuracy of his or her perceptions and assertions ('truth claims', in linguistic terms). Bourne, for example, is taken to task over his methods and attitudes at more than one point in the narrative. His actions, however, prove appropriate to the extremity of the situation in which he and Kreutz find themselves. In fact, the point of the disagreement is to validate the social role of the male hero. The introduction of material that interrogates his heroic status remains an underdeveloped counter-point to the dominant course of the narrative. There are places where Kreutz questions the story (or alibi) that Bourne produces as an explanation for his conduct, but the audience is, perhaps, most willing to give credence to Bourne's perspective, because it has been prepared in advance by the opening sequences. Kreutz, meanwhile, has already been portrayed as confused and inefficient.

During an early conversation, as Kreutz drives Bourne to Paris, the 'master narrative' is preoccupied with establishing the hero's calibre and lack of guile. In the following passage, the 'rational' explanation for Kreutz's verbosity, that she is nervous, competes with another perspective; that this is a *gendered* account of behaviour which refers to female volubility and male *inexpressiveness*:

Bourne: And what?
Kreutz: What do you mean what? Listen to me. I've – I've been speed-talking for about 60 kilometres now. I talk when I'm nervous. I mean, I talk like *this* when I'm nervous. I'm gonna shut up now.
Bourne: No. Don't do that. I haven't talked to anybody in a while.
Kreutz: Yeah, but *we're* not talking. I'm talking. You've said, like, ten words since we left Zurich.

This exchange reveals certain features that can be attributed to the roles each character plays; Kreutz produces an *expressive* utterance, revealing aspects of her psychological state, while Bourne responds with an *invitation* to her to continue talking. Significantly, in the light of later developments, this invitation assumes the form of a *directive*, a form of utterance that can be read as a request or a command (Price, 1996: 153). In her reply, Kreutz points out the difference between talking as the production of conversation and an utterance as a monologue. Here, too, it may be possible to discern the recursion of stereotypical speech-behaviours and the assignation of distinct traits to gendered individuals. Bourne goes on to provide his companion with a *physiological* explanation for his preference that she continue speaking: 'Well, listening to you, um, it's relaxing. I haven't slept in a while and – and I've had this headache.' Kreutz then agrees to continue talking but the next exchange becomes uncomfortable because, instead of telling a story, she interprets Bourne's request as an opportunity to make a conversational opening:

> Kreutz: What kind of music do you like? Huh? What do you like? Come on. Um – [turns on radio]
> Bourne: You know what, never mind.
> Kreutz: No. It's fine. Tell me [switching channels]. What do you want to listen to?
> Bourne: I don't know.
> Kreutz: Come on. It's not that hard. What do you like? Tell me.
> Bourne: I don't know.

In contrast to the tale of sociability, adventure, friendship and risk that Kreutz produces at the beginning of this scene, in which she reminisces about her dissatisfaction with Amsterdam and her move to begin a new venture with friends in Biarritz, Bourne has nothing to offer. His heroic individuality is protected by his memory loss. His lack of family and friends, or of any interesting tales, even his inability to name the kind of music he likes, presents the viewer with another insight into gendered behaviour. This is the suggestion that Bourne is the unsocialised male, whose recourse is to *pathological* and neurotic behaviour, devoted to detailed planning, violence and unceasing activity, all of which are used to constrain Kreutz's personal trajectory of random but productive encounters.

Once again, the narrative or ideological 'project' insists on a simple explanation; Bourne has no identity, only abilities, and thus cannot be held responsible for his instinctive responses to events. His 'paranoia' is legitimate; 'they' are indeed out to get him. Increasingly, therefore, he exerts forms of discipline on Kreutz, which began with the initial act of bribery that buys the escape from Geneva and which, in effect, becomes the down payment that 'purchases' the relationship. Kreutz's question, 'Who pays $20,000 for a ride to Paris?' is eventually answered when they discover Bourne's combined occupation and identity, that of assassin. Even before the discovery, the 'unknowing' Bourne is allowed to exert pressure on the disorganised Kreutz, always apparently for her own benefit ('I'm trying to do the right thing for you', he says). Returning from his mission to secure money from a deposit box in a station locker, he finds that she is not waiting in her assigned place and remonstrates with her:

> Bourne: Hey. I told you to stay in the car. Jesus Christ. I told you to stay in the car.
> Kreutz: I needed a drink. I didn't think you would come back.

In effect, what an audience witnesses is the odd proposition that training, ability and worldly insight are not the detritus which covers an essential identity, but the true components of masculine character. In contemporary society, however, with its formal adherence to notions of equality and opportunity, the unabashed promotion of the retrogressive male, without qualification or irony, can only take place where the protagonist is fundamentally innocent, and when he faces an enemy that threatens his destruction.

Throughout the movie, even during the most traumatic episodes, Bourne must remain an *innocent*, presented in some essential way as a decent person, at whom an *undeserved* evil is directed. He does not initiate violence and his response is, given the situation, proportionate. Yet, once again, the reservations expressed by Kreutz provide an alternative point of view. Bourne's amnesia, for instance, is all along an excuse for the reappearance of an unreconstructed masculinity, a justification provided by the narrative but not attributed to the character:

> Bourne: Fuck it. I can't remember anything that happened before two weeks ago.
> Kreutz: Lucky you.

Kreutz's reply reveals the deviant perspective which may already have occurred to the viewer; Bourne is provided with all the necessities for a highly mobile contemporary lifestyle, including a large supply of currency (disposable income), multiple nationalities (alternative identities), fashionable surroundings and a high level of physical and mental aptitude. He has shed, again in all *innocence*, the social constraints which many might gladly abandon in return for mobility and freedom. Bourne's loss of identity might be interpreted by the unscrupulous commentator as nothing less than an immense *relief*: 'Lucky you', as his companion says. What, however, does this say about the moral universe inhabited by the characters and, by implication, about the enterprise of self-preservation in a real world of agents and operatives?

THE ALIENATED MALE

Writing about the reproduction of role identity in the film *Courage Under Fire* (dir. Zwick, 1996), Tasker notes that the 'prevailing stereotype' of the veteran soldier has been 'an alienated, violent male' whose physical and mental scars 'operate as marks of (masculine) character' (Tasker, 2004: 95). In certain respects, the central character in *The Bourne Identity* inherits this persona. He carries both kinds of disfigurement, but is removed from responsibility by the narrative device of memory loss. He becomes, therefore, an *innocent*, capable of (but not culpable for) immoral activities. His *limited* verbal interventions return the hero to the classic period of authoritative, muscular masculinity, as opposed to the period in which uncertainty produced a *rhetorical* variant. Isolated from the alibi provided by amnesia, and read at the level of the individual scene, Bourne engages in bribery, assault, manslaughter (in self-defence), destruction of property, illegal surveillance, theft and dangerous driving!

These transgressions may be valued as essential ingredients of the 'thriller' genre, but it is their production *in opposition to social forces portrayed as less trustworthy*, which secures Bourne's position as the centre of heroic agency. Tasker notes in her analysis of military masculinity that it is defined not primarily against 'the enemy' but in opposition to 'the insubstantial world of politicians and the domestic media' (Tasker, 2004: 96). Similarly, the most significant threat in *The Bourne Identity* is the power of bureaucracy and the *coercive* apparatus of the 'secret state'. The Bourne character does not, initially at least, take a principled stand against this coercive authority; he responds to its attacks without understanding their motivation.

ISSUES OF POWER AND EFFECT

The concentration of emotional and narrative resource on the perpetrators rather than the victims of violence, allows the military in general (the armed forces operating in the real world) to evade the charge of criminality. This, I would argue, is why the appearance of such narratives in the story-world matters; not because they produce definite ideological outcomes in audiences *at the time of circulation*, but because they act as preparatory models for other excursions into public consciousness. My contention here is that narrative forms of meaning are not confined to fictional scenarios but are reproduced in other contexts. These include, most significantly, news stories, in which the public is often placed in the moral and executive position of individual state operatives (police, military, secret agents) when they carry out armed or aggressive actions against (in many cases) civilian opponents.

Within the espionage drama, issues of power and effect are presented within a context that displays antagonism between distinct forms of contemporary agency. In essence, the free activity of individuals like Kreutz who appear to create, in a haphazard way, their own destiny, is set against the deep, hidden structures of the government 'agency'. In the embassy scene, Kreutz encounters obdurate reality in the form of bureaucratic procedure and rules, together with their accompanying mentality. The film does not, however, choose to develop the dilemma of this particular 'refugee', nor does it make a real attempt to examine the repressive character of everyday bureaucracy. Instead, it chooses to assign all illicit and oppressive activity to a secret condition – the existence of a parallel state which works through surveillance and the application of ruthless force. Yet the apparatus of this shadowy institution can be 'shut down' and its operatives disowned. Just as any unofficial programme within the security state is useful because of its deniability, so its fictional counterpart is equally valuable; it too can take the blame for a situation that might otherwise be assigned to the 'democratic' order itself. An objective analysis of effective agency depends, therefore, on understanding the true character of the institutional structures that human beings inherit. Bourne and Kreutz are shown acting within situations and structures which are, in common with most institutional settings encountered in everyday life, not of their making.

A study of the gendered inflection of agency in narrative forms provides a useful insight into the difference in operational power assigned to characters that are meant to be fighting on the same side. In effect, however, the gendered protagonist in the protected space of the adventure genre remains an essentially masculine figure: despite the limited critique of formal power offered in movies like *The Bourne Identity*, traditional gender roles seem to remain largely undisturbed. Addressing the question of gender and the state, Wendy Brown makes the argument that both state activity and masculine performance have much in common. In recent years, she believes, both have offered an insincere repudiation of their power, in an attempt to disguise political dominance and social privilege. Therefore, according to Brown, the 'central paradox of the late modern state ... resembles the central paradox of late modern masculinity' (Brown, 1995: 18). Perhaps, however, as Susan Faludi (2008) has noted, the situation after 9/11 has changed, in the sense that few of those in positions of power attempt to offer excuses for the concentration of authority and the narrative dramatisation of coercive force.

6
Economic Transformation, Protest and the State

> Any Government that thinks it can go it alone is wrong.
> If the markets don't like your policies they will punish you.
> (Blair, *Doctrine of the International Community*,
> 24 April 1999)

> Destroyed, the once towering symbols of capitalism.
> (*Daily Mail*, 11 September 2001: 12)

On 11 September 2001 it seemed as though the first great economic shock of the twenty-first century had been delivered by an act of terror. 'World financial markets were sent into turmoil by yesterday's terrorist attacks', read an article in the *Telegraph*, which also noted that the fall in share prices did not affect 'oil and gold prices', which 'soared' (Trefgarne and Litterick, 12 September 2001). Another piece in the same newspaper ran under the headline: 'World pays the terrible price for globalisation' (Collins, 12 September 2001). Its author argued that 'in 90 terrible minutes, the same technology that allows us to ... jump on to an aircraft ... was turned into an agent of mass destruction' (*ibid*). According to another journalist, September 11th was 'the day capitalism stopped', and the terror attacks were 'deadly assaults on the nerve centre of global markets and the military-industrial complex' (Brummer, 12 September 2001: 79).

This economic setback should not, however, create the impression that only an external assault could damage the system. In January 2001, for example, financial analysts had been expressing doubts about the strength of the market. One group of journalists had identified 'the growing weakness of the US economy' (Crooks et al., 5 January 2001), while others examined the fear that the UK was on the brink of a 'full recession' (Doward and Ryle, 22 July 2001). Eventually, as the 'credit crunch' seven years later seemed to demonstrate, it was the system's own 'asymmetrical' threat to the social order – its piratical drive to exploit any situation that could create profit – which proved more devastating, in economic terms, than 9/11.

The idea that al-Qaeda had targeted, not only people and buildings, but the representative institutions of the world's foremost capitalist power, clearly demanded some kind of evaluative response from the 'captains of industry'. Putting economic considerations to the fore, however, would seem heartless – when for example the insurance organisation Lloyd's of London (see the Conclusion) issued a report to its members which described the 'terrorist attacks in the United States' as an 'opportunity' because 'rates have shot up to a level where very large profits are possible', a number of British Members of Parliament raised objections (Manning and Gilfeather, 29 October 2001: 11).

It would be difficult, therefore, to imagine national newspapers giving undue prominence to an economic perspective when so many individuals had been killed in an obscene act of violence. Editions of UK newspapers appearing on 12 September did, however, print references to the financial character of the attack, but carried them on inside pages. The *Daily Mirror*, for instance, identified the World Trade Center as an 'ICON OF WEALTH' (Merrett, 12 September 2001: 21), while the *Daily Mail* published a list of '110 facts about the World Trade Center' under the title, 'Destroyed, the once towering symbols of capitalism' (*Mail*, 12 September 2001). The anonymous article was carried on page 10, rather than the front page, where its appearance might have created offence. The *Mail*'s front page read 'APOCALYPSE New York. September 11, 2001', while the *Mirror* opted for 'WAR ON THE WORLD'.

Over the next few years, however, not only was the destructive force of terrorism posited as the enemy of democracy and consumer culture, but capital itself continued to be described as a devastating force; the effects of both phenomena were measured against their ability to disrupt everyday life through violent and unexpected shocks. Yet mainstream commentators seemed reluctant to argue that capitalism was the enemy of democracy, in the same way that terrorism was imagined as an anti-democratic force. It was left to the satirists to make the connection between terror and exploitation. In 2002, for example, in a reference to corporate fraud, one magazine carried a picture of Osama bin Laden on its cover, with the caption 'NEW OSAMA THREAT TO AMERICA', and a speech bubble emerging from the al-Qaeda leader's mouth which read, 'Forget terrorism, I'm going to become an accountant' (*Private Eye*, 12 July 2002). In a testimony to the scale of the damage caused by

Figure 3   An economic perspective: *Daily Mirror*, 12 September 2001.

recession, the language of mass destruction and war began to feed into economic analysis. In 2009, for instance, a piece on European responses to the crisis appeared under the headline 'Europe's stockmarkets go to war over control of "financial WMDs"' (Gow, 20 February 2009). A few months earlier, an academic study of the downturn had been published called 'Financial Regime Change?' (Wade, 2008: 5).

COMPLIANCE AND PUNISHMENT

In the speech cited at the head of this chapter, delivered 'on the eve of a new Millennium', Blair set out a model of globalisation that emphasised its economic character, while claiming that it was also 'a political and security phenomenon' (Blair, 24 April 1999). In suggesting that governments must recognise the disciplinary power of markets, he followed an unremarkable though also expedient line of argument. Blair was not trying to be alarmist: in a globalised economy, governments that run trade deficits are indeed 'punished savagely' (Turner, 2008: 53), and those who fail to observe other 'international policy norms' are definitely 'punished by capital flight' (Kirshner, 2003: 6).

Blair's accurate reading of the market as an independent force capable of undermining the wishes of elected authority might therefore suggest some critical perspective on its 'impersonal "laws"' (Wood, 2003: 11). His speech, however, suggests no resentment of, or opposition to, the relentless activity of economic forces. Such apparent indifference to the negative effects of 'globalisation', from a leading member of the political class, may in part explain the rise of resistance among other public groups, who feel that their interests are not being represented. Intended as a warning against protectionism, Blair's portrayal of elected governments as helpless victims was probably intended to flatter his listeners, but also demonstrates a readiness to take advantage of the dominant neo-liberal mindset, confirming that the New Labour administration would welcome US investment.

Indeed, Blair is in places quite specific about the influx of American capital, noting that 'nearly half the $124 billion US firms spent on foreign acquisitions last year went on British companies', and 'we would like it to be even more' (Blair, 24 April 1999). Once again, the dynamic actor in this scenario is the private sector, rather than the state; though an admission that the UK prime minister was eager to encourage the sale of assets to foreign concerns would not necessarily go down well in a domestic context. In the speech, Britain was also represented as being a major conduit for the unregulated flow of capital. According to Blair, 'about one trillion dollars moves across the foreign exchanges, most of it in London' (*ibid*).

Blair's description of the iniquitous relationship between capital and governments was not unusual in this period; as Boyer remarked, 'competition in world markets' was 'perceived as a strong constraint' upon national forms of organisation (Boyer, 1996: 85). In the meantime, the belief that 'capital flows should not be regulated' was not only 'the express policy of powerful states like the U.S.', but was also followed by those international institutions that were 'supposed to oversee the smooth functioning of the global economy' (Kirshner, 2003: 4). This testified not simply to a lack of control, but to the exercise of a conscious policy. As Gowan argues, 'both regulators and operators' actively generated price bubbles, inflating estimations of market value (in housing, for example), which were created so that a profit could be made from their eventual collapse (Gowan, 2009: 9). The financial institutions on Wall Street would 'enter a particular market, generate a price bubble within it, make big speculative profits, then withdraw' (*ibid*).

When Blair does identify problems in economic globalisation, they do not include questionable practices such as 'light touch' regulation, short-selling, insider trading or asset-stripping. He described instead volatile or criminal activities which are the result of uncontrolled or *illicit* globalisation – i.e. those forms of exchange that lie, rhetorically at least, beyond the power of western influence. These included 'financial instability in Asia' which 'destroys jobs in Chicago and in my own constituency in County Durham', and challenges like 'poverty in the Caribbean' which 'means more drugs on the streets in Washington and London' (Blair, 24 April 1999).

Blair's observations are designed to suggest that the infection comes from outside the US/UK system: America, for example, is not accused of destroying British jobs when it acquires UK companies. Poverty, on the other hand, is an attribute of 'underdeveloped' countries, and is undesirable only because it creates negative effects in the heartland; it is not supposed to exist within the west because that might contradict the narrative of prosperity and growth. On the whole, Blair might seem to recognise 'the reified generality of "the market"' (DeLanda, 2006: 18), and to accept its disciplinary effects, yet, unlike those who actually receive the 'punishment' described, and who fall victim to the 'systemic requirements of competition' (Wood, 2003: 11), he does not consider it in any way oppressive.

ECONOMIC COMPLEXITIES

While an 'economy' is often presented in neutral terms, as the administration of the affairs of a state or nation, it is clearly more than this. It is not only 'a complex of social institutions and practices', but also 'a set of concepts and theories' that construct 'the market' as an object of enquiry (Aldridge, 2005: 81). Irvine reinforces this point, arguing that linguistic 'goods' may enter a marketplace 'as objects of exchange' and that 'linguistic signs are part of a political economy, not just vehicles for thinking about it' (Irvine, 1989: 1). A similar position is taken by Graham in his work on the knowledge economy, when he argues that 'the products of the human imagination, including particular types of thought, the language used to convey these, and the perceived value of these two socially inseparable phenomena, are commodities' (Graham, 1999: 487).

Ideas themselves are 'fashioned into capital' (Turner, 2002: 18/29) while capital – as a social and economic force – depends on representation and the use of symbols. The 'signs' of the market appear as *a type of control*, and are used to defend, enhance or realise *forms of value* through expressions of 'confidence'. This in turn depends on the degree to which the political sphere is able to provide favourable conditions for the commercial exploitation of resources. It is clear, therefore, that no economic theory is composed simply of market strategies, as they will necessarily be framed within a 'rhetoric' of explanation.[1] As Blyth argues, the 'political power of financial ideas' is seen in their ability to 'dictate specific governance solutions' and in their simple use as 'valuable political weapons' (Blyth, 2003: 239). Of course, when Dowd notes that 'economic arguments naturally tend to carry the most weight' (Dowd, 2000: 3) in a capitalist society, this does not mean that economic motives are presented by politicians, public-relations wonks and think-tanks in their true guise; moral positions are often used to obscure underlying pragmatic causes (Thussu, 2006: 14).

However the relationship between representation and moral and economic value is conceived, the problem lies in the fact that the free market model, circulated by 'elite' social actors, contributes not just to the creation of inequality but also to the 'regulation of *social relations*' (Wood, 2003: 11). In other words, class stratification within the 'globalised' world order is reinforced through economic strategy and its attendant alibis. Those in power are of course unwilling to frame their intentions in such stark terms, because that would contradict the notion of free choice and social mobility in a market economy. This is one of the reasons why the economic is presented as a neutral arena of activity, and why 'political struggles about money' are often disguised in 'economic terms' and then 'veiled by a cloak of *economic legitimacy*' (Kirshner, 2003: 3, my emphasis). In the international context, Kirshner argues that 'uninhibited financial liberalisation is the most obvious example' of this deceitful practice (*ibid*: 3).

DEFENSIVE EXPLANATIONS

Discussing the economic functions of globalisation in his 'Doctrine of the International Community', Blair included both hidden and explicit references to the political, talking of 'free trade' as a desirable goal, and describing the gradual 'spread of democracy' (Blair, 24 April 1999). He accompanied this with anodyne and internally inconsistent prescriptions of belief, such as the notion 'that partnership and co-operation' – between states rather than communities – 'are essential to advance self-interest' (*ibid*). Although Blair recognised that governments are constrained by the markets, he did not examine the fact that the political class was responsible for placing itself in a position of subservience. As Boyer points out, 'the final factor in the revival of the market' was the 'adoption of free market ideology and economic recipes by *governments and policy-makers*' (Boyer, 1996: 85). Having aligned themselves with the neo-liberal economic model, ruling elites were unable to change direction, despite clear evidence that the regime of liberalised and integrated markets was both 'inefficient and crisis-prone' (Blyth, 2003: 239).

Once committed to a particular economic course, however, the political elite found that it had to justify its choice during a period when other fundamental assumptions – like the security of the 'homeland' and its citizens – also had to be revised. Key political utterances tended towards *defensive* explanation rather than evaluative enquiry. So, for example, when President Bush declared in 2001 that the US economy was 'fundamentally strong' despite the decline in the value of shares held by American citizens (Anon, *Mail on Sunday*, 23 September 2001: 8), this might be described as an attempt to shore up economic confidence, rather than to calculate, however inadequately, the actual economic effects of terrorism and the war which seemed increasingly to be fought *in the name of terror*. Defensive remarks are therefore broadly rhetorical in character, made in the knowledge that financial value is indeed partly maintained through the positive declarations of faith made by influential individuals. Peter Mandelson's statement that the 9/11 terrorists 'could not have timed their attacks at a more fragile point in the world's business cycle' (Mandelson, 23 September 2001), serves as a useful counterpoint, as it is more clearly evaluative.

In some political formations, the connection between expression and particular economic values is made explicit. This was the case with the Bush administration, where the re-imagining of American values[2] after September 11th involved the mobilisation of existing principles in the service of an information 'war'. In 2001, Charlotte Beers, who had once promoted the shampoo 'Head and Shoulders', was drafted in from the war on dandruff to become George W. Bush's Under Secretary for Public Diplomacy. She described her task as follows: 'the burden is now on us to act as though no-one has ever understood the identity of the U.S., and redefine it for audiences who are at best cynical' (Benady, 8 November 2001: 27). Her role was further described by the then head of the State Department, Colin Powell, who revealed that he 'wanted one of the world's greatest advertising experts, because ... we're selling a product' (*ibid*). In Powell's words, there was no difference between political and economic conceptions of freedom. 'That product we are selling', he declared, 'is democracy ... the free enterprise system, the American value system ... it's a product very much in demand' (*ibid*). The strong relationship between 'democratic', commercial and military discourse remains a powerful indicator of how each contributes to an overall system of belief.

Such discourse, in the United States at least, moves between the permeable barriers of public relations firms, transnational corporations, government institutions, the armed forces and entertainment capital. As General Tommy Franks declared, America wished to tighten the net around bin Laden, in order to fulfil 'the core values of this campaign' (BBC News, 16 November 2001). In this case, one of the central practices in contemporary governance, public relations in its 'political' mode, provides the essential terms for the concentration of force, just as Rumsfeld drew upon managerial discourses when he advocated the use of 'flexible force' (Thomas and Barry, 3 March 2003) against the Iraqi army. Flexibility, a notion which disguises a managerial edict 'in the guise of an emancipatory practice' (Price, 2006b: 67), provided Rumsfeld with the principle he needed to dominate opposition within the US military hierarchy, which was still attached to the principle of 'overwhelming' force.

Not all political elites, however, engage so directly in these comparisons between democratic values and commercial goals. Where discursive norms exclude the possibility of moral references, or make their expression too risky, the consequence is a more constrained mode of speech. British political discourse is characterised by a greater reluctance to vocalise the integration of fiscal and moral standards that American politicians take for granted. When UK ministers do emphasise economic concerns, their utterances tend to create unease.

Take, for example, the remarks made by Jack Straw when challenged over the lack of progress in establishing a 'government of national unity' in Iraq. Straw, then Foreign Secretary, insisted that progress must be made because of the coalition's political efforts and 'the huge amount of money that has been spent' (BBC Radio 4 News, 2 March 2004). Similarly, David Miliband, Foreign Secretary under Prime Minister Gordon Brown, described the handover of Basra to Iraqi forces (in December 2007) by noting that 'we've got a political agreement ... that allows people to see politics as the way they divide the spoils, rather than violence' (in Oborne's documentary *Iraq: The Betrayal*, 17 March 2008, Channel 4). Here, an insight into the instrumental purpose of formal politics emerges from the simple reference to 'spoils' rather than, for example, the usual allusion to democracy or participation.

QUESTIONS OF VALUE

In Swedberg's view, contemporary economics has reduced studies of 'interest' and value to a narrow, financial conception which divorces the economic world from its social context (Swedberg, 2003: 1). The wider meaning of the term 'value' encompasses worth, desirability and utility (Concise OED, 1964), suggesting moral, aesthetic and functional standards. Used with reference to human beings, value represents an estimation of both individual and a more general social worth. Calculating human value seems, however, to present difficulties for the free market theorist.

Therefore, when trade is described as the fulfilment of genuine needs, this should be recognised as an attempt to provide the absent 'moral' rationale for the operation of the free market, feeding the myth that the only problem with capitalism is that it does not operate on a human scale. Although the size and apparent ubiquity of large corporations does indeed give them a strategic advantage, there is a more fundamental reason for their ability to dominate the mechanisms of exchange. They are able to manipulate the abstraction of *value*, guaranteeing that neither 'real' needs nor ethical standards need govern economic relationships. With the onset of new technology (Kirshner, 2003: 12), the capitalist has been further removed from the realm of actual goods and is better able to oversee the electronic management of capital (Schoonmaker, 1994: 172). In this sense, it is correct to say that *number* rather than need 'governs the economy' (Badiou, 2008a: 3).

A common misconception is that financial systems are used to assist the 'operations of the real economy' (Gowan, 2009: 9) rather than to exploit its weaknesses. The process of trading, for example, though it suggests equal exchange and some form of commitment, does not necessarily mean that it provides financial support for companies, or that 'long-term investment' is taking place (*ibid*). Gowan gives the example of the 'massive bubble in oil prices' that grew between 2007 and 2008, a phenomenon which was not caused by supply and demand, but by 'financial operators' who 'blew the price from $70 dollars a barrel to over $140 in less than a year', before letting the value of the commodity collapse (*ibid*: 6). The scale of the profits made through such manoeuvres can be appreciated when 'most integrated oil majors are geared up to make money even if it trades at $10 a barrel' (Dewson, 31 January 2006). With the ability to move swiftly and in a coordinated fashion, raids on commodities can therefore yield substantial returns for the predatory trader.

The financial sector has the ability to turn all kinds of material, from oil to bundles of debt, into tradeable commodities. In the meantime, neo-liberal ideologues have been eager to hasten the symbolic/material decline of the industrial base and its 'outmoded' structures, because it represented stable employment and thus a high degree of class and community solidarity. The apparent transition from the paradigm of a *productive/material* national base characterised by 'solidity' to a model of *abstract* market internationalism required some ideological clothing. In justifying this development, *neo-liberalism*, with its doctrine of individuation and self-reliance, became a general social doctrine.

NEO-LIBERALISM

Harvey defines neo-liberalism as 'a theory of political economic practices' which insists that the interests of humanity are best served by 'liberating individual entrepreneurial freedoms and skills' (Harvey, 2005: 2). It does not, therefore, begin from the conviction that the goal of economic endeavour is a general or collective movement towards equality, whether or not that is possible to attain in absolute terms. The emancipation of human energy is instead supposed to take place within 'an institutional framework characterised by strong private property rights, free markets and free trade' (*ibid*). The role of the state in the production of economic freedom is simply to guarantee 'the quality and integrity of money' (though this is less of a burden where nations share a common currency) and to construct 'military, defence, police, and legal structures' in order to protect the operation of markets. Where markets do not exist they should, according to this doctrine, be created – if necessary 'by state action' (*ibid*).

This observation, that it is the state which has to intercede on behalf of the market principle, is of particular significance when considering not only the economic 'determinants' of the 'war on terror', but a larger proposition: that the whole *rationale* of the neo-liberal project is based on the production of various forms of disintegrative violence. This includes the drive to war and the application of a social-economic 'shock' (Klein, 2007) to any structures that stand in the way of the neo-liberal reordering of society. This suggestion, that the role of the political executive is to create favourable conditions for the aggressive recomposition of the social order, has serious implications for any model of the state which argues that it is 'peculiarly charged with overall responsibility for maintaining the cohesion of the social formation of which it is part' (Jessop, 2008: 79). Instead of meeting these imagined responsibilities, in free market theory the state acts as the overseer (though not necessarily the direct beneficiary) of economic exploitation.

This is not to argue that the state is unable to make positive interventions in the social realm (Poulantzas, 1978a: 30), but rather that this tendency has been countered by the growth of market fundamentalism. The public avowal of faith in the market has meant that, where politicians do act to improve the lives of the subaltern, such activity must not seem to be part of a redistributive or 'socialist' agenda. Instead, the rhetorical pronouncements of the political elite characterise such activities as part of a commitment to 'doing the right thing'. In turn, the deregulation of the public sector is presented as not only a pragmatic, but a *moral* response to those supposedly irresistible forces (globalisation, restructuring, flexibility) that form the new 'realities' of modern life.[3]

Having discarded many of their own structural responsibilities, and having ceded a decisive role in public life to capital interests, the representatives of government have now to pretend that the systemic failure of the system they helped to construct was caused by a blunder committed somewhere overseas, or in the hidden recesses of the financial sector. The dissolution of those 'oppositional' social structures that might have resisted the power of capital has in the meantime led to two parallel developments: the reappearance of social discontent and protest, and the strengthening of the 'repressive' apparatus. The collision between these forms of power has reappeared, with the state taking 'pre-emptive' measures wherever possible. The existence of such a clash, however, is not the simple product of the 'war on terror'. It represents the resurgence of an antagonism that was based on an objection to the entire panoply of western authoritarianism – but in particular to the *structural* iniquities built into the economic system of the west. This hostility began to appear in the streets of those cities chosen to host the various international summits devoted to the structural adjustment of the international system.

FROM 'DOOMSDAY' TO GENOA: PROTEST AND RESISTANCE

During a news conference before the G8 summit of July 2001, Tony Blair acknowledged that there would be 'people there who will be making their protest', before saying that he hoped 'they do so peacefully' (Blair, 19 July 2001). The championing of peaceful activity by warmongers, explains why some regard such exhortations with scepticism, and why they try instead to ensure an impact by making a physical impression on their surroundings. In response, the state is then able to fulfil its legitimate desire to meet force with its own forms of violence.

Increased (para)militarisation of the repressive function was, however, planned long before the 'war on terror' and even before the anti-globalisation protests of the late 1990s. A *Sunday Times* article of 8 April 1990, for example, revealed that 'secret plans to use SAS-trained armed police in riots have been approved' (Sunday Times Insight Team, 1990: 1). The basis for this development was the production of a particular *scenario*: in this case, it was called 'Doomsday', and centred on the notion that the authorities would have to deal with an armed assailant who would use a disturbance as cover for an attack against police.

'In essence', one Chief Constable said of this procedure, it was 'a shoot-to-kill policy' (Sunday Times Insight Team, 1990: 1). This kind of warning, replicated after the Stockwell incident of 2005

(Price, 2009a), was actually intended to emphasise the determination of the authorities, not always to shoot individuals, but to use the 'full range' of available techniques up to and including pre-emptive assaults. Meanwhile, a number of undesirable groups were measured up for the role of villain, including animal rights protestors, football hooligans and 'anti-capitalist' campaigners. Over ten years after the Doomsday scenario was revealed, the protestors who congregated in Genoa in July 2001 provided an opportunity for the vilification of the political activist.

Restrictions on the free movement of European radicals were reported in the *Guardian* in June 2001, under the headline 'Travel ban to block "anarchist" leaders' (www.guardian.co.uk, 18 June 2001). While the political executives of the G8 nations could move without hindrance, the governments of the 'leading industrialized states' used 'a detailed police dossier on the "travelling anarchists' circus"' which had 'disrupted the EU's Gothenburg summit' (Black and White, 18 June 2001). The paper reported that 'ringleaders are likely to be treated like football hooligans – and kept at home', and noted that officials had been studying a 'coordinated and hard response to this new form of extremist, cross-border criminality' (*ibid*). Meanwhile, Swedish police in Gothenburg had already been responsible for shooting three demonstrators during the protests in the city.

It seems clear that peaceful opposition to the state, unless it is on a grand scale, is not given the degree of prominence accorded to more dramatic forms of protest. 'Violent' activities achieve extensive press and television coverage, and in every case reveal a practice that extends throughout the mainstream right-wing media – the moral condemnation of radical groups. This is not to suggest that demonstrations never attract organisations which believe in creating disorder. However, public authority shies away from trying to justify its own use of violence, by presenting repression as the just deserts of all; the first task is to identify some collective or individual opponent that can be made to represent a grave challenge to the fundamental values of democracy.

Press use of human interest stories, where individual demonstrators are profiled and interviewed, risks producing a sympathetic portrayal, so the preferred practice is often to spy on protestors, emphasising their apparent naivety or their supposedly sinister beliefs. In the case of Genoa, the British tabloid the *Daily Mail* not only reported the controversy but helped to compose a particular view of the demonstrators. One journalist, Lucie Morris, described how, 'posing as a student' she 'infiltrated [a] London-based direct action group' dedicated to 'civil disobedience' (Morris, 21 July 2001). Her article appeared under the headline 'The graduate, the banker and the doctor's son ... introducing Britain's middle-class revolutionaries' (*ibid*).

The technique used in this type of writing is to confine moral judgement to the subjects of the article. Morris does not describe her method of entry to the group as subterfuge, nor her claim to be an activist, as an outright lie. Instead, it is the demonstrators who are vilified. Pen portraits of the protestors included one that described 'Becky, who has just been awarded a 2:1 BA degree in English and History at Goldsmith's College', while an activist called Justin revealed that 'you'll find a lot of us who enjoy coming on things like this are pretty normal really' (*ibid*).

Morris was also responsible for the article 'ARMED GUARD ON BRITON WHO LED RIOTERS', a piece which distorted the role of the activist Mark Covell (Morris, 23 July 2001: 1). Covell was described as a 'sociology graduate ... known to British police', who was 'arrested during the May Day riots in London for possessing cannabis' (*ibid*). The accusation directed at Covell was that he was '*said to be in charge* of computer systems used to coordinate attacks on the G8 summit by anarchist groups and could spend five years in jail' (*ibid*, my emphasis). Morris reproduced the opinion of the Italian police without question, noting that they believed that Covell 'was using his computer skills to help the Genoa Social Forum' (*ibid*, 6–7). The Social Forum, it should be noted, offers an arena for debate, rather than violent activity.

Seven years later, the methods employed to frame Covell as a violent ringleader were described in an article written by Nick Davies. Davies, working for the *Guardian*, reported that 'lying in San Martino hospital the day after his beating', Covell came round 'to find his shoulder being shaken by a woman who, he understood, was from the British embassy' (Davies, 17 July 2008). This person, most likely to have been Lucie Morris, was only revealed to be a reporter from the *Daily Mail* when 'the man with her started taking photographs' (*ibid*). Covell, a freelance journalist himself, posed no threat to the authorities in Genoa, but had the misfortune to be attacked, together with over 90 others, by the Italian police during a night-time raid on a school being used to provide accommodation for protestors. His injuries included a broken rib-cage, a punctured lung, a broken hand, a damaged spine and the loss of twelve teeth (*ibid*). In their final communiqué, the leaders of the G8 declared that 'we will defend the right of peaceful protestors to have their voices heard but, as democratic leaders, we cannot accept that a violent minority should be allowed to disrupt our discussions' (MacAskill et al., 23 July 2001). When actual examples of the abuse of power are brought to public attention, however, it becomes particularly difficult for political leaders to characterise their conduct as ethical.

SECRECY AND POWER

One attempt to provide a rationale for the increased strength of the repressive apparatus is the insistence that a 'new protective state' has been constructed, in which government agencies are supposed to act, not as the persecutors of the citizen, but as a bastion against the threat of terrorist attacks. One of the individuals supporting this conception, is Sir Kevin Tebbit who, in a piece on 'Ethics and Intelligence', recognises first that the 'operations ... methods and techniques' employed by intelligence services 'are to some degree impaired by open public debate about them' (Tebbit, 2007: 170). This opening move in Tebbit's argument rests on the undeniable fact that transparency may reduce the effectiveness of an intelligence agency, but his point is only valid if the citizen accepts assurances that the role of MI5 is really to prevent 'terrorist attacks' against the public, and not for example to dress up dissent as potentially 'terrorist'.

Tebbit, aware of the need to achieve some kind of balance in the debate, asks how far the intelligence community should go in attempting to 'convince the public that the operations of the intelligence agencies' are in line 'with what people expect them to be, not just in law, but in terms of ethics' (*ibid*: 171). On the face of it, this sounds like an impulse to make genuine progress towards bringing the powers of the secret state into line with public expectations. Of course, it is perfectly possible to use language to obscure all types of nefarious activity, but it is more instructive to take Tebbit at his word. The curious aspect of this line of reasoning is that his apparently enlightened statement is actually the prelude to a different kind of argument. He goes on to say that intelligence officers are, in fact, already moral individuals, and that they 'need to be satisfied, more than anybody else, that they're operating within an accepted body of guidelines' (*ibid*). The point, however, is not whether the 'spooks' have a sense of morality, but *i*) whether their moral sense is comparable with public expectation, and *ii*) whether this ethical compass is strong enough to prevent them from carrying out immoral acts, such as collaborating with agencies that use torture and lying about their involvement in such activities (see Norton-Taylor, 21 April 2009).

No solution to these questions is offered, because Tebbit ends this part of his discussion by declaring that 'the idea that we need to impose such a framework on them ... is mistaken' (Tebbit, 2007: 171). Instead of answering his earlier question, he turns instead to what he regards as a greater problem; this is his belief that intelligence agencies 'are not equipped to meet and face the challenges that twenty-first-century threats pose' (*ibid*). His penultimate conclusion is essentially to maintain secrecy, or as he puts it: not 'to provide many more details in public about the operations and methods' (*ibid*). The interesting aspect of this position is that Tebbit is also opposed to the assumption that security officers operate in an environment 'less principled or ethical than the one lived in by society as a whole' (*ibid*: 175). Considering the types of corruption that are to be found within the social order, this provides no form of reassurance whatever.

'A CAREFULLY CRAFTED IMAGE'

Overall, the accusation that clandestine developments represent the secret concentration of repressive powers is dismissed by Tebbit on the grounds that it exaggerates the real state of affairs, either because of 'ideological' prejudices, or because people are simply not in possession of the facts. The detailed exposure of 'inside' information is the preferred technique of retired police officer Michael Waldren (2007) who, in contrast to the vague reassurances offered by commentators like Tebbit, tries to correct enduring misapprehensions about the British police force. Its much vaunted status as an unarmed organisation has now disappeared forever, but Waldren insists that it was 'always a manufactured myth' (Waddington, cited in Waldren, 2007: x). In his preface, he notes that 'the carefully crafted postwar image of the police was one of a benign unarmed service', but later describes how weapons had been available to the Metropolitan force almost from its inception in 1829 (*ibid*: 3). It had always from that time on had access to firearms for certain duties like protection of dignitaries, the guarding of bullion, or the apprehension of dangerous criminals.

Waldren's approach to the question of confidentiality and secret knowledge is to compare the speculation characteristic of many newspaper reports with the actual situation experienced within the police service. In other words, specific examples of media exaggeration or inaccuracy are contrasted with a rather more mundane 'reality'. The verifiable existence of 'inside information', however antique, is therefore supposed to disprove the validity of critical perspectives, including the idea that the police have become a paramilitary force. Unlike Tebbit, therefore, Waldren provides concrete examples in order to support his position, though they do tend to prove the opposite case.

At one point, Waldren notes that a major economic summit to be held in London in June 1984 caused public controversy when details of security arrangements appeared in the press. Ronald Reagan, the US President at the time, was due to attend. Claims that the Americans had expressed serious reservations about the standard of British security began to circulate. Waldren recalls that 'the decision was taken to train a small number of protection officers in the use of the Heckler and Koch MP5K 9mm sub-machine gun' (Waldren, 2007: 98). He denies, however, that this was due to Reagan's participation in the conference, going on to cite the *Daily Mail* of 2 April 1984, which reported that 'British policemen are to carry automatic sub-machine guns for the first time after training by the SAS' (*ibid*). Contesting the idea that the firearms instruction was to be conducted by the Special Air Service, Waldren demonstrates that both the Home Office and the Prime Minister of the day, Margaret Thatcher, denied SAS involvement. Thatcher insisted that the police 'will not be trained by the military' (*ibid*).

Waldren's use of another newspaper story allows him to highlight what he sees as the misconceptions surrounding the paramilitary education of the police. In this case, the *Daily Mirror* is his target, because it ran an article which combined reference to the new weapons with a more general argument about the political trajectory of the police. 'Our so-called unarmed police force', the *Mirror* announced, 'is now to be issued with SAS-style sub-machine guns' (cited in Waldren, 2007: 99). The paper took this development as evidence of a downward path towards 'a semi-military constabulary', and warned that 'arming the police adds to the dangers to innocent people rather than reducing them' (*ibid*). The *Mirror* went on to offer the reasonable opinion that no extra protection ought to be offered to President Reagan, and that he should be content with the level of security provided for the Queen. At this point, Waldren tells the reader that 'the *Daily Mirror* would presumably have been mortified' if it had known that part of the Queen's security detail was to be issued with MP5K's, the weapon referred to in the news reports. The ignorance of the *Mirror* provides Waldren with some wry satisfaction. There is no doubt that, at least with regard to operational matters, police officers like Waldren often have access to more accurate information than do journalists. The supposed misperception of police intent is therefore attributed to the inadequacy of the press, and *not to public concern about the development of a paramilitary capability*. This, however, is a function of the officers' institutional position, rather than testament to the undoubtedly substantial failings of the media.

Journalists are, nonetheless, capable of creating 'exclusives' in which genuine insights can be discovered. The *Sunday Times*' front page report on the Poll Tax 'riot' of March 1990, referred to above, is a case in point. The headline 'Police plan a "shoot to kill" policy in riots', followed by the sub-heading 'SAS trained marksmen would "take out" gunmen in crowd', demonstrates the antecedents of policies that some commentators imagine were confined to military conflict in Northern Ireland, or were only brought onto the mainland after September 11th, or first applied during the Stockwell shooting in July 2005.

The *Sunday Times* claimed that 'it is the first time that police on the mainland have considered using firearms during outbreaks of public disorder' (Sunday Times Insight Team, 8 April 1990: 1). The policy was contained in the Public Tactical Options Manual of the Association of Chief Police Officers, a document that had apparently been compiled after the riots that took place in British cities in 1981 (Emmerson and Shamash, 1987: 20). Information about a version of such a manual had in fact been revealed during the trial of the Orgreave pickets in 1986, mentioned during cross-examination by an ex-police officer called Clements (Jackson and Wardle, 1986: 68). In this case, the incident that brought this detail to light was the practice of beating truncheons on shields (*ibid*). While the authorities had to contend with the difficulty of controlling the appearance of confidential information, the problem faced by their opponents was the challenge of making their perspective heard at all, not only within the media but within the public realm in general.

THE REALM OF THE 'LEGITIMATE': PROTEST AND EFFECT

The title of a book called *The War We Could Not Stop* (Ramesh, 2003), seemed to reveal something of the mood that prevailed among British opponents of the Iraq war. A similar observation, noting that 'masses of people' had tried, without success, to 'stop a war before it began', was made by a group of American-based authors (Boal et al., 2005: 5). Another writer argued that 'the combined efforts of anti-war movements around the world' had, in fact, nearly derailed the plans of the Bush administration (Rai, 2003: xix). However close this enlightened but protean 'multitude', often organised through web-based groups (Boal et al., 2005: 4; Gillan et al., 2008: 29) had come to achieving its primary goal, the fact remains that it did not succeed. Of course, not all the participants in the anti-war movement really expected to prevent the onset of hostilities; for many individuals and groups, the point was to make a principled stand, or to increase the strength of alternative forms of political association. Any assessment of informal political opposition to state policies must, therefore, recognise the variety of stances and attitudes that could be adopted, not just with regard to particular tactics, but in some cases to the principal rationale that was supposed to motivate the protests.

When new threats emerged, however, those organisations formed to oppose the first phase of the offensive (the attack on Afghanistan), redoubled their efforts. The UK's 'Stop the War Coalition', for example, had been founded on 21 September 2001 in order to resist 'the war currently declared by the United States and its allies against "terrorism"' (stopwar.org.uk, 2001). In 2003, the threat to invade Iraq drew more people into the protestors' ranks. Yet the growth of this emergency also exacerbated a tactical problem: how to characterise the activity of the belligerent powers. Immediately after 9/11, it had seemed entirely logical to respond to events by using the frame of reference (the 'war on terror') invented by the US administration. The drawback then had been that the critics of military force found themselves using an 'amorphous abstraction' (Holloway, 2008: 4), an *alibi* designed to allow those in authority freedom of manoeuvre (see Chapter 1). In the next phase of 'imperial' aggression, this conceptual frame had undergone some changes.

PRESERVING THE PEACE?

Unlike the pronouncements issued after the attack on the US mainland, which were clearly based on mobilising the symbolic resonance of a 'just war' (see Chapter 2), the political leaders of Britain and America were more circumspect about their intentions with regard to Iraq. This was because they wished to place the emphasis on Saddam Hussein's supposed reluctance to comply with United Nations demands, which asked for full access to Iraq's military installations. In seeking international cover for their plans, the US and UK executives were unable to return to the aggressive language employed after the 9/11 attacks. In order to maintain this more moderate façade, Bush and Blair had to show restraint, while reinforcing the widely shared perception that the Iraqi leader was brutal and intransigent. Addressing both domestic and overseas audiences, the leading functionaries of the pro-war faction acted as though they were fully engaged in the rituals of public persuasion; for this reason, war was not their preferred term, and the concept was actively denied or suppressed.

A couple of examples will demonstrate this point. Speaking to the UN Security Council on 5 February 2003, US Secretary of State Colin Powell referred to resolution 1441. This document, produced by the UN Security Council on 8 November 2002, called upon the Iraqi regime to allow full access to UNMOVIC (UN Monitoring, Verification and Inspection Commission) and IAEA (International Atomic Energy Agency) inspectors, and noted that it had 'repeatedly warned Iraq' that 'it will face serious consequences' as a result of its repeated violations (UNSC Resolution 1441, 2002: 5). This reference to the previous behaviour of the Security Council did not really constitute a threat to impose any future penalty (Rai, 2003: 55), and should not have provided a sufficient reason for an invasion. Powell, however, in his speech to the Council, tried to turn the imprecision of such language to his advantage, declaring that 'we wrote 1441 not in order to go to war' but 'to try to preserve the peace' (cited in Prados, 2004: 225).

Evidence of evasive utterance was also recorded in the UK. Blair, responding to a parliamentary question on Iraq on 15 September 2002, insisted that it was not true 'that the Americans had decided to take military action come what may' (Kilfoyle, 2007: 78). Here, again, war was not mentioned. Six months later, the same reluctance to draw attention to the condition was apparent, at the moment when Blair announced the beginning of the attack. 'On Tuesday night', he said, 'I gave the order for British forces to take part in military action in Iraq' (Blair, 20 March 2003). 'British servicemen and women', he declared 'are engaged from air, land and sea' (*ibid*). When the term 'war' did appear in this speech, it was relegated to an historical context, reassuring the listener that 'war between the big powers is unlikely' and noting that 'the cold war' was 'already a memory' (*ibid*).

The effect of this extensive subterfuge was, as suggested above, to present the political Left with a problem; in the interests of exposing the hypocrisy of the Right, it had to draw attention to the 'true' circumstance underlying the rhetorical manoeuvre. The advantage of assigning the term 'war' to this condition, from the radicals' point of view at least, was that their supporters would be in no doubt as to the devastation that would ensue. For the Left, contemporary manifestations of war are not interpreted as armed confrontations between evenly matched enemies. Instead, it signifies the destruction of weaker opponents, including non-combatants, through the use of advanced technology and bombing. As Slim argues, 'with air power, the business of killing civilians slipped easily into the grand strategic realm'; this means that it can be subsumed within military and political objectives (Slim, 2007: 53). Assaults on civilians are sewn into the fabric of war but are interpreted by soldiers as its unfortunate by-product: hence the proposition that 'each loss of an innocent life is a tragedy'.

In trying to bring the 'actual' case into focus, at a time when the architects of the conflict were being coy about their aims, the dissenters had to avoid the notion that the aggressors really were about to engage in an equal struggle. Meanwhile, their opponents in government were torn between representing their triumph as a foregone conclusion, in order to reassure their audiences that their own casualties would be light, and the need to exaggerate the threat in order to justify the use of force.

A PRACTICAL DILEMMA

The rhetorical tactics of the aggressors seemed transparent and at times risible. How then should the failure of the anti-war camp to prevent the invasion of Iraq be understood? One obvious answer is that its enemies were able to initiate events which the dissidents *were not in a position to stop*; this is explored below. In the meantime, the protestors were forced into a contest without being able to appropriate the practical and symbolic tools needed to project their argument; broadcast reports of demonstrations provided only fragmentary accounts of their position (see Gillan et al., 2008). The Left's anti-war case had to begin with the simple demand that the invasion should be prevented; yet the logic of opposition to this threat meant identifying a number of other disorders, all of which were inextricably linked to this new phase of imperial expansion. Many other pressing domestic and global controversies were thus automatically drawn into the equation, because all were important indicators of the social and economic costs of the 'war on terror'. The various dissidents involved in the protests had, therefore, to attack what they perceived as the root of the problem.

In the UK, 'Justice Not Vengeance' called for the creation of a 'UN Transitional Authority to assist Iraqi political groupings' to develop democracy (Justice Not Vengeance, 24 September 2003). The standard approach among many of those opposed to the war, at least in the period before the conflict began, seemed to be a vague faith in the progressive character of the UN. On 15 February 2003, for example, during the biggest of the UK's anti-war mobilisations,[4] some protestors were calling for a second UN resolution before any further action was taken, rather than for outright opposition to the invasion, arguing that 'the UN inspectors should be given more time to do their job' (BBC News online, 15 February 2003). Others emphasised their political moderation, celebrating 'the fact that it's people of all ages not just extremists' which had 'made this a really powerful rally' (*ibid*). One man placed his faith in the symbolic power of the demonstration itself. In an interview given to camera he expressed the hope that 'Tony Blair will see sense ... and it will make him aware of what the public mood is like and basically make him realise that ... going to war is just a big mistake' (Padilla, 2003).

In this case, a clear link is imagined between public activity and the idea that the question could be decided by moral example. It is interesting to note that this view is predicated on the belief in an open, democratic exchange of opinion, a model of interaction promoted by Blair himself in order to demonstrate that some national debate had taken place. This passed over the essential feature of executive rule: the obligation to act without restraint in pursuit of a goal, once the principles of 'free speech' have been aired and exercised. Therefore, at the beginning of the war, when it had the numbers to make an impact, the Left had to contend with the fact that many of its supporters remained unwilling to move beyond the most limited of demands. It did not help that, once the troops were engaged, mainstream political parties which had opposed the military build-up (like Britain's Liberal Democrats), fell into line with the government.

When the invasion had been initiated, and the scale of protests began to diminish, it seemed as though the authorities were better able to determine the conditions under which protest could take place; the physical and ideological boundaries of opposition could be managed more easily. The exercise of greater internal control was, in fact, one of the aims of 'the war on terror', which was used to increase 'the militarisation of law enforcement' (McCulloch, 2002: 55). The later wave of protests, by comparison, faced with the need to maintain pressure as the Iraq conflagration showed no sign of abating, required the production of an uncompromising attitude and the mobilisation of a more determined base;[5] this in turn helped the police to justify the development of tighter security. The use by the state of surveillance and 'paramilitary' tactics very much depends on being able to characterise all protests as capable of degenerating into a state of anarchy; protestors enter a situation in which their actions are determined as a potential threat to public order. The various groups demanding an end to 'war' found that they could not easily offset the binary division (determined by formal authority and reinforced in moral discourse) between legitimate and illegitimate conduct.

PEACEFUL AND VIOLENT PROTEST

According to this perspective, 'peaceful' manifestations are forever in danger of being spoiled by a 'violent minority'. The alternative stance, adopted by some revolutionary organisations, is that effective action is smothered by an unwarranted regard for respectability; this provides the mirror image of the 'moderate' position, but neither discursive frame need be taken at face value. So, for example, not every lawful, peaceful protest simply feeds the system, nor is all violent activity guaranteed to shake the foundations of the neo-liberal state (see the discussion in *Aufheben*, 10, 2002: 1–17). The anti-war alliance was, after all, flexible enough to allow a number of tactics to be deployed, from peaceful direct action and civil disobedience to the use of petitions and orderly processions through public space; each of these actions could draw upon features of the material-symbolic environment, creating a mix of practical and theatrical statements during the course of their exposition or performance.

If, however, the media are to be understood as 'the subtler instrument of the same homogenisation of force' (Baudrillard, 2005: 77), then nothing that the Left presents for mediation will be interpreted in ways it would prefer. One way of trying to overcome this impasse was attempted during the anti-war campaign. The idea was to deploy established media images in an alternative context, in order to recapture the public imagination through symbolic means.

An example of this occurred nine months after the huge February demonstration, in November 2003, when George W. Bush visited the UK and a protest was organised against his presence. The route taken by marchers to Trafalgar Square was almost hermetically sealed by crash barriers, creating a long, winding corridor, with few spectators in evidence. Arriving in the Square from darkened streets, the scene resembled a floodlit pen in which a gigantic crèche had been organised – a feverish atmosphere prevailed as protestors set up and then toppled an outsize statue of Bush. This piece of theatre, a reference to the demolition of Saddam Hussein's statue earlier in 2003, was designed to generate media coverage. In one sense, it answered the earlier event; yet it is possible to argue that it was conducted for the cameras within an equally sterile arena.

STRUCTURAL POSITION AND OPPORTUNITY

In essence, the radicals' potential for success was circumscribed by their place within the overall disposition of forces. Jessop argues that a productive analysis of power depends on examining the 'organisation, modes of calculation, resources, strategies [and] tactics ... of different agents', including for example 'unions, parties, departments of state, pressure groups, police', and so on. It is then important to consider 'the relations among these agents' (Jessop, 2008: 29). In other words, the operation of influence is multi-dimensional; it is not enough to imagine a straightforward clash of ideas or a confrontation between diametrically opposed forces, which merely fulfils the drama of opposition. A significant factor in determining the outcome of the contest between the executive authority and its opponents, therefore, lay in the *structural location* of the antagonists. They operated within distinct, though *rhetorically interdependent* spheres of action; they had access, however, to different types of *practical* resource.

The structural or institutional opportunities available to specific actors help to shape the type of practical/symbolic effects they are able to produce, while the need to dramatise the contest for a 'public', and to answer the accusations and feints of the opponent, means that they are forced to draw meanings from the same lexicon. This serves as a reminder that, despite the formal differences between the opposing sides (the advocates of 'military action' and those who spoke out against this option), there remains an ideological continuum; this runs, for example, through the appeals made on all sides to notions of 'peace', 'democracy', 'justice' and so on.

This begins to fracture when 'unanswerable' demands are made or the language begins to include terms only available to authority: few protestors for example would have argued that they went on demonstrations in order to defend 'national security'.

Ultimately, though many of the Left's interventions were highly effective as propaganda, and made good use of discursive/practical resources, they could not match the fundamental capacity of the executive power to dominate the airwaves and to issue *legitimate* commands. On the other hand, while the authorities could monitor, they could much less easily command the online and mobile media networks used by protestors to organise their public events (Gillan et al., 2008).

Conclusion
Democracy and the Terror War

The Iraqi people do not yet fully understand the implications of
the gift we have chosen to bestow upon them.

(Staff Sergeant Brian Sipp, 3rd US Infantry
Division Public Affairs Office, 2003)

Nothing produces greater satisfaction on the part of the oppressors,
than to hold elections everywhere, to impose them, by war if need
be, on people who did not ask for them.

(Badiou, 2008b: 32–3)

DEMOCRACY, WAR AND THE BURDEN OF SECURITY

Since elections are generally regarded as an essential expression of
the popular will, Badiou's contention that the oppressors are those
who provide access to the ballot, rather than those who deny it,
presents a clear challenge to established wisdom. One well-known
response to this kind of argument is that the 'subjugated' masses
living under foreign dictatorships deserve, at the very least, the
same opportunities and liberties that are taken for granted in the
west: freedom of association, free speech and the chance to cast a
vote, for example.[1]

This position must, in its turn, address two substantial difficulties:
it should describe the mechanism through which this model of
democracy will be delivered, since the oppressed often live under a
sovereign government that is hostile to the whole proposition; and it
must take account of the failings of democracy itself. Beginning with
the latter, it seems first that democracy is restricted to the political
realm, and is separated from economic life; there is no such thing,
for example, as 'economic democracy'. The second problem lies in
the paucity of choice, since all mainstream parties are 'incorporated
into a form of state' that is 'appropriate for the maintenance of the
established order' (Badiou, 2008b: 34). Third, many voting systems
are designed to exclude minority perspectives. Fourth, once the
electors have made their choice, the political class takes this as a

general mandate for all its subsequent activities, including the use of war as an instrument of policy.

Drawing attention to such deficiencies seems to cause right-wing commentators considerable annoyance: of course the system is not perfect, they contend, but it remains of exceptional value, exactly because it is more than the sum of its parts, and represents a higher principle, based on the laudable effort to improve the human condition. This brings the discussion back to the question of how the champions of democracy imagine that it could be 'exported' abroad.

Badiou referred to its dissemination by war. Yet war was not the primary focus of his remarks, which were directed at the uncritical celebration of electioneering that typified the French media's response to Sarkozy's victory in the French presidential contest of May 2007. War seems therefore to be presented as a last resort, as an extreme way of spreading the electoral principle. According to this perspective, the process of 'democratisation' may involve war, but presumably it is also possible to achieve the same end using other means. Distinguishing between the various methods of exerting pressure on a recalcitrant, 'non-democratic' state, depends therefore on understanding what the term *war* is meant to include.

Iraq provides a useful example, since it had long been the object of western hostility, ostensibly based on attempts to curb the power of Saddam Hussein. Two periods of 'open war' were initiated by the west, in 1991 and 2003, but other forms of aggression were also employed. These included preparatory assaults like the enforcement of 'no-fly' zones, the use of propaganda, diplomatic manoeuvres and the maintenance of economic sanctions. Some of the individual elements that make up the overall strategic repertoire of 'war' seem therefore to typify the state's behaviour during those periods rather casually designated as 'peace'.[2] Or, as Bull noted, 'war in the material sense' is sometimes 'hard to distinguish from peace' (Bull, 1977: 179). The launch of an open, supposedly 'all-out' war is itself often a means of creating an artificial distinction between this condition and peace, preserving the latter as the normative condition. This suggests that, rather than an 'extraordinary' measure which may be brought into play at the end of a process, war informs the logic of the process from the very beginning.

Drawing on the case of Iraq, a first period of material degradation (blockades, air strikes, etc.), gives way to a second (the 'shooting' war), in order to prepare in turn for a third phase – the creation of democratic institutions and procedures.[3] In effect, therefore, all three stages contribute to the enlargement of the same universal process – the coercive production of order. The construction of democratic structures represents the 'mature' period of the imperial project (Ayers, 2009), in which the new economic colony is provided with a form of organisation determined by the occupier. Having designed the protocols for political behaviour, the latter then tries to set up a relatively compliant national leadership, standing ready to intervene on behalf of the new 'sovereign' body.

This development is represented as an advance on the eccentric arrangements of the past, and is accompanied by an attempt to spread 'civic' consciousness (in Ayers' words: 'mentalities and consent' [2009: 6]). It also comes with a warning – that democracy has enemies and must be defended by force. When elections are held, police and paramilitaries appear on the streets to guard the polls. The institutional bequest of the conqueror consists, therefore, of two elements – electoral democracy, and *the burden of security* that accompanies it. The overall intention is to regulate the social order by forcing those who want less (or more) democracy to become the enemy of this new, 'constitutional' freedom.

NOMINATING THE ENEMY

The concept of democracy has long been the reflex reference of the political class, because it suggests full commitment to an egalitarian social order. The citizens of an occupied nation-state are, however, invited to support an authoritarian, 'national' version of this democracy, on the grounds that it represents the consolidation of their natural rights. This tactic, used to encourage the indigenous population to believe that they have a substantial stake in society, also reinforces the view that outsiders do not deserve access to the same rights or resources. When this implication is made explicit in the right-wing press,[4] the ruling party, happy to manipulate xenophobia but careful not to appear explicitly racist, points to the economic benefits of immigration while offering no moral defence of immigrants.[5]

Meanwhile, the dispossessed in general are subject to forms of control that can be 'rolled out' for the population as a whole. This repressive process is then presented to the citizen as a positive development, an *opportunity* for residents to assert their 'full' citizenship – by, for example, volunteering to carry identity cards. This, in turn, reinforces the notion that the aim of the 'un-naturalised' resident is to steal identity, exploit the benefits of modernity, and perhaps even to carry out acts of terror.

The hasty initiation of a general war on terror, however, produces another problem. In the rush to justify the policy, *too many enemies are nominated*. This was the case in the US after September 11th. As Richard Perle declared, 'this is total war' in which the US had to fight 'a variety of enemies'; there were 'lots of them out there', he said (cited in Wood, 2003: 151). These foes were not simply threatening in numerical terms, but also occupied a bewildering number of categories: Ba'athist 'dead enders', nationalists, religious zealots, al-Qaeda, Iranian agents, criminals, errant tribes and the Taliban all required suppression. This attitude weakened, rather than reinforced, the attempt to compose a unitary ideological position. There were indeed real opponents to be faced, but they were not all driven by the same motives.

Instead of fighting all comers, therefore, the new US administration of 2009 attempted to concentrate its efforts and thus, so it hoped, end the internal confusion over principles. This explains the overtures made to the Iranian leadership, and the co-option of the Sunni insurgency in Iraq.[6] The shift in influence from Republican ideologues to their more pragmatic realist associates, was of course prefigured by the advocates of the 'surge', which took place nearly two years before the official handover to Barack Obama occurred. The retreat from 'the war on terror' can be explained therefore as an attempt to *rationalise* the coercive effort. However, in moving to a bureaucratic position, one major rationale for war had to be abandoned: the exalted cause of democracy itself.[7]

ABANDONING DEMOCRACY?

The sudden omission of references to democracy was picked up in the press: 'notable by its absence in any of the speeches by the US team', one journalist observed, was 'any mention of building democracy in Afghanistan' (Traynor, 9 February 2009: 18). This report also cited a 'senior NATO official' who expressed the opinion that 'it [Afghanistan] doesn't need to be a democracy, just secure' (*ibid*). General Jones, one of Obama's special envoys, noted that the president 'is a pragmatist' who 'knows we must deal with the world as it is' (*ibid*). This perception, borne out by a study of the president's early political career (see Leslie, 2009: 188), provides a stark contrast to the promotion of social change that lay at the heart of the Democrats' election campaign. The reversion to less illustrious goals emerged, moreover, from military experience, particularly the (anti)democratic doctrine of counter-insurgency (see Chapter 1).

Obama's commitment to a limited form of democracy was, however, clear before he came to office. His concern was to rebuild the moral and therefore *technical* authority of the powerful.[8] The sharp contrast Obama drew between the honest, put-upon voter and a remote, disengaged national leadership, was not designed to liberate the people from their servitude as electoral drones, but to reinforce the position of a new set of political managers.[9] The sobering reality was that, in trying to describe their policy in bureaucratic terms, realists like Obama also sent a subliminal message to the US population: *that democracy within the homeland was also in effect a technicality*, a routine process more concerned with the ceremonies of leadership than effective representation. The movement of the democratic trope to the background merely reinforced the perception that the capitalist social order is not 'truly' democratic, and even perhaps that 'war is the global perspective of democracy' (Badiou, 2008b: 14).

'WAR ON TERROR': THE *INSIDIOUS PRINCIPLE OF REPRESSION*

The relief that greeted the Obama ascendancy was based in part on two perceptions: that the 'war on terror' had been a disaster[10] and the Bush administration an abject failure. If, however, the war is understood, not just as one 'phase' in a long conflict, but as the *insidious principle of repression* that continues to support an 'informal' mode of 'non-territorial' imperialism (Ayers, 2009: 1), then the Republicans helped to construct a durable framework for the production of force. It is also important to note that the neo-conservative cabal was not solely responsible for undertaking the 'war on terror'; it had to enter into alliances with other powerful interest groups inside the US (Holloway, 2008: 35–6), before turning outward to reliable supporters within the transnational bourgeoisie. The Americans and their overseas allies, such as the UK executive, may have differed over the exact nature of the future threats to US hegemony, but they shared a vision of political power that was essentially devoted to *pre-emptive action* both on the global stage and within the borders of their own states.

If some belligerent demonstration of power was required to put this policy into practice, then the Bush cohort was ideally suited to the task, since only the bold and ignorant could rise to meet the challenge. The first phase of the terror war was undermined, however, by the contradiction that lay at the heart of the enterprise. Set alongside an apparent commitment to the expansion of an effective security apparatus was the neo-liberal principle of 'doing more with less'. While the executive leadership of the US paid lip-service to the value of the armed forces as a social institution, the vision of a military able to respond to the challenges of the post-Soviet world led to a preference for a 'lighter' force. Therefore, when it came to road-testing their beliefs, the neo-conservatives and their allies did so with relatively limited resources, allowing them to make an *excessive investment in privatised capacity*[11] to make up the shortfall they had created. Although this matched their economic convictions, it drained resources from civil 'reconstruction' and bypassed formal controls.

However, at least until the later stages of the Iraq debacle, the dominant group in the US establishment was immune to criticism because it operated according to an agenda that subsumed all unexpected outcomes within an ideological frame *that accepted contingency* and saw chaos as part of an inevitably messy but cathartic process. Therefore, to the faction concerned, the collapse of public infrastructure, fatal assaults on the occupiers, the murder of civilians by US soldiers, and the growth of sectarian killings, did not indicate flawed planning, but represented instead elements of a necessary readjustment, one that would eventually produce a balance in social relations and new opportunities for exploiting Iraq's resources. The 'war on terror' was therefore not only adaptable enough to contain a host of strategic errors but, more to the point, leading elements of the Bush administration did not care, *at the time of their commission*, whether or not their actions might be defined as 'mistakes'. The Bush White House might have become the victim of its own ideological *laissez-faire*; but by that time, it had served its purpose.

THE CONCEPTION OF WAR

Eventually, it became obvious that the Iraq campaign, rather than being a struggle against terrorism, more closely resembled the imposition of an imperial/commercial discipline on a weaker, strategically important state. After the invasion, the Iraqi economy served 'US political and economic interests within the global economy' (Herring and Rangwala, 2006: 211). The ubiquitous use of the expression 'war on terror', meanwhile, began to seem inappropriate. It became apparent that the war included a general drive against internal dissent, that the strategy in Iraq had failed to establish security, and that various overseas governments had seized the opportunity to re-brand a number of nefarious activities under the aegis of anti-terror campaigns.

As Chapter 1 attempted to demonstrate, the relentless promotion of a particular term can, in the right circumstances, secure a number of political or commercial benefits; yet no single intervention can dominate a conceptual field indefinitely. So it was with the 'war on terror', which had offered the initial advantage of being vague enough to defy semantic constraints. By 2004, however, every malevolent deed enacted by a vengeful state – torture, kidnapping, illegal imprisonment and assassination – came to be associated with this policy. Eventually, those who coined the phrase argued that they had mis-named their own strategic goals, while other public functionaries (who made no apology for the Iraq invasion), expressed regret for its over-use, and were belatedly convinced that it had helped to unite a previously divided enemy. Yet the 'war on terror' continued to provide a useful service: it became the repository for all the bad publicity generated by the exercise of US power, while continuing to provide the underlying rationale for the aggressive projection of force.

This is why the Democrats tried to draw a line under some of the PR disasters made by 'Team Bush'. The closure of the prison at Guantanamo Bay in 2009, signed off with a flourish for the global television networks, was a significant act. It was undertaken, however, because the facility had achieved notoriety in a way that the detention centre at Bagram air base, due for expansion under Obama, had managed to avoid (Foley, 22 February 2009: 33). The trash-can labelled 'war on terror' received, from that time on, only the most conspicuous failures and the more thoroughly exhausted ploys of the Bush presidency.

'THERE IS NO WAR ON TERROR': NOT DENIAL BUT QUALIFICATION

Not content with an alteration in terminology, leading members of the political class began to describe the entire concept of a 'war on terror' as little more than a fantasy. In a speech made to members of the Criminal Bar Association in 2007, the UK's director of public prosecutions, Ken Macdonald, argued that there was 'no such thing as a "war on terror"' on the streets of London, just as there 'can be no such thing as a "war on drugs"' (cited in Dyer, 24 January 2007:

1). The notion of 'an open-ended and permanent state of emergency' (Townshend, 2002: 1) had indeed been circulated throughout the British social order, in a rather uncomfortable imitation of rhetorical utterances generated by factions within the American state.

In essence, Macdonald's observation represented an attempt not so much to make a denial as to offer a *qualification*; in other words, his intervention takes issue with the referential accuracy and therefore usefulness of the term, attempting to imbue it with a sense of the real in order to produce a more reliable form of association. 'London', he declared, 'is not a battlefield', and the casualties of 7 July were not in his opinion 'victims of war' (Dyer, 24 January 2007: 1). The fight against terrorism was 'not a war' but the 'prevention [*sic*] of a crime' (*ibid*). The identification of insurgent activity as a crime is clearly intended to reconstruct the legal authority of the state. Macdonald remained convinced, however, of the reality of a 'new form of terrorism', popularly associated with suicide bombing; indeed, he saw this activity as a more dangerous threat than that once posed by the IRA (*ibid*).

Nearly two years later, the British Foreign Secretary, David Miliband, also declared that the 'war on terror' was in some respects wrong. He argued, however, that the phrase had once 'had some merit' because it captured both the seriousness of the threat and 'the need to respond urgently – if necessary, with force' (Miliband, 15 January 2009: 29). In effect, this was a late acknowledgement that the *efficacy* of the term had declined. In the new formulation, the British government was trying to 'prevent extremism' and 'its terrible offspring, terrorist violence' (*ibid*). Extremism had thus become the ideological 'parent' of terrorism.[12] The truly disingenuous part of this assertion is the idea that the principles of the 'war on terror' allowed for the occasional use of coercion, suggesting that this was some painful last resort, rather than an essential characteristic of the entire enterprise. Miliband's chief reservation was based not on a moral assessment, but rather on the belief that the whole concept 'gave the impression of a unified, transnational enemy, embodied in the figure of Osama bin Laden and al-Qaeda' (*ibid*). He then went on to list all the organisations that were *not* similar to al-Qaeda, in order to prove that there was no unified opposition, a tactic which actually tends to reinforce the idea that there is really a 'core' threat, and that a committed enemy of some sort really does exist.

Miliband criticised the notion that 'battle lines' could be drawn 'as a simple binary struggle between moderates and extremists, or between good and evil' (*ibid*). His objection was based on the suspicion that this belief simply played into the hands of those *who seek to unify terrorist groups* – it was not meant to undermine the idea that the west had right on its side. In support of this general approach, none other than General Petraeus is cited: he is supposed to have told Miliband that 'the coalition [in Iraq] could not kill its way out of the problems of insurgency and civil strife' (*ibid*). This amoral conception may be read as: there are too many to kill, and killing too many only produces more opposition. Counter-insurgency, a *civil/military* policy, directed against *civil society*, had apparently become the touchstone not only of the hardened military operative but also of the cosseted bureaucrat.

According to Miliband, the correct response to terrorism was therefore to champion 'the rule of law' because that 'is the cornerstone of the democratic society' (*ibid*). He had in effect made a clear alignment with a new political reality, represented by the election of Barack Obama. Positioning himself as the champion of democratic modernity, Miliband described the best course of action: to uphold 'our commitments to human rights' and 'civil liberties' (*ibid*). This he considered 'was surely the lesson of Guantanamo' and why the UK government welcomed 'Obama's commitment to close it' (*ibid*).[13] In other words, the use of torture in the terror war should not be advertised with a neon sign.

REALMS OF ACTIVITY: POLITICS, MEDIA AND BUREAUCRATIC RULE

When national political executives engage in wars, they provide a running commentary on the worthiness of their motives. Official announcements, speeches and press conferences offer 'moral' accounts of pragmatic activities, specifically tailored for public consumption. Formal interventions of this type represent, therefore, the theatrical regulation of meaning. Yet, in accepting the amplification of their communicative power by those media forms that possess a clearly delineated hierarchical structure, representatives of government realise that they cannot control the presentation of their messages. Unable, therefore, to rely on the media to convey an exact reproduction of their intended meaning, the formal rhetoric they employ anticipates the *mediated abbreviation of its own content*. It is this material, a condensed variety of 'elite' political activity, which is presented for interrogation within the public domain.

Traditional media (unlike less hierarchical networks used in social networking) offer the opportunity to construct events which dramatise the democratic condition, staging a 'frank exchange of views' between adversaries who are meant to display a high degree of respect both for their opponents and for the various institutions in which the encounter is set. For politicians, conducting a mediated public discussion provides one major advantage: the exchange between leaders and led is removed from the realm of *immediate practical effect*, taking place in a 'spectral' realm that offers a 'cultural vision of a physical space' (Couldry and McCarthy, 2004: 2). This does not mean that it is 'unreal', simply that it is part of a process of *disassociation* between expression and practical action.[14] The argument is *expanded discursively* without making any difference to the subsequent activities of political leaders. The laziness of the 'terror' rationale is suited to this kind of public forum: it absorbs the blows of the opposition and is designed to frustrate critique, which can be drawn into answering a series of absurd propositions. There is no doubt that the public alibis for the Iraq war, for instance, were substantially undermined, but it did not seem to matter.

The reason for this is simple: although it can influence other forms of social action, formal politics and dissent are both *functionally distinct* from the technical management of economic life.[15] The difference is that once a debate has been aired, the political leader can leave the symbolic arena and grapple with the levers of power, while the public has to find ways of creating effective networks (see Chapter 6). Bureaucratic rule (see Cardan, 1965: 53), upon which the political class ultimately depends, is by contrast a largely confidential process. It is this systemic condition which constitutes the *foundational* practice of the contemporary state, and which is clothed in the language of democracy.

THE MYTH OF RESTRAINT

The notion that the western powers and their allies have been forced to engage in a defensive struggle, in order to protect an entire way of life, represents a distorted recognition of the moral principles that are supposed to govern the social order.[16] Ethical references are designed to counter the accusation that the true reason for overseas aggression lies in what Boal and his co-authors call the 'primitive accumulation' of capital assets (Boal et al., 2005: 52). Yet when the stakes are apparently so high that national survival itself is threatened, the executive will announce that it must reconsider its supposedly unshakeable commitment to decency and the rule of law.

This tactic has a long history. Curtis cites the content of a declassified US government report from 1954, in which the author notes that 'hitherto accepted norms of conduct do not apply ... to survive, long-standing American concepts of "fair play" must be reconsidered' (Curtis, 1998: 16–17). In fact, the idea that there was ever a time when ethical standards held sway is used only to mark the onset of extraordinary circumstances where moral qualms can be abandoned. The notion that a 'state of emergency' has come into force, in which the due process of legal accountability has had to be rescinded, is no more than an 'ideological sham' (Neocleous, 2008: 72). The appearance of emergency and extraordinary modes of governance is, in Neocleous' opinion, 'not an exception but ... part and parcel of the political administration of contemporary capitalist states' (*ibid*), just as the shadow banking system was 'not in competition with the regulated system', but was an 'outgrowth of it' (Gowan, 2009: 13).

THE CONCENTRATION OF POWER AND THE DIFFUSION OF RESPONSIBILITY

However it is justified, warfare in the contemporary period is loosely based on the traditional division between two spheres of activity – combat overseas and activity on the 'home front'. The difficulty in making this distinction meaningful, and thus of creating a shared sense of purpose, is partly explained by the core executive's general preference for an apolitical citizenry, one that can be managed without too much effort (see the Introduction). In times of war, this inertia has to be replaced by useful forms of solidarity, such as expressions of support for 'our troops'.

The use of authoritarian measures is supposed, meanwhile, to 'secure the homeland': in other words, to induce a condition in which awareness of disciplinary structures is made general. This, in turn, leads to accusations that western nations are becoming 'police states', reinforced by the suspicion that the repressive function is assuming near universal proportions. There are, however, significant differences between the 'total' societies of the past and the present condition.

First, the repressive capacity of the state has been enlarged through technological advances (with a concomitant development of technological resistance); and second, this enhancement of power has been achieved without abandoning references to fair play, tolerance, democracy and so forth, just like Miliband's commitment to 'the rule of law' mentioned above. The gutter press can be allowed to pursue the authoritarian agenda to its logical conclusion but, within mainstream British society at least, the repressive condition is not celebrated in its own right: there is no formal glorification of a single leader, no exultation of the people through reference to racial characteristics, and no slavish worship of power as such.

In Britain, the development of a powerful authoritarian faction within the social order would not be served by unnecessary populist agitation. The repressive condition is built up gradually, through the bureaucratic accumulation of powers and the paramilitary training of 'special units' – a kind of *licensed fascism*, which does not require the manufacture of communal enthusiasm or any form of public hysteria. This is exactly the lesson that the governments of the US and UK learned from their clash with the Axis powers during the Second World War: that the fascist bands must be subsumed into *official* organisations, formally subjected to discipline, and thus incorporated into the state. One essential achievement of the 'war on terror', together with its antecedents and successors, is not therefore the production of a single, dramatic outlook aligned with the wishes of one party, nor the permanent elevation of an entirely visible elite to positions of power. It is rather the concentration of executive authority, the diffusion of responsibility for that power,[17] and the dissolution of public agency.

THE OVERPRODUCTION OF FORCE: CENTRE AND PERIPHERY

The extension of coercive influence is therefore not just devoted to the suppression of foreign insurgency. When lethal force is delivered at the *periphery* through the prosecution of a counter-insurgency war, this entails a 'double-headed' move, in which the compliance of the home population is partly achieved through the spectacular repression of various threats marked as either foreign or treacherous. The twofold effort to exert control, however, suffers from a particular contradiction characteristic of contemporary power.

Since it is easier to dominate the relatively passive (including those who have at some point demonstrated their consent to be governed), it would seem logical to expect that only very small amounts of hardware (weapons and technology) would be needed to keep domestic nationals under some form of discipline. Yet this perception is challenged by the regular intervention of 'law enforcement' agencies, in which serious threats to public order are anticipated and new supplies of equipment are said to be required.[18]

Yet the full consequences of this concentration of materiel are only made fully apparent when a crisis within the 'homeland' is met with the dramatic *overproduction of force*,[19] where police and other agencies overwhelm their targets with the threat and actual use of violent compulsion (Price, 2009a). In contrast, the narrative woven around the activities of the armed forces, fighting a determined enemy at *the periphery*, is that they are supposed to be *under-resourced*.

It is this 'deficient' element of the security equation that the Obama administration has acknowledged, without admitting that it is only one part of the fault-line that runs through the twin approaches that together make up a larger campaign of repressive violence.[20] The bulk of the western forces are indeed placed under duress, in the sense that they are offered as targets of insurgency, while special forces are given the resources they need and permission to act in whatever way they see fit. In sum, as the failure to spread their 'principles' to the deprived periphery becomes more apparent, political leaders alter their *domestic* rhetoric, seeking to 'redress' the supposed imbalance between liberty and security,[21] but also suggesting that the democratic narrative has been supplanted by the discourse of security. In the process, freedom, democracy and justice began to appear as formal adjuncts to the actual core of the system – the bureaucratic management of the security regime.

Yet the provision of 'real' security is itself uncertain (see Chapter 5). Any failure in its provision is usually regarded as an indication of a major deficiency in the system of governance, which was once supposed to characterise 'underdeveloped' nations. Beetham, for example, argued that 'in many regions of the Third World especially', the management of 'security has been *only partially under the control of the supposedly sovereign state*' (Beetham, 1991: 140, my emphasis). Although this shortcoming was attributed to the poorer regions of the world, the US government not only deliberately 'outsourced' its security needs to private companies, but itself appeared to be a partially privatised entity, a *mercenary state* dependent on Chinese creditors, making it necessary to ask on whose behalf the US military actually fights.

In addition, the constant drive to war presents a considerable risk, because the fundamental constraint on expansion was exactly the kind of economic weakness that an uncertain external adventure might exacerbate. The American empire for example was, according to Todd, undergoing 'a process of decomposition' (Todd, 2003: 192). It was in his opinion only the fall of the Soviet bloc that gave the impression that the United States had risen to 'a level of absolute power' (*ibid*). Unable to establish economic dominance over Europe or Japan, or achieve the final dissolution of Russian military power, the US made, in Todd's opinion, 'a show of empire' by conducting attacks against militarily inconsequential nations (*ibid*: 193).[22] This notion, however, does not explain why America needs to maintain a military capability that, according to some calculations, is greater than that possessed by all other states combined (Wood, 2003: 143).

THE SYSTEM OF STATES: COMPETITION AND IMPERIAL POWER

One explanation for the apparently excessive growth of the United States military can be found within studies of the 'modern states system' (Bull, 1977: 180). Without a global centre of political authority that could enforce international law, universal principles must be upheld by 'particular states able and willing to take up arms' to defend them (*ibid*: 182). The US leadership, however, though it has paid lip service to the rule of law, has also clearly acted against its precepts, and did not moderate its plans to take account of bodies like the UN when it invaded Iraq. US executive power must, therefore, be motivated by some other principle. Wood argues that the answer can be found in the development of a 'new' imperialism, which does not depend on the acquisition of territory or the subjugation of serious rivals to exercise power (Wood, 2003). The occupation of Iraq, however, does in some ways resemble colonial occupation and the primitive seizure of resource (Boal et al., 2005).

More persuasive is Wood's observation that it 'may be precisely because the new imperialism has no clear and finite objects' that 'it requires such massive military force' (Wood, 2003: 144). If the goal is simply to maintain unfettered pre-eminence, then this 'boundless domination' will require 'military action without end' (*ibid*: 144). The lack, among America's economic rivals, of any serious opposition to this belligerent stance, may seem puzzling. Yet the reason for such acquiescence is not difficult to find. The extensive dominance of the US does not represent a threat to national 'elites', because they are able to use the free market agenda for their own purposes.

If the neo-liberal creed has really been consolidated as 'an institutionalised global regime' (Albo, 2003: 106), then the bourgeoisie appears in most instances to have adapted to the circumstance.

Ruling cabals have used the twin weapons of economic liberalisation and pre-emptive coercion to suppress the economic demands of their own working class. The 'national' bourgeoisie is thus able to sustain 'the international circuits of capital' in which it has a stake (Albo, 2003: 106). While workers experience the 'systematic dismantling' (Turner, 2008: 18) of their protective structures, the ruling elite uses its intellectual and managerial subordinates (state bureaucrats and commercial executives) to carry out the task of restructuring.[23] The aim is the gradual destruction of established patterns of life and the political perspectives that grow from them.

THE MYTH OF DISORDER: *SUBSTANTIATING* THE TERROR THREAT

Resistance to the process of liberalisation has taken many forms. In response, authority has pretended that any form of protest is a manifestation of *general* social breakdown, and an unholy alliance of bureaucrats, politicians and market privateers talk up the prospect of serious disorder.[24] For any ruling alliance the challenge is to ensure that social disintegration, caused by the application of capitalist principles, can be used as evidence to support another rationale: that disruption is the fault of the dispossessed. Any response from the subaltern (political, criminal, cultural) is used to justify the application of repressive modes of social control.

In Britain, the fact that the old, predictable enemies (trade unions, radical political parties, and even the 'new' social movements) had been weakened meant that the growth of 'disorganised' dissent could be represented as a serious threat to authority. Criminal gangs from overseas, 'terror' suspects, militant environmentalists, anarchists, benefit fraudsters, asylum seekers and other groups were all distinguished from law-abiding citizens, not in order to reassure the conformist, but to demonstrate to all that no form of dissent would go unnoticed.[25]

Yet, having assembled a huge array of weapons and an extensive repertoire of techniques, the police and paramilitary arm of the state could only be exercised against a comparatively feeble opposition which was, even when all groups were combined, often only a few thousand strong, supposedly containing an even smaller 'hard core' of committed agitators. Awareness of this deficiency and the urgent need to *substantiate* the terror threat forced the security regime to repeat the strategic error made in the US at the beginning of the 'war on terror' – to generate numberless enemies.[26] There is only one place where such multitudes can be found, however – amongst the general public. In other words, 'populations themselves' come to represent 'a terrorist threat to the authorities' (Baudrillard, 2005: 120).[27] The terror campaign reveals as a consequence its true disposition: it is the state's 'war against civil society' (Bull, 2006: 25).

The terror war might therefore appear both dangerous and absurd; but then it would be a mistake to expect it to follow a 'rational' path. This is because it is at root an aggressive attempt to reassert the contradictory interests of a transnational elite, *the effective composition of which alters according to the particular alignment of forces called into being by particular events.* This unstable cabal is governed by a simple impulse: to maintain its influence and to counter those forces that threaten to constrain its power.[28] The fact that, as an alliance of groups, it cannot always establish a reliable sense of where these interests lie, or how they should be pursued, does not mean that its drive to accumulate resources and deploy coercive force is diminished. This war is at heart a *terror enterprise*, a multi-faceted political and economic project that continues to produce new victims and opponents. Its architects have yet to encounter, however, a truly implacable enemy. The greatest threat to the security regime would be a political force capable of attacking the structures that underpin the state's ability, not just to conduct a war, but to determine the fate of an entire social order.

Notes

INTRODUCTION

1. This loose designation refers to the leading powers providing the infrastructure for the production of coercive force: the discussion in this book focuses on the US and the UK, rather than NATO or ISAF, as the 'prime movers' in the recent wars.

2. George W. Bush was still using this formula during his second term. Baker, in *The Times*, noted that 'Mr. Bush placed the current war in Iraq, and the wider War on Terror, as the natural successor to the struggles ... fought to advance liberty – the Civil War, the Second World War and the Cold War' (21 January 2005: 1). Chapter 2 describes Mazower's perspective on the Allied powers' attitude to Nazism.

3. In his programme 'Afghanistan: Siege City' for Channel 4's *Unreported World* (1 May 2009), Peter Oborne encountered a number of Kabul residents who wanted the Taliban to return to power, so that they could bring *order* to the city.

4. For the composition of this administration, see Johnson and Leslie, *Afghanistan: the mirage of peace*, 2008: 6.

5. See for instance, Poole (2003), West and Smith (2003), and Wright (2004).

6. The use of the term 'terror war' serves the following purpose: it recognises the transition from the 'war on terror' to other designations and makes terror not the target of western policy, but its operational practice. See Kellner (2003) for an early use of the term.

7. See for example 'Obama bid to turn to moderate Taliban "will fail"' (Boone, 9 March 2009). A particularly challenging category problem arose when John Walker Lindh was called the 'American Taliban': BBC News online, 'America's home-grown Taleban fighter', http://news.bbc.co.uk/1/hi/world/south_asia/1689138.stm 3 December 2001 (accessed 2 July 2009).

8. See Woods, '26 Top Anomalies of 9/11', in *Global Outlook*, 8, Spring 2004: 32.

9. The use of the term 'bourgeois' in this book does not indicate 'the holders of commercial property' *per se* (Catephores, 1989: 227), nor is it meant as a slur on the cultural behaviour of the various factions that compose the western 'ruling class'; rather, it is supposed to indicate *i*) the leading political/bureaucratic representatives of those factions devoted to the active maintenance of capitalism as an economic, social and political system; and *ii*) the relational position of this dominant political caste (the 'governing' fraction; see Poulantzas, 1978a: 189) to other, structurally subordinate social groups. Gramsci described the 'capitalist entrepreneur' as 'an organiser of the "confidence" of investors in business' – this designation can be applied to the political executive, which organises confidence on behalf of the capitalist/patriarchal system (Gramsci, 1971: 5).

10. The political process was in fact intensified under the sign of 'suspension' and compassion. This had a populist variant, expressed through the notion of

observing a brief period of 'mourning' before embarking on the task of revenge; see for example the UK's *Sun* newspaper, which printed a leader entitled 'A short silence ... then we have a job to do' (*Sun*, 14 September 2001: 10).

11. Not all postings on the web were quite so unambiguous or offensive, though of course it was just this kind of material that was deemed unsuitable: in the early days after 9/11, a series of images based on the notion that Sesame Street's Burt was 'evil', including one where he appeared in a turban behind bin Laden's shoulder, achieved great popularity, until such objectionable items were removed by their creator.

12. When the weak eventually demonstrate their 'ingratitude', this feeds the conviction that the goodwill of the US has once again been exploited. Then the complaints about the US doing all the 'heavy lifting' begin.

13. The social order is capitalist in so far as the private ownership and operation of the means of production, and the drive to maintain profitability, gives rise to a system of rationalisation intended to justify the inequality and division which it creates. The social order is patriarchal, not simply because it is dominated by men who reproduce structures designed to give them a material advantage, but because patriarchal values are the normative inheritance of both men and women – both groups are drawn into the ideological orbit of gendered relations and both use a variety of strategies to increase or mitigate its effects. Within the general order of patriarchy, not all men will be opposed to the 'progression' of women, and not all women will try to make a general emancipatory effort on behalf of all classes of female. It is quite possible for men to argue that women should be 'admitted' to some prestigious inner circle, just as it is conceivable that women will seek advancement by trying to conform to expectations that might be regarded as 'normal'.

14. Coercive power does not necessarily assume the form of physical force or violence, yet the knowledge that certain actors have the right and/or ability to apply force, constitutes an often 'unspoken' threat – the guarantee of social order is founded on the assurance that all citizens may be treated equally harshly should they fail to observe certain norms. The notion that democratic power can only operate within the context of a general social 'consent', is valid only if all parties have an equal opportunity to determine the conditions under which they are governed. Under the present system of temporal and spatial constraint, in which democracy expresses itself as a concentrated electoral spasm, consent is not renewed in a timely manner. In addition, consent may be said to be genuine only where it can be distinguished from those forms of compliance that are *an integral part of the structures that individuals must of necessity occupy* in order to survive within a complex social order.

15. Since the measure of success is commercial, the appearance of 'subversive' texts is not impossible.

16. By 'symbolic function' I mean the human capacity to communicate a (structural) intention through any system that conveys meaning, including speech, diagrammatic illustration, and narrative forms of various kinds.

17. This is not meant to exclude speech, but only that offered as a rationalisation for an activity. On the London G20 mobilisation in April 2009, for example, some demonstrators heard police talking about 'level one', 'level two', or 'level three', without realising that this referred to the three types of public order response that could be deployed. The terms used were not 'secret', but were organisational categories used as internal forms of code.

18. 'Imperial' is used here in the sense of an impulse to conduct an 'informal' or 'deterritorialised' expansion of state power: see Ayers (2009) and Wood (2003).

19. See the Conclusion for an assessment of the dangers posed by different threats.

CHAPTER 1

1. Both terms emerge from a common root: the Greek 'idios' meaning 'own' or 'private'. The intellectual limitations of the 'GWOT' ('global war on terror') were *productive* in the sense that they allowed room for manoeuvre.

2. See Chandrasekaran's account of those who ran the occupation in Iraq, individuals who 'went out there because of their political leanings' (Chandrasekaran, 2007: 104). The tide began to turn against the reckless Bush administration in 2006, when a third group, composed of bi-partisan realists, used to the pragmatic adjustment of power, issued the Iraq Study Group report on the costs of the American occupation (Ryan, 2007: 117).

3. I follow Rhodes and Dunleavy in describing the core executive as 'all those organisations and procedures which coordinate central government policies, and act as final arbiters of conflict between different parts of the government machine' (Rhodes and Dunleavy, 1995: 12).

4. Neocleous provides a similarly trenchant critique when he argues that the distinction between illicit and legal activity is a convenient fiction, designed to provide the executive with power to act in a 'crisis', while the emergency itself is 'what *emerges* from the rule of law when violence needs to be exercised' (Neocleous, 2008: 72, my emphasis).

5. The effort to transform the 'war on terror' into a less ideologically strident procedure was first mooted in 2006, when talk of 'the long war' was introduced. This designation seemed to promise only relentless and unending effort and thus was of little use in the propaganda effort known as public diplomacy. In other words, the 'long war' was deemed unfit for public consumption, though it was used to initiate debate within a more academic context (Williams, 2007: 275; Ricks, 2009).

6. It also appeared as a solemn caveat running alongside more assertive utterances like 'smart power', the term used to describe the Obama/Clinton approach to foreign policy (Usborne, 14 January 2009: 19). 'Smart power' was intended to create the impression that the Republicans had been too dim-witted to attain their goals, while drawing attention to the intellectual credentials of the Democratic leadership. It was an attempt to mark a departure from a contaminated brand, while retaining many of the old attitudes and practices.

7. See also the Reuters article which notes that 'Israel had withdrawn most of its forces before Obama was sworn in on Tuesday, in a move analysts saw as an attempt to avoid early tensions with his administration' (Heller, 21 January 2009).

8. See Bromley (2008: 71) on 'cooperative bargains and coercive power'.

CHAPTER 2

1. Ten days after 9/11, the architect Charles Jencks announced: 'this is a war of symbolism' (Jencks, 2001).

2. See for example Hale, 'Five Muslims in "terror material" case are freed', in *Daily Mail*, 14 February 2008.

3. *Informal* military discourse can, however, suggest the brutality of war. Wright reports a Marine officer noting that, during the 2003 war in Iraq, he had been advised by his general that 'division-wide, we're shooting more civilians than we should' (Wright, 2004: 248).

4. 'Things' here can mean an 'object, entity, idea, action' (Dillon, 1995: 167), some form of phenomena which exists within the symbolic/material condition which is human life.

5. A unit of meaning indicates the existence of something recognisably coherent through a combination of internal structure (endophoric or grammatical consistency) and exophoric gestures (external reference) to a world beyond the text.

6. The idea that an essential meaning can be identified in terms of basic content, and that the same position can appear in different grammatical formations.

7. See Price (1996); 'social narratives' are stories told to achieve general outcomes – they are tales with an ideological purpose.

8. Burke et al. note that 'Derrida's concept of "différance" is a term derived from the French "différer", which means both to defer and to differ; it is used to express the idea that signification can never be fully achieved or arrived at. This is because meaning ... does not exist within the sign itself, but is an effect of the differential relations between signs; it cannot, therefore, ultimately be fixed or stabilised' (Burke et al., 2000: 223).

9. In this chapter, the *provisional* is related to that condition I have called the 'alibi', and is aided by use of a professional language that *is devoted to* the production of ambiguous statements.

10. In their critique of postmodern theorising, MacCannell and MacCannell ask 'how do certain individuals and classes remain in power ... even after the mechanisms of power are revealed to be arbitrary social constructs?' (in Rojek and Turner, 1993: 126).

11. See also Glaister on the character of 'coalition' air-strikes, 'High-profile air strikes "killed only civilians"', *Guardian*, 14 June 2004.

12. Perhaps the best thing to have done in this case, was to have arrested the officials who produced the alarming diagrams of Iraqi WMD capability.

13. 'British born Steve Allinson, a team leader with the UN chemical inspection group, said: "People would laugh at times because the information he was presenting just didn't mean anything – had no meaning."' In Scheer, 2006, 'Now he tells us', 12 April 2006, in Alter Net at http://www.alternet.org/waroniraq/34861/.

14. Hansen and Salskov-Iversen identify 'managerial patterns of political authority' (2002: 4), while Dahlgren calls elections 'consumer choice in the rotation of elites' (Dahlgren, 1995: 3).

15. See for example George W. Bush's speech of 9 May 2002, in which he contrasted the 'free market's invisible hand, which improves the lives of people', and 'the government's invisible foot' which 'tramples on people's hopes and destroys their dreams' ('Remarks by the President in Tribute to Milton Friedman', 9 May 2002, in www.freetochoosemedia.org/freetochoose/tribute_pres.php).

16. A typical example may be found on the website of the Global Knowledge Partnership, which describes its commitment to 'flexible, efficient decision-making' (see Hansen and Salskov-Iversen, 2002: 7).

17. In the British context, the development of full citizenship may be limited by 'continued allegiance to a constitutional monarchy' which 'is bound to exert a powerful influence on public consciousness' (Price, 2006c). As Coleman argues, 'historically the British were subjects and that status needed little elaboration' (Coleman, 2001: 109).

CHAPTER 3

1. An endophoric element within a sentence is one which gains its meaning from an internal rather than an external, or exophoric, reference (Brown and Yule, 1983, cited in Price, 2007: 55). In practice however, the two forms of reference are difficult to separate.
2. A referential alibi is essentially an explanation that makes reference to real events, but in an inappropriate context, often used to disguise a strategic decision.
3. Indeed, the 'coalition' led by the US clearly expected to prove or fabricate the existence of at least one element of this multiple category, in order that the entire proposition about Iraqi intentions could be proved (Price, 2007: 7). If for example some minor chemical component had been found, then this would have been paraded in the media as conclusive evidence that the WMD 'programme' was a material reality.
4. In advocating this perspective, I would argue that the formal requirement for the successful circulation of 'meaning', however inconsequential or debased the actual content, depends on media outlets that are *structurally* subservient to a political-commercial nexus.
5. The academic author Snow identifies the existence of 'a global information war' (Snow, 2006: 45).
6. The interface between politics, economics and culture is permeable, so that the existence of practices like torture is inevitably recognised and discussed, but the act itself is assigned, not to the actual perpetrators, but to the imagined enemies of America (see Chapter 5).
7. An overriding interest in the dramatic re-presentation of conflict is based on the notion that the armed forces will eventually 'play out' one or other of the strategic game-plans that are designed to *cover all the bases*; in other words, to meet all eventualities. The appearance of language drawn from competitive sports is only one instance of a common parlance deployed without embarrassment by representatives of the state. If a major aspect of governance is directive or persuasive address, then many expressions are derived from the terminology used by the private sector.
8. See also the Conclusion.
9. Cruse gives an account of the 'descriptive' in the following terms; it is '*objective* in the sense that it interposes a kind of distance between the speaker and what he says ... *displaced* in [the] sense of not being tied to the here and now of the current speech situation' and 'fully *conceptualised*' because it provides 'a set of conceptual categories into which aspects of experience may be sorted' (Cruse, 2000: 47).
10. The *Daily Mirror* columnist Tony Parsons, for example, wrote that the Towers 'demanded your attention, like the most beautiful women in the world' (Parsons, 20 September 2001).

11. See, for example, the two separate *Daily Mirror* articles by Routledge and Carroll (both 29 March 2003).

CHAPTER 4

1. Goold contends that the arguments about CCTV tend to become polarised, with 'those strongly against the use of public area surveillance' being disinclined to point to 'the fact that most CCTV schemes are in reality quite limited in ... their surveillance capacity', while proponents of surveillance avoid focusing on the shortcomings of the technology 'or its potential threat to civil liberties' (Goold, 2004: 11).

2. Lyon calls surveillance 'the focused, systematic and routine attention to personal details for purposes of influence, management, protection or direction' (Lyon, 2007: 14).

3. Lyon is of the opinion that the 'watching' may be 'metaphorical ... as well as literal' (Lyon, 2007: 50).

4. The international popularity of reality TV and the *Big Brother* phenomenon attests to this transition towards a 'hybrid performance genre' (Mathijs and Jones, 2004: 1), based on the willingness of individual subjects to pursue the 'project of the self' (Fowles, 1996) within a commercial framework.

5. An example was the appearance in 2006 of the Peugeot 207 TV commercial, which showed the car being driven through an urban landscape while being monitored by an array of CCTV cameras. The voiceover, replicated by an on-screen display, was as follows: 'The new Peugeot 207. You are caught on camera over 300 times a day. Give them something to watch. The drive of your life.'

6. The 2007 RAC advertisements feature the ex-footballer and actor Vinnie Jones being located by a rescue vehicle, by tracking his mobile phone signal.

7. Corporate Social Responsibility or CSR is a 'philosophy' of attitudinal address in which socially progressive messages are composed as part of a wider concern with 'reputation management' (see Price, 2007: 115–18).

8. The actual purpose of some of these forms of address, particularly of those campaigning against 'benefit cheats', may be identified as 'promotional' rather than truly functional, i.e. as designed to draw attention to political positions rather than achieve actual effects. Other campaigns use direct reference to surveillance technology, such as the vehicle tax TV 'commercial' shown on 22 July 2005, which tried to demonstrate that the DVLA, the UK Licensing Authority, does not need to 'look' for offenders in the physical environment but only in its database, which will 'automatically issue an £80 penalty'.

9. To frame an event is to select some elements of social, practical, or natural reality (Archer, 2000) and to use these as the primary determinants of meaning.

10. This position would seem to contradict Gill's assertion that 'in most instances the state does not seek to enter the moral realm' (Gill, 2003: 5).

11. Escolar, in presenting his argument that it was 'the absolute states which began to develop in Western Europe during the Late Middle Ages', and which laid 'the political and institutional foundations of the different types of representative democratic states which evolved after the last quarter of the eighteenth century', notes that they 'were distinguished by the fact that they exercised the power of political domination uniformly and on an exclusive basis throughout the territory'. He identifies among five requirements 'the building up of state power in the absolute states of Western Europe entailed ... the institutional

consolidation of a centralised political and administrative apparatus' and 'the legitimisation of the political rights of the people both within and beyond the borders of the state' (Escolar, 2003: 29–30).

12. Poulantzas also warns against 'a topological representation of "base" and "superstructure": namely, the conception of the State as a mere appendage or reflection of the economic sphere' (Poulantzas, 1978a: 15).

13. Pierson speaks of 'a unitary order of violence' (Pierson, 1996: 11).

14. An example of the interrelationship between *normative* and *coercive* power is the requirement to use a recognised currency for the payment of services. The *norm* is that one should pay for facilities (when 'free' they are represented as exceptional), but any deviation from the norm results in coercive action (arrest, prosecution, fines, etc.).

15. Beetham notes that 'power relations are almost always constituted by a framework of incentives and sanctions, implicit if not always explicit, which align the behaviour of the subordinate with the wishes of the powerful' (Beetham, 1991: 27).

16. Reporting the 'final verdict on a two-year saga', the *Guardian* noted that 'De Menezes, 27, who was making his way to work, was shot seven times in the head by an armed police surveillance team after being mistaken for one of the July 21 suicide bombers' (Laville, 1 August 2007). It should be noted that the bombers did not commit suicide, since they failed to carry through their mission.

17. In making this observation, I follow Oakes et al. in their description of stereotypes as 'social categorical judgements' that are 'fluid, variable and context-dependent' and also 'the product of a dynamic process of social judgement and meaningful inference' (Oakes et al., 1994: 211).

18. See Therborn on the constitution of classes through the ideological training of individuals and groups (Therborn, 1980: 86).

19. The first type of category, *natural kind*, is described as having relative autonomy from the human sphere and includes objects or animals that appear in nature without requiring human intervention. The second, *human artefact*, represents things made by human endeavour. The third, *social categories*, refers to the divisions used to make distinctions between 'types' of people, from occupation to personality.

20. Sir Ian Blair, then Chief Constable of the Metropolitan Police, made the following declaration at the press conference of 22 July 2005: '*Met police officers* have shot a man inside Stockwell Underground Station at approximately 10 a.m. this morning.' This statement was reproduced in various forms; the *Guardian* reported that 'a man was chased by *officers* and shot around five times in the head at point-blank range' (Cobain et al., 23 July 2005).

21. For instance, the *Daily Mirror* of 29 July 2005 declared in a headline over a page ten article that the 'BRAZILIAN'S VISA 2 YEARS OUT OF DATE' (Roberts, 2005: 10).

22. During the 10.30 p.m. ITV News bulletin of 18 August 2005, Dan Rivers concluded his report by noting that 'we must remember the circumstances in which this operation was taking place; it happened just one day after those failed attacks on the Tube ... police only had a matter of minutes to make life and death decisions'.

23. See for example the front page of the *Daily Mirror*, 18 December, 2002. The headline reads 'Warkies!' and shows Bush holding his Scots Terrier Barney, with

the face of Blair superimposed. This predates the use of the epithet 'poodle', now regularly assigned to Blair when discussing his relationship with the US president.

24. Tolson notes that in broadcast talk interviewees are on the one hand 'on display, rather like actors, for an audience' while also being required to 'speak to, or for, that audience in a listener-friendly (and not actorly) manner' (Tolson, 2006: 11).

25. The notion of belief gives rise to the question of position, or the notion of activity carried out on behalf of another individual, or in support of a moral and/or social order.

26. See Tolson (2006) for an account of such behaviours.

27. Goffman describes this aspect as 'evidence of some failing in the intellectual grasp and achievement required within official or otherwise cultivated circles' (Goffman, 1981: 209).

28. White House Press Conference, 20 November 2003. See www.talkleft.com for the view that Bush's phrase was a deliberate attempt to re-categorise prisoners.

29. This is further refined in Bach and Harnish (1979), who examine *intention* and theorise the hearer's inferences.

30. Searle does, however, go on to list more developed acts including utterances that constitute 'referring and predicting' (Searle, 1969: 16).

31. Note here how the correspondent summarises Bush's attitude by assuming his subject-position and presenting 'propositional content' within a 'conversational' response.

32. I use 'ideological' here in the sense of a consistent but limited 'worldview', not necessarily one which is conspiratorial or poisonous.

CHAPTER 5

1. 'Unitary' in an ideological sense, where texts appear to encourage a particular reading of the material they present.

2. A scene is composed, in Branigan's view, of variables that include the quantity and *plausibility* of information (Branigan, 1993: 148).

3. As a linguistic category, 'textual cohesion refers to the arrangement of words (surface lexis) and obedience to the rules of grammar'. Any larger 'propositional development' (Stubbs, 1983: 9) is dependent on the intelligibility of basic linguistic reference.

4. Explanations may emerge from either diegetic or non-diegetic sources.

5. Resonance is the attainment of emotional recognition, where a display 'strikes a chord' with an audience, as distinct to the process of rationalisation based on a 'logical' justification for narrative development.

6. The programme or film is *paid for* within a larger field of consumption.

7. Parallels exist in the political realm; see for example the current controversy over 'foreign' re-offenders. Woodward, in the *Guardian* (18 May 2006), gives an account of how issues in the public realm are turned to the political advantage of authoritarian politicians: 'Tony Blair insisted yesterday he would press ahead with plans to deport "the vast bulk" of foreign prisoners after their sentences, regardless of the threat they face in their home countries. The prime minister upped the ante by telling the Commons: "There will be an automatic presumption to deport and the vast bulk of those people will be deported."'

CHAPTER 6

1. It is relatively easy to identify instances of 'economic' discourse, within both formal and informal expression, but less than clear how to analyse the relationship between such references and the stated or presumed intention of political actors, quite apart from their questionable ability to 'manage' the economic sphere itself.

2. See Faludi (2008) for an analysis of retrogressive measures that attempt to justify a return to 'traditional' types of gendered behaviour.

3. In a parallel development, 'soft skills' were (until recently) offered to the workforce as the path to survival. The individual was supposed to bear responsibility for their own 'career', in an economy apparently devoted to service, but which actually produced nothing more than a functional and perfunctory interaction at the 'point of sale'.

4. The huge size and vast social mix of the February 2003 demonstration, together with the great range of opinions on display, made the event hugely impressive yet also relatively inoffensive; the BBC cited a senior Metropolitan Police officer, who said that the crowd had been 'tolerant and patient' (BBC News online, 'Million march against Iraq war', 16 February 2003).

5. A year and a half after the big demonstration, the Socialist Party demanded 'working class unity ... in Iraq', together with 'democratically organised workers' defence forces' in order to 'provide real security for all ethnic and religious sections of society' (Socialist Party, 19 March 2005). Unfortunately, as the leaflet recognised, the subjective self-conception of factions within the armed Iraqi resistance tended to follow a religious or nationalist pattern, rather than the paradigm of class solidarity.

CONCLUSION

1. Ayers describes the standard or orthodox notion of democracy as 'a (neo) liberal, procedural model of democracy', that includes 'periodic election[s] ... constitutionalism, the rule of law and respect for a particular conception of "human rights"; "good governance" ... and a pluralist, "independent" civil society' (Ayers, 2009: 7).

2. For a discussion of the use of 'emergencies' to provide states with the means of waging a social war during peacetime, see Neocleous (2008: 52–3). The index to Neocleous' book reveals his perspective: under the heading 'peace' the entry is 'see *war*'.

3. In the case of Iraq, a hybrid civil-military institution, the Coalition Provisional Authority, carried out this task.

4. See, for example, Rice and Broster 'TALIBAN GET ASYLUM BUT STILL HATE US', in *Daily Express*, 17 February 2003.

5. See the remarks of Piero Fassino, an Italian politician who spoke out against Prime Minister Berlusconi's attack on 'multi-ethnicity', arguing that 'without immigrants, Italy's productive system would have serious gaps', in Hooper, 'We don't want multi-ethnic Italy, says Berlusconi', *Guardian*, 11 May 2009.

6. These actions suggest the use of the ancient battlefield technique in which some (though not all) of the city-state's more powerful adversaries are allowed to escape physical encirclement; the remainder of the enemy is more easily suppressed and the allies suffer fewer losses.

7. Of course, it might be possible to argue that the neo-conservative attachment to the democratic principle was no more than a form of hypocrisy, and that 'true' democracy need not be sullied through a process of association. If, however, an authoritarian model of capital interest *still holds sway*, then the democratic process will continue to be used as a mechanism for ensuring that the market finds its 'natural' level: government bailouts and takeovers do not alter this basic assumption. According to the original scenario described by Klein (2007), social chaos would merely be the precursor to an eventual economic settlement.

8. His speeches and party propaganda reveal an obsession with the 'inclusive *we*' (Atkinson, 1984), and the '*multiple* you' (Price, 2009b).

9. He referred for example to 'Americans who still believe in an America where anything's possible', but argued that 'they just don't think their leaders do' (Russell, 2009: 52).

10. The terror war was indeed a catastrophe for those injured, killed, displaced, tortured or exploited, yet for the many individuals and institutions that profited from the war (Armstrong, 2008; Stiglitz and Blimes, 2008), it provided a safe haven during the storms of recession.

11. In other words, capacity mobilised by the private sector.

12. While terrorists are supposed to *groom* subordinates, democrats are said to do no more than *mentor* theirs.

13. See Norton-Taylor, 'Miliband's lawyers try to block CIA report on torture claims', in *Guardian*, 2 May 2009.

14. The notion that political capability can become the undifferentiated property of all social actors during the course of 'democratic exchange', may perhaps be answered by the suggestion that power is indeed dispersed, but largely because different types of effect occur within distinct physical and conceptual locations.

15. Jessop, referring to insights of Marx, describes the 'rigorous distinction' he made between 'the political scene, the institutional architecture of the state', and the 'embedding of the state within a broader ensemble of economic and political forms' (Jessop, 2008: 94).

16. Civilian deaths, for example, are presented as the 'tragic' but necessary by-product of actions taken to secure the democratic order/security regime.

17. In the de Menezes case (when a man was shot dead by specialist firearms officers in July 2005), police were protected by systemic failure and the subsequent difficulty of establishing who bore responsibility for the death of the victim.

18. The resource demanded is partially based on an economic imperative, as the burgeoning security industry benefits from official depictions of social crisis and draws capital from the public sector in the form of orders for its products.

19. See the attempts to justify these policies, in for example, Lewis, 'Britain faces summer of rage – police', in *Guardian*, 23 February 2009, and for comments on the growth of surveillance, see Sengupta, 'Unmanned spy planes to police Britain', in *Independent*, 6 August 2008.

20. The reason for this reluctance to address the domestic question is precisely because it would draw attention to the authoritarian stance of the Democratic Party leadership, revealed when Obama voted for the Bush administration's bill to formalise its policy of electronic eavesdropping without requiring a legal warrant (Leslie, 2009: 192).

21. See Neocleous (2008), and by way of contrast the standard treatment of this issue, in Cottey (2007).

22. The shortcoming of Todd's analysis is not only the suggestion that this was mere 'show', but also his notion that the level of risk for the US military 'is almost non-existent' (Todd, 2003: 193); in a volunteer army, the death rate in Iraq and Afghanistan is actually regarded as considerable.

23. The role of the amorphous collection of publicists, journalists, party officials and other functionaries, who together form the ranks of the professionally opinionated, is to ensure the reproduction of plausible *moral* reasons for reform.

24. See for example the scenario reported in the *Independent* newspaper, through the UK's Freedom of Information Act, in which British authorities gave permission for security forces to shoot civilians under 'extreme' circumstances (in Milmo, 'Shoot to kill, Britain's answer to massacre at the Munich Olympics', in *Independent*, 9 May 2009).

25. A particular event is often chosen, in order to represent a larger chaos that would undermine the nation's economic base if not kept in check. The incident can then be met with repressive force by the paramilitary apparatus of the security state, itself heavily reliant on the assumptions created by a private sector devoted to making vast profits from the paranoia of public officials.

26. Since October 2007, for example, the UK's Metropolitan police carried out 154,293 'stop and searches' under the provisions of the Terrorism Act, 2000. See Anon, 'Police restrict anti-terrorism search powers', in *Independent*, 8 May 2009.

27. See the argument that the use of police in Athens during the 2004 Olympics, though justified as necessary to meet the terrorist threat, was actually used to control working-class demonstrations, called to protest against the government's failure to honour promises to give bonuses to key workers (Price, 2008).

28. Beetham notes that 'those who hold power, or seek to do so, are themselves frequently at odds with one another over the scope of their power and the control over their subordinates' (Beetham, 1991: 3).

Bibliography

9/11 Commission Report (2004) www.9-11commission.gov/report/911Report.pdf (accessed 22 July 2004).

Abercrombie, N., Hill, S. and Turner B.S. (1980) *The Dominant Ideology Thesis*, London: Unwin Hyman.

Ahearn, L. (2001) 'Language and Agency', *Annual Review of Anthropology* 30: 109–37.

Albo, G. (2003) 'The Old and New Economics of Imperialism', in Panitch, L. and Leys, C. (eds) *The New Imperial Challenge*, London: Merlin Press.

Aldridge, A. (2005) *The Market*, Cambridge: Polity Press.

Alexander, Y. and Latter, R. (eds) (1990) *Terrorism and the Media*, London, Washington, DC.

Allan, S. (ed.) (2005) *Journalism: Critical Issues*, Buckingham: Open University Press.

Almond, M. (2001) 'Solidarity or Appeasement: Europe's Dilemma', *The European Journal* 9 (1): 5–6.

Altschull, J.H. (1995) *Agents of Power*, New York: Longman.

Anderson, P. (2002) 'Force and Consent', *New Left Review* 17, September–October.

Anon (2001a) 'Reading the Leaders' Minds', *Newsweek*, 8 October.

Anon (2001b) 'Economy Strong "Despite Losses"', *Mail on Sunday*, 23 September.

Anon (2009) 'Police Restrict Anti-terrorism Search Powers', *Independent*, 8 May.

Archer, M. (1995) *Realist Social Theory: The Morphogenetic Approach*, Cambridge: Cambridge University Press.

Archer, M. (2000) *Being Human: The Problem of Agency*, Cambridge: Cambridge University Press.

Archer, M., Bhaskar, R., Collier, A., Lawson, T. and Norrie, A. (eds) (1998) *Critical Realism: Essential Readings*, London and New York: Routledge.

Armstrong, S. (2008) *War PLC*, London: Faber.

Ashdown, P. (2009) BBC Radio Four *Today* programme, 29 April.

Atkinson, M. (1984) *Our Masters' Voices*, London: Methuen.

Aufheben (2002) Article on Protest in UK, *Aufheben* 10: 1–17.

Austin, J.L. (1975) *How to Do Things with Words*, Oxford: Clarendon Press.

Ayers, A. (2009) 'Imperial Liberties: Democratisation and Governance in the "New" Imperial Order', *Political Studies* 57 (1): 1–27.

Axford, B. and Huggins, R. (2001) *New Media and Politics*, Thousand Oaks, London, Delhi: Sage.

Bacevich, A. (2009) 'The Long War', *London Review of Books*, 26 March.

Bach, K. and Harnish, R.M. (1979) *Linguistic Communication and Speech Acts*, Cambridge, MA: MIT Press.

Badiou, A. (2008a) *Number and Numbers*, Cambridge: Polity Press.

Badiou, A. (2008b) *The Meaning of Sarkozy*, London and New York: Verso.

Bailey, O.G. and Harindranath, R. (2005) 'Racialised "Othering": The Representation of Asylum Seekers in News Media', in Allan, S. (ed.) *Journalism: Critical Issues*, Buckingham: Open University Press.

Baker, G. (2005) 'His Second-term Mission: To End Tyranny on Earth', *The Times*, 21 January.

Barber, B.R. (2003) *Jihad vs. McWorld*, London: Corgi Books.

Barker, M. (1989) *Comics*, Manchester: Manchester University Press.

Baudrillard, J. (2003) *The Spirit of Terrorism*, London and New York: Verso.

Baudrillard, J. (2005) *The Intelligence of Evil or the Lucidity Pact*, Oxford and New York: Berg.

Bauman, Z. (2004) *Identity*, Cambridge: Polity Press.

Bavelas J.B., Black A., Chouil, N. and Mullet, J. (1990) *Equivocal Communication*, Thousand Oaks, London, Delhi: Sage.

BBC News (2001) Bulletin on US Policy in Iraq, 16 November.

BBC News online (2001) 'America's Home-grown Taliban Fighter', news.bbc.co.uk/hi/English/world/south_asia/newsid_1689000/1698138.stm3 (accessed 3 December 2001).

BBC News online (2003a) 'The UN Inspectors Should Be Given More Time To Do Their Job', news.bbc.co.uk, 15 February (accessed 16 February 2003).

BBC News online (2003b) '"Million" March Against Iraq War', 16 February, news.bbc.co.uk/1/hi/uk/2765041.stm (accessed 11 February 2009); opinions on 'Million' article, news.bbc.co.uk/1/hi/uk/2765549.stm (accessed 11 February 2009).

BBC World News (2006) Bulletin on Blair's Declining Influence, 19 November.

BBC News (2007) Bulletin on the Stockwell Shooting, 18 July.

Beaumont, P. (2009) 'Gaza War Crime Claims Gather Pace as More Troops Speak Out', *Observer*, 22 March.

Beetham, D. (1991) *The Legitimation of Power*, London: Macmillan.

Bell, A. (1991) *The Language of News Media*, Oxford: Blackwell.

Bellah, R. (1970) *Beyond Belief: Essays on Religion in a Post-traditional World*, New York: Harper and Row.

Benady, D. (2001) 'Fighting Talk', *Marketing Week*, 8 November.

Bennis, P. (2007) 'And the Name for our Profits is Democracy', in Vanaik, A. (ed.) *Selling US Wars*, Moreton-in-Marsh: Arris.

Berenskoetter, F. (2007) 'Thinking about Power', in Berenskoetter, F. and Williams, M.J. (eds) *Power in World Politics*, London and New York: Routledge.

Berenskoetter, F. and Williams, M.J. (eds) (2007) *Power in World Politics*, London and New York: Routledge.

Billig, M. (1991) *Ideology and Opinions*, Thousand Oaks, London, Delhi: Sage.

Billig, M. (1999) 'Whose Terms? Whose Ordinariness? Rhetoric and Ideology in Conversation Analysis', *Discourse and Society* 10 (4): 543–82.

Birks, J. (2008) 'The Professional Ideology of Campaign Journalism', in Ross, K. and Price, S. (eds) *Popular Media and Communication*, Newcastle: Cambridge Scholars Publishing.

Black, I. and White, M. (2001) 'Travel Ban to Block "Anarchist" Leaders', *Guardian*, 18 June, www.guardian.co.uk/world/2001/jun/18/globalisation.eu.

Black, J. (2001) *War in the New Century*, London and New York: Continuum.

Black, I. (2009) 'A Week is an Eternity as Diplomats Strive to Keep the Peace', *Guardian*, 19 January.

Blair, T. (1999) 'Speech: Doctrine of the International Community', 24 April, www. pm.gov.uk/output/Page1297.asp (accessed 2 August 2006).

Blair, T. (2001a) Interview, BBC *Newsnight*, 4 June.

Blair, T. (2001b) 'Full Text of Blair's Speech to the House of Commons', 14 September, www.guardian.co.uk/politics/2001/sep/14/houseofcommons.uk1 (accessed 23 April 2009).

Blair, T. (2001c) G8 News Conference, 19 July, in 'Bush to Confront G8 Summit', 23 July, archives.cnn.com/2001/WORLD/europe/07/20/bush.blair/index.html (accessed 29 April 2009).

Blair, T. (2003a) 'Address to the Nation', 20 March, www.number10.gov.uk/ Page3327 (accessed 17 April 2009).

Blair, T. (2003b) 'Full Text: Blair's Speech in Iraq', 29 May, www.guardian.co.uk/ politics/2003/may/29/iraq.iraq1 (accessed 23 April 2009).

Blair, T. and Bush, G.W. (2001) 'News Conference', 10 July, www.bulk.resource. org/gpo.gov/papers/2001/2001_vol2_873.pdf (accessed 6 April 2009).

Blair, T. and Bush, G.W. (2003) 'Press Conference', 31 January, www.number10. gov.uk/Page1767 (accessed 17 April 2009).

Blondheim, M. and Liebes, T. (2003) 'From Disaster Marathon to Media Event', in Noll, A.M. (ed.) *Crisis Communications*, Maryland: Rowan and Littlefield.

Blyth, M. (2003) 'The Political Power of Financial Ideas', in Kirshner, J. (ed.) *Monetary Orders: Ambiguous Economics, Ubiquitous Politics*, Ithaca and London: Cornell University Press.

Boal, I., Clark, T.J., Matthews, J. and Watts, M. (2005) *Afflicted Powers: Capital and Spectacle in a New Age of War*, London and New York: Verso.

Bobbitt, P. (2008) *Terror and Consent: The Wars for the Twenty-first Century*, London and New York: Penguin, Allen Lane.

Boehlert, E. (2004) 'Team Bush Declares War on the New York Times', 19 October, www.guardian.co.uk/media/2004/0ct/19/pressandpublishing1 (accessed 6 March 2009).

Bogard, W. (1996) *The Simulation of Surveillance*, Cambridge: Cambridge University Press.

Bonner, D. (2007) *Executive Measures, Terrorism and National Security*, Aldershot, Burlington: Ashgate.

Boone, J. (2009) 'Obama bid to turn moderate Taliban "will fail"', 9 March, www. guardian.co.uk/world/2009/mar/09/obama-taliban-talks (accessed 10 March 2009).

Boone, J. (2009) '"Worse Than the Taliban": New Law Rolls Back Rights for Afghan Women', *Guardian*, 31 March.

Boyer, R. (1996) 'State and Market: A New Engagement for the Twenty-First Century?', in Boyer, R. and Drache, D. (eds) *States Against Markets*, London and New York, Routledge.

Branigan, E. (1993) *Narrative Comprehension and Film*, London, New York: Routledge.

Brenner, N., Jessop, B., Jones, M. and MacLeod, G. (2003) *State/Space: A Reader*, Oxford: Blackwell.

Brewin, C. (2003) *Post-traumatic Stress Disorder: Malady or Myth?* New Haven: Yale University Press.

Bromley, S. (2008) *American Power and the Prospects for International Order*, Cambridge: Polity Press.

Bromwich, D. (2009) 'Responses to the War in Gaza', *in London Review of Books*, 29 January.

Brown, D. (2008) 'Vote Zippy', cartoon in *Independent*, 31 December.

Brown, G. and Yule, G. (1983) *Discourse Analysis*, Cambridge: Cambridge University Press.

Brown, W. (1995) 'States of Injury: Power and Freedom in Late Modernity', in Murphy, T. and Whitty, N. (eds) *Crowning Glory: Public Law, Power and the Monarchy*, Princeton: Princeton University Press, 2000.

Brubaker, R. (1992) *Citizenship and Nationhood in France and Germany*, Cambridge, MA: Harvard University Press.

Brummer, A. (2001) 'The Day Capitalism Stopped', *Daily Mail*, 12 September.

Bull, C. and Erman, S. (2002) *At Ground Zero*, New York: Thunder's Mouth Press.

Bull, H. (1977) *The Anarchical Society: A Study of Order in World Politics*, London: Macmillan.

Bull, M. (2006) 'States of Failure', *New Left Review* 40, July–August: 5–25.

Burbach, R. and Clarke, B. (2002) *September 11 and the US War*, San Francisco: City Lights.

Burds, J. (2009) 'Sexual Violence in Europe in World War II, 1939–45', *Politics and Society* 37 (1), March: 35–73.

Burke, L., Crowley, T. and Girvin, A. (2000) *Language and Cultural Theory Reader*, London and New York: Routledge.

Burkeman, O. (2009) 'War on Terror is Over, Overseas Contingency Operations Begin', *Guardian*, 26 March.

Bush, G.W. (2001) Speech to Congress and the Nation, 20 September, *Time US*, www.time.com/time/nation/article/0,8599,175757,00.html (accessed 29 April 2009).

Bush, G.W. (2002) 'Remarks by the President in Tribute to Milton Friedman', 9 May, www.freetochoosemedia.org/freetochoose/tribute_pres.php (accessed 19 April 2009).

Bush, G.W. (2003a) Interview, *Breakfast with Frost*, ITV, 16 November.

Bush, G.W. (2003b) White House Press Conference, 20 November, www.accessmylibrary.com/coms2/summary_0286-2363992_ITM (accessed 26 April 2009).

Bush, G.W. and Blair, T. (2003) 'Press Conference', 31 January, www.number10.gov.uk/Page1767 (accessed 17 April 2009).

Buxton, D. (1980) *From the Avengers to Miami Vice: Form and Ideology in Television Series*, Manchester: Manchester University Press.

Calvert, C. (2004) *Voyeur Nation*, Boulder: Westview Press.

Campbell, J. (2005) *Film and Cinema Spectatorship*, Cambridge: Polity Press.

Campbell D. (2009) 'Pakistan Terror Accused Acted in Self-defence, Court Hears', *Guardian*, 6 January, www.guardian.co.uk/uk/2009/jan/06/pakistan-terrorism-internet-balach-warna (accessed 29 April 2009).

Cardan, P. (1965) *Modern Capitalism and Revolution*, London: Solidarity.

Carroll, S. (2003) 'The Families Want Respect For Their Dead', *Daily Mirror*, 29 March.

Cassidy, R.M. (2008) *Counterinsurgency and the Global War on Terror*, Stanford: Stanford University Press.

Catephores, G. (1989) *An Introduction to Marxist Economics*, London: Macmillan.

Cerny, P.G. (1990) *The Changing Architecture of Politics: Structure, Agency and the Future of the State*, London, Newbury Park, New Delhi: Sage.

Chandrasekaran, R. (2007) *Imperial Life in the Emerald City*, London, New York, Berlin: Bloomsbury.

Chayes, S. (2007) *The Punishment of Virtue*, London: Portobello Books.

Chomsky, N. (2009) '"Exterminate All the Brutes": Gaza 2009', *ZNet*, www.zmag. org/znet/viewArticle/20316 (accessed 30 January 2009).

Chomsky, N. and Herman, E.S. (1988) 'Manufacturing Consent', in Tumber, H. (ed.) *News: A Reader*, Oxford: Oxford University Press 1999.

Churchill, W. (1999 [1940]) 'Speech to the House of Commons', in MacArthur, B. (ed.) *The Penguin Book of Twentieth-Century Speeches*, London and New York: Penguin Books.

CNN (2002) 'Rice: Iraq Trained al Qaeda in Chemical Weapons', 26 September, edition.cnn.com/2002/US/09/25/us.iraq.alqaeda (accessed 30 September 2002).

Cobain, I., Cowan, R. and Norton-Taylor, R. (2005) 'They Held the Pistol to Him and Unloaded Five Shots', *Guardian*, 23 July.

Cockburn, P. (2009) 'Warning to the US: Beware Treating Afghanistan Like Iraq', *Independent*, 26 February.

Coleman, R. (2004) *Reclaiming the Streets*, Portland: Willan Publishing.

Coleman, S. (2001) 'The Transformation of Citizenship?', in Axford, B. and Huggins, R. (eds) *New Media and Politics*, Thousand Oaks, London, Delhi: Sage.

Collier, A. (1998) 'Language, Practice and Realism', in Parker, I. (ed), *Social Constructionism, Discourse and Realism*, London, Newbury Park, New Delhi: Sage.

Collins, N. (2001) 'World Pays the Terrible Price of Globalisation', *Daily Telegraph*, 12 September.

Concise Oxford English Dictionary (1964) Oxford: Oxford University Press.

Cottey, A. (2007) *Security in the New Europe*, Basingstoke and New York: Palgrave Macmillan.

Couldry, N. and McCarthy, A. (eds) (2004) *Mediaspace: Place, Scale and Culture in a Media Age*, London and New York: Routledge.

Coulthard, M. (1985) *An Introduction to Discourse Analysis*, London: Longman.

Crooks, E., Despeignes, P. and Barber, T. (2001) 'Jitters Return After US Rate Cut', *Financial Times*, 5 January.

Crossley, N. (1995) 'Body Techniques, Agency and Intercorporeality: on Goffman's *Relations in Public*', *Sociology* 29 (1): 133–49.

Cruse, A. (2000) *Meaning in Language*, Oxford: Oxford University Press.

Curtis, M. (1998) *The Great Deception: Anglo-American Power and World Order*, London: Pluto Press.

Culler, J. (1985) *On Deconstruction*, London and New York: Routledge.

Dagenais, B. (1992) 'Media in Crises: Observers, Actors or Scapegoats?' in Raboy, M. and Dagenais, B. (eds) *Media, Crisis and Democracy*, London, Newbury Park, New Delhi: Sage.

Dahlgren, P. (1995) *Television and the Public Sphere*, London, New Delhi, Thousand Oaks: Sage.

Daily Express (2005) 'They Were All Sponging Asylum Seekers', 27 July.

Daily Mail (2001) 'Destroyed, the Once Towering Symbols of Capitalism', 11 September.

Daily Mail (2005) 'Comment: Another Victim of the Terrorists', 25 July.

Daily Mirror (2002) 'Warkies!', 18 December.

Davies, N. (2008a) *Flat Earth News*, London: Chatto and Windus.

Davies, N. (2008b) 'The Bloody Battle of Genoa', 17 July, www.guardian.co.uk/world/jul/17/italy.g8 (accessed 15 April 2009).

DeLanda, M. (2006) *A New Philosophy of Society*, London and New York: Continuum.

Dewson, A. (2006) 'Prospect of Bumper Profits Lifts the Oil Giants', *Independent*, 31 January.

Dillon, M.C. (1995) *Semiological Reductionism*, New York: State University of New York Press.

Doward, J. and Ryle, S. (2001) 'UK "on brink of full recession"', *Observer* Business Section, 22 July.

Dowd, D. (2000) *Capitalism and its Economics*, London: Pluto Press.

Dyer, C. (2007) 'There is No War on Terror', *Guardian*, 24 January.

Edles, L.D. (2002) *Cultural Sociology in Practice*, Oxford: Blackwell.

Emmerson, B. and Shamash, A. (1987) *A Report on the Policing of the News International Demonstration at Wapping*, London: Haldane Society.

English, R. and Townshend, C. (eds) (1999) *The State*, London and New York: Routledge.

Enloe, C. (1989) *Bananas, Beaches and Bases: Making Feminist Sense of International Politics*, Berkeley: University of California Press.

Entman, R. (1993) cited in Simons, H.W., 'What's in a News Frame?', Paper for ATINER conference, 22–24 May 2006.

Ericson, R.V., Baranek, P.M. and Chan, J.B.L. (1991) *Representing Order*, Milton Keynes: Open University Press.

Escolar, M. (2003) 'Exploration, Cartography and the Modernization of State Power', in Brenner, N., Jessop, B., Jones, M. and MacLeod, G. (eds) *State/Space: A Reader*, Oxford: Blackwell.

Etzioni, A. (1961) *A Comparative Analysis of Complex Organizations: On Power, Involvement, and Their Correlates*, New York: Free Press of Glencoe.

Fairclough, N. (1989) *Language and Power*, London and New York: Longman.

Fairclough, N. (2000) *New Labour, New Language?* London and New York: Routledge.

Faludi, S. (2008) *The Terror Dream*, London: Atlantic Books.

Fenton, B. (2001) 'This is War and We'll Win it, Say Pentagon Staff', *Daily Telegraph*, 12 September.

Ferudi, F. (2007) *Invitation to Terror*, London and New York: Continuum.

Feury, P. (2000) *New Developments in Film Theory*, London: Macmillan; London, New Delhi: Sage.

Fisk, R. (2009a) 'Wherever I go, I hear the same tired Middle East comparisons', 10 January, www.independent.co.uk/opinion/commentators/fisk/robert-fiskrsquos-world-wherever-i-go-i-hear-the-same-tired-middle-east-comparisons-1297595.html (accessed 20 January 2009).

Fisk, R. (2009b) 'So, I asked the UN secretary general, isn't it time for a war crimes tribunal?', 19 January, www.independent.co.uk/opinion/commentators/fisk/robert-fisk-so-i-asked-the-un-secretary-general-isnt-it-time-for-a-war-crimes-tribunal-14 (accessed 20 January 2009).

Fiumara, G.C. (1992) *The Symbolic Function*, Oxford: Blackwell.

Fletcher, V. and O'Grady, S. (2001) 'British Shoppers Defy the Terrorists', *Daily Express*, 19 October.

Flynn, B. (1982) 'ITN: Mutton Dressed as Lamb?', in Blanchard, S. and Morley, D. (eds) *What's This Channel Fo(u)r?*, London: Comedia.

Foley, S. (2009) 'Obama Denies Terror Suspects Right to Trial', *Independent*, 22 February.

Foreign Staff (2007) 'Sunni Dissidents in Iraq to be Given Arms by US', *The Times*, 12 June.

Foucault, M. (2001) *Fearless Speech*, London: MIT Press.

Fowles, J. (1996) *Advertising and Popular Culture*, Thousand Oaks, London, New Delhi: Sage.

Frankel, B. (1983) *Beyond the State?*, London: Macmillan.

Freedland, J. (2006) Analysis of Bush/Blair Exchange, *Guardian*, 18 July.

Frum, D. (2003) *The Right Man*, New York: Random House.

Ganser, D. (2005) *NATO's Secret Armies*, London and New York: Frank Cass.

Gardner, H. (2005) *American Global Strategy and the 'War on Terrorism'*, Aldershot and Burlington: Ashgate.

Gareau, F.H. (2004) *State Terrorism and the United States*, Atlanta and London: Zed Books.

Garton-Ash, T. (2004) 'Let's Rock the Boat', *Guardian*, 5 August, www.guardian.co.uk/world/2004/aug/05/usaelections2004.usa1.

Gerbner, G. (1992) 'Violence and Terror in and by the Media', in Raboy, M. and Dagenais, B. (eds) *Media, Crisis and Democracy*, London, Newbury Park, New Delhi: Sage.

George, S. (2002) 'Clusters of Crisis and a Planetary Contract', in Burbach, R. and Clarke, B. (eds) *September 11 and the US War*, San Francisco: City Lights.

Gibb, J. (2005) *Who's Watching You?*, London: Collins and Brown.

Gill, G. (2003) *The Nature and Development of the Modern State*, Basingstoke and New York: Palgrave Macmillan.

Gillan, K., Pickerill, J. and Webster, F. (2008) *Anti-War Activism: New Media and Protest in the Information Age*, Basingstoke and New York: Palgrave Macmillan.

Glaister, D. (2004) 'High-profile Air Strikes "Killed Only Civilians"', *Guardian*, 14 June, www.guardian.co.uk/world/2004/jun/14/iraq.usa (accessed 12 July 2009).

Global Outlook (2004) '26 Top Anomalies of 9/11', *Global Outlook* 8, Spring: 31–4.

Goffman, E. (1981) *Forms of Talk*, Oxford: Blackwell.

Goldenburg, S. (2004) 'Democrats Show No Mercy', *The Hindu*, 2 August, www.hindu.com/2004/08/02/stories/2004080201341400.htm (accessed 29 April 2009).

Goldenburg, S. (2009) 'Activist or Terrorist? Mild-mannered Eco-militant Serving 22 Years for Arson', *Guardian*, 25 March.

Goold, B.J. (2004) *CCTV and Policing*, Oxford: Oxford University Press.

Goulden, H., Hartley, J. and Wright, T. (1982) 'Consciousness Razing: Channel Four, News and Current Affairs', in Blanchard, S. and Morley, D., *What's This Channel Fo(u)r?*, London: Comedia.

Gow, D. (2009) 'Europe's Stockmarkets Go to War Over Control of "Financial WMD's"', *Guardian*, 20 February.

Gowan, P. (2009) 'Crisis in the Heartland: Consequences of the New Wall Street System', *New Left Review* 55, January–February: 5–29.

Graham, P. (1999) 'Critical Systems Theory: A Political Economy of Language, Thought, and Technology', *Communication Research* 26 (4): 482–507.

Graham, P., Keenan, T. and Dowd, A.M. (2004) 'A Call to Arms at the End of History: Discourse-historical Analysis of George W. Bush's Declaration of War on Terror', *Discourse and Society* 15 (2–3): 199–221.

Gramsci, A. (1971) *Selections from Prison Notebooks*, London: Lawrence and Wishart.

Green, P. (1990) *The Enemy Without*, Buckingham and Bristol: Open University Press.

Greenberg, K.J. and Dratel, J.L. (eds) (2008) *The Torture Papers: The Road to Abu Ghraib*, Cambridge: Cambridge University Press.

Grice, P. (1989) *Studies in the Ways of Words*, Cambridge, MA: Harvard University Press.

Grice, A. (2001) 'Bush's Speech to Congress', *Independent*, 22 September.

Gupta, S. (2002) *The Replication of Violence*, London: Pluto Press.

Habermas, J. (1991) *Communication and the Evolution of Society*, Cambridge: Polity Press.

Hale, B. (2008) 'Five Muslims in "Terror Material" Case are Freed', *Daily Mail*, 14 February.

Hall, M. (2006) 'Bush and Blair's Toe-curling Chat', *Daily Express*, 18 July.

Halliday, F. (2002) *Two Hours that Shook the World*, London: Saqi Books.

Haney, E. (2002) *Inside Delta Force: The Story of America's Elite Counterterrorist Unit*, New York: Delacorte Press.

Hansen, H.K. and Salskov-Iversen, D. (2002) 'Managerialised Patterns of Political Authority', *Critical Quarterly* 44 (3), Autumn.

Harris, P. (2006) 'No Civil War in Iraq, Insists Bush – But Pentagon Differs', *Guardian*, 3 September, www.guardian.co.uk/world/2006/sep/03/usa.iraq (accessed 17 April 2009).

Harvey, D. (2005) *A Brief History of Neoliberalism*, Oxford: Oxford University Press.

Heller, J. (2009) 'Israel Completes Gaza Troop Withdrawal', 21 January, www.reuters.com/articlePrint?articleID=USLL17859 (accessed 2 February 2009).

Heritage, J. (1985) 'Analyzing News Interviews', in van Dijk (ed.) *Handbook of Discourse Analysis*, Vol. 3, London: Academic Press.

Herring, E. and Rangwala, G. (2006) *Iraq in Fragments: The Occupation and its Legacy*, London: Hurst.

Hewitt, S. (2008) *The British War on Terror*, London and New York: Continuum.

Hirsch, A. (2009) 'Police Accused of Misusing Terror Laws Against Peaceful Protests', *Guardian*, 23 March.

Hobsbawm, E. (2008) *Globalisation, Democracy and Terrorism*, London: Abacus.

Hobson, D. (2008) *Channel 4: The Early Years and the Jeremy Isaacs Legacy*, London and New York: I.B. Tauris.

Holloway, D. (2008) *9/11 and the War on Terror*, Edinburgh: Edinburgh University Press.

Hooper, J. (2009) 'We Don't Want Multi-ethnic Italy, Says Berlusconi', *Guardian*, 11 May.

Horton, D. and Wohl, R. (1956) 'Mass Communication as Para-social Interaction', *Psychiatry* 19 (3): 215–29.

Hoskins, A. and O'Loughlin, B. (2007) *Television and Terror*, Basingstoke and New York: Palgrave Macmillan.

Houen, A. (2002) *Terrorism and Modern Literature*, Oxford: Oxford University Press.

Hughes, S. (2007) *War on Terror Inc.*, London and New York: Verso.

Hulsse, R. and Spencer, A. (2008) 'The Metaphor of Terror: Terrorism Studies and the Constructivist Turn', *Security Dialogue* 39 (6): 571–92.

Hunt, K. and Rygiel, K. (eds) (2007) *(En)Gendering the War on Terror*, Aldershot and Burlington: Ashgate.

Hutchby, I. and Wooffitt, R. (1998) *Conversation Analysis*, Cambridge: Polity Press.

Hutton, J. (2009) BBC Radio 4 news, 15 March.

Independent Editorial (2009) 'Obama, Tell Us the Whole Truth', 22 February.

Independent Television News (2003) 'Breakfast with Frost', 16 November.

Independent Television News (2005a) Bulletin on the Stockwell Shooting, 16 August.

Independent Television News (2005b) Bulletin on the Stockwell Shooting, 18 August.

Independent Television News (2006) Bulletin on the G8 'Open Microphone', 17 July.

Independent Television News (2007) Bulletin on the Stockwell Shooting, 2 August.

Irvine, J.T. (1989) 'When Talk Isn't Cheap: Language and Political Economy', *American Ethnologist* 16: 248–66.

Ivie, R.L. (2005) *Democracy and America's War on Terror*, Tuscaloosa: University of Alabama Press.

Jackson, B. and Wardle, T. (1986) *The Battle for Orgreave*, Brighton: Vanson Wardle Productions.

Jencks, C. (2001) 'Chris Jencks' Column', *Building Design* 1502, 21 September.

Jensen, K.B. (1995) *The Social Semiotics of Mass Communication*, Thousand Oaks, London, New Delhi: Sage.

Jessop, B. (2008) *State Power: A Strategic-Relational Approach*, Cambridge: Polity Press.

Johnson, C. and Leslie, J. (2008) *Afghanistan: The Mirage of Peace*, London and New York: Zed Books.

Joint Chiefs of Staff (2000) *Joint 20/20 Vision*, Washington, DC: US Government Printing Office.

Judd, T. and Sengupta, K. (2006) 'Poor Planning in Iraq to Blame for Soldiers' Deaths, Says Coroner', 3 October, www.independent.co.uk/news/world/middle-east/poor-planning-in-Iraq-to-blame-for-soldiers-deaths-says-coroner-418518.html (accessed 15 June 2009).

Jusdanis, G. (2001) *The Necessary Nation*, Princeton: Princeton University Press.

Justice Not Vengeance (2003) Leaflet: 'Transitions and Priorities', 24 September.

Kalita, S.M. (2002) 'Seeking Solace in my Notebook', in Bull, C. and Erman, S. (eds) *At Ground Zero*, New York: Thunder's Mouth Press.

Kastiaficas, G. (2006) *The Subversion of Politics: European Autonomous Social Movements and the Decolonisation of Everyday Life*, Oakland and Edinburgh: AK Press.

Kavoori, A.P. and Fraley, T. (2006) *Media, Terrorism and Theory*, Oxford and Lanham: Rowan and Littlefield.

Keane, J. (1992) 'The Crisis of the Sovereign State', in Raboy, M. and Dagenais, B. (eds) *Media, Crisis and Democracy*, London, Newbury Park, New Delhi: Sage.

Kellner, D. (2003) *From 9/11 to Terror War Theory*, Oxford and Lanham: Rowan and Littlefield.

Kilfoyle, P. (2007) *Lies, Damned Lies and Iraq*, Petersfield: Harriman House.

King, O. (2006) 'Blair to Fly to US for Middle East Talks', *Guardian*, 27 July, www.guardian.co.uk/politics/2006/jul/27/foreignpolicy.usa (accessed 5 May 2009).

Kirshner, J. (2003) 'Explaining Choices About Money', in Kirshner, J. (ed.) *Monetary Orders: Ambiguous Economics, Ubiquitous Politics*, Ithaca and London: Cornell University Press.

Klaidman, D. and Thomas, E. (2000) 'A World on Alert', *Newsweek*, 3 January 2000.

Klein, N. (2007) *The Shock Doctrine*, London and New York: Penguin, Allen Lane.

Labov, W. (1972) 'Rules for Ritual Insults', in Sudnow, D. (ed.) *Studies in Social Interaction*, Mouton: The Hague.

Lambert, S. (1982) *Channel Four: Television With a Difference?*, London: BFI.

Laquer, W. (1986) 'Reflections on Terrorism', *Foreign Affairs*, Fall: 86–100.

Latour, B. (2005) *Reassembling the Social*, Oxford: Oxford University Press.

Laville, S. (2005) 'De Menezes Shooting: UK's Top Anti-terror Officer is Singled Out', 1 August, www.guardian.co.uk/uk/2007/aug/01/topstories3.menezes (accessed 29 April 2009).

Lazuka, A. (2006) 'Communicative Intention in George Bush's Presidential Speeches', *Discourse and Society* 17 (3): 299–330.

Leishman, F. and Mason, P. (2003) *Policing and the Media*, Abingdon: Lawrence and Erlbaum.

Leslie, I. (2009) *To Be President*, London: Politico's.

Levin, C. (1996) *Jean Baudrillard: A Study in Cultural Metaphysics*, London: Prentice Hall.

Lewis, J. (2005) *Language Wars*, London: Pluto Press.

Lewis, P. (2009) 'Britain Faces Summer of Rage – Police', *Guardian*, 23 February.

Lister, D. (2001) 'Army Calls up Film-makers to Provide Tactical Advice', *Independent*, 10 October, www.independent.co.uk/news/world/America/army-calls-up (accessed 17 April 2009).

Lucas, E. (2006) 'Yo Blair!' *Daily Mail*, 19 July.

Lyon, D. (2003) 'Surveillance Technology and Surveillance Society', in Misa, T.J., Brey, P. and Feenberg, A. (eds) *Modernity and Technology*, Cambridge, MA: MIT Press.

Lyon, D. (2007) *Surveillance Studies*, Cambridge: Polity Press.

MacAskill, E. (2008) 'Obama Briefed by Rice on Conflict but Declines to Comment on Future Policy', *Guardian*, 29 December.

MacAskill, E. and McCarthy, R. (2009) 'Mitchell Hopes for Israel–Hamas Peace Talks', *Guardian*, 28 January.

MacAskill, E., Vidal, J. and O'Carroll, R. (2001) 'Riots Force Review of Summits', *Guardian*, 23 July, www.guardian.co.uk/world/2001/jul/23/usa.russia1 (accessed 12 July 2009).

MacCannell, D. and MacCannell, J.F. (1993) 'Social Class in Modernity', in Rojek, C. and Turner, B.S. (eds) *Forget Baudrillard?*, London and New York: Routledge.

McClellan, S. (2008) *What Happened*, New York: Public Affairs.

McCulloch, J. (2002) '"Either You Are With Us, Or You Are With the Terrorists": The War's Home Front', in Scraton, P. (ed.) *Beyond September 11th*, London: Pluto Press.

McGreal, C. (2009) 'Israel Looks to Drive Out Hamas', *Guardian*, 6 January.

Macintyre, D. (2009a) 'Military Condemns Soldiers' Shocking T-shirts', *Independent*, 22 March.

Macintyre, D. (2009b) 'Israeli Military in PR Offensive to Explain Civilian Deaths in Gaza', *Independent*, 30 March 2009, www.independent.co.uk/news/world/middle-east/israeli-military-in-pr-offensive-to-explain-civilian-deaths-in-gaza-1657050.html (accessed 12 July 2009).

McNair, B. (2003) *An Introduction to Political Communication*, London and New York: Routledge.

McQuire, S. (1998) *Visions of Modernity*, Thousand Oaks, London, Delhi: Sage.

Mandelson, P. (2001) 'How Good Could Still Come Out of This Evil', *Mail on Sunday*, 23 September.

Manning, C. and Gilfeather, P. (2001) 'SICKENING: Lloyd's Report Boasts September 11 is "Historic Chance" For Rich to Get Richer', *Daily Mirror*, 29 October.

Mansoor, P.R. (2008) *Baghdad at Sunrise*, New Haven: Yale University Press.

Mathijs, E. and Jones, J. (2004) *Big Brother International*, London, New York: Wallflower Press.

Mattern, J.B. (2007) 'Why "Soft Power" Isn't So Soft: Representational Force and Attraction in World Politics', in Berenskoetter, F. and Williams, M.J. (eds) *Power in World Politics*, London and New York: Routledge.

Mazower, M. (2008) *Hitler's Empire: Nazi Rule in Occupied Europe*, London and New York: Allen Lane.

Mearshimer J.J. (2009) 'Responses to the War in Gaza', *London Review of Books*, 29 January.

Mearshimer, J.J. and Walt, S.M. (2008) *The Israel Lobby and US Foreign Policy*, London and New York: Penguin Books.

Merrett, J. (2001) 'Icon of Wealth: The World Trade Centre', *Daily Mirror*, 12 September.

Meyers, P.A. (2008) *Civic War and the Corruption of the Citizen*, Chicago: Chicago University Press.

Mikula, M. (2008) *Key Concepts in Cultural Studies*, Basingstoke and New York: Palgrave Macmillan.

Miller, G.R. and Stiff, J. (1993) *Deceptive Communication*, Thousand Oaks, London, New Delhi: Sage.

Miliband, D. (2009) 'War on Terror was Wrong', 15 January, www.guardian.co.uk/commentisfree/2009/jan/15/david-miliband-war-terror (accessed 20 January 2009).

Milmo, C. (2009) 'Shoot to Kill, Britain's Answer to Massacre at Munich Olympics', *Independent*, 9 May.

Misa, T.J., Brey, P. and Feenberg, A. (2003) *Modernity and Technology*, Cambridge, MA: MIT Press.

Montgomery, M. (2005) 'Talking War', in Allan, S. (ed.) *Journalism: Critical Issues*, Buckingham: Open University Press.

Morris, C. (2002) Interview with Matt Damon, www.webwombat.com.au/entertainment/movies/bourne_int.htm (accessed 6 September 2008).

Morris, L. (2001a) 'The Graduate, the Banker and the Doctor's Son ... Introducing Britain's Middle-class Revolutionaries', *Daily Mail*, 21 July.

Morris, L. (2001b) 'Armed Guard on Briton Who Led Rioters', *Daily Mail*, 23 July.

Morse, M. (1985) 'Talk, Talk, Talk', *Screen* 26 (2): 2–15.

Mosco, V. (1996) *The Political Economy of Communication*, Thousand Oaks, London, Delhi: Sage.

Nagl, J.A. (2002/2005) *Learning to Eat Soup with a Knife: Counterinsurgency Lessons from Malaya and Vietnam*, Chicago: University of Chicago Press.

Neocleous, M. (2008) *Critique of Security*, Montreal and Kingston, Ithaca: McGill-Queen's University Press.

Newby, H., Bujra, J., Littlewood, P., Rees, G. and Rees, T.L. (1985) *Restructuring Capital: Recession and Reorganisation in Industrial Society*, Basingstoke and London: Macmillan.

Nofsinger, R.E. (1991) *Everyday Conversation*, Thousand Oaks, London, Delhi: Sage.

Noll, A.M. (ed.) (2003) *Crisis Communications*, Maryland: Rowan and Littlefield.

Norton-Taylor, R. (2009a) 'MI5 Officer Gave False Evidence in Guantanamo Detainee Case', *Guardian*, 21 April.

Norton-Taylor, R. (2009b) 'Miliband's Lawyers Try to Block CIA Report on Torture Claims', *Guardian*, 2 May.

Nussbaum, B. (2001) 'Liberation', *Business Week*, 3 December.

Oakes, P.J., Haslam, S.A. and Turner, J.C. (1994) *Stereotyping and Social Reality*, Oxford: Blackwell.

Obama, B. (2009) 'Inauguration Address', *Guardian*, 20 January.

Oborne, P. (2008) 'Iraq: The Betrayal', documentary, 17 March, Channel 4.

Offe, C. (1984) *Contradictions of the Welfare State*, Cambridge, MA: MIT Press.

Ogilvy 'Topoff' Exercise for Department of Homeland Security, www.ogilvypr.com, 'case studies' (accessed 1 March 2006).

Outhwaite, W. (1994) *Habermas: A Critical Introduction*, Cambridge: Polity Press.

Padilla, N. (2003) (video) Anti-war Demonstration, 15 February.

Panitch, L. and Leys, C. (eds) (2003) *The New Imperial Challenge*, London: Merlin Press.

Parker, I. (ed.) (1998) *Social Constructionism, Discourse and Realism*, London, Newbury Park, New Delhi: Sage.

Parsons, T. (2001) 'Out of a Clear Blue Sky', *Daily Mirror*, 20 September, www.mirror.co.uk/news/allnews/page.cfm?objectid=11314790&method=full (accessed 13 February 2002).

Perkins, A. (2006) *A Very British Strike*, Basingstoke: Macmillan.

Pierson, C. (1996) *The Modern State*, London and New York: Routledge.

Poole, O. (2003) *Black Knights: On the Bloody Road to Baghdad*, London: Harper Collins.

Poulantzas, N. (1978a) *State Power Socialism*, London: Verso.

Poulantzas, N. (1978b) *Classes in Contemporary Capitalism*, London: Verso.

Prados, J. (2004) *Hoodwinked*, New York and London: The New Press.

Prescott, J. (2004) Interview, BBC Radio 4 *Today* programme, 24 November.

Price, S. (1996) *Communication Studies*, Harlow: Longman.

Price, S. (1997) *Complete A–Z Media and Communication Handbook*, London: Hodder and Stoughton.

Price, S. (2005) 'American Mentality? Trauma, Imperialism and the Authentic Veteran', *Journal of Media Practice* 6 (2): 83–91.

Price, S. (2006a) 'Conceptions of Democracy', in Pappas, N. *3rd International Conference on European History*, Athens: ATINER.

Price, S. (2006b) 'Brute Reality: Television, War and Timeliness', in Barker, A. (ed.) *Television, Aesthetics and Reality*, Newcastle: Cambridge Scholars Press.

Price, S. (2006c), 'From Media Studies for Some to Media Education For All: Towards a New Citizenship?' in Breslin, A. and Dufour, B. (eds) *Developing Citizens*, London: Hodder Murray.

Price, S. (2007) *Discourse Power Address: The Politics of Public Communication*, Aldershot and Burlington: Ashgate.

Price, S. (2008) 'Missiles in Athens, Tanks at Heathrow: Urban Security and the Materialisation of "Global" Threat', *Social Semiotics* 18 (1): 1–16.

Price, S. (2009a) 'The Mediation of "Terror": Authority, Journalism and the Stockwell Shooting', in Boehmer, E. and Morton, S. (eds) *Terror and the Postcolonial*, Oxford: Blackwell.

Price, S. (2009b) 'The Audacity of Rhetoric: Barack Obama and Moral Authority', paper for *British Association of American Studies*, 19 April.

Private Eye (2002) 'New Osama Threat to America', Front cover, 12 July.

Raboy, M. and Dagenais, B. (1992) *Media, Crisis and Democracy*, London, Newbury Park, New Delhi: Sage.

Rai, M. (2003) *Regime Unchanged: Why the War on Iraq Changed Nothing*, London: Pluto Press.

Ramesh, R. (2003) *The War We Could Not Stop*, London: Faber and Faber.

Rashid, A. (2001) *Taliban*, London, Basingstoke and Oxford: Pan Macmillan.

Rettburg, J.W. (2008) *Blogging*, Cambridge: Polity Press.

Reuters.com (2009) 'U.S. Senate Supports Israel's Gaza Incursion', 8 January, www.reuters.com/article/politicsNews/idUSTRE5075JG20090108 (accessed 30 January 2009).

Rhodes, R.A.W. (1995) 'Prime Ministerial Power to Core Executive', in Rhodes, R.A.W. and Dunleavy, P. (eds) *Prime Minister, Cabinet and Core Executive*, London and New York: Macmillan.

Rhodes, R.A.W. and Dunleavy, P. (eds) (1995) *Prime Minister, Cabinet and Core Executive*, London, New York: Macmillan.

Rice, D. and Broster, P. (2003) 'Taliban Get Asylum But Still Hate Us', *Daily Express*, 17 February.

Ricks, T.E. (2006) *Fiasco: The American Military Adventure in Iraq*, London: Penguin Books.

Ricks, T.E. (2009) *The Gamble*, London: Allen Lane.

Roberts, B. (2005) 'Brazilian's Visa 2 Years Out of Date', *Daily Mirror*, 29 July.

Rojek, C. and Turner, B.S. (eds) (1993) *Forget Baudrillard?*, London and New York: Routledge.

Routledge, P. (2003) 'Blair Has Hit New Low by Exploiting the Dead', *Daily Mirror*, 29 March.

Ross, K. and Price, S. (eds) (2008) *Popular Media and Communication*, Newcastle: Cambridge Scholars Publishing.

Russell, H. (2009) *The Politics of Hope*, London, Sydney, Cape Town, Auckland: New Holland Publishers.

Ryan, D. (2007) *Frustrated Empire*, London: Pluto Press.

Sands, P. (2005) *Lawless World*, London and New York: Penguin Books.

Scanlan, M. (2001) *Plotting Terror*, Virginia: University of Virginia.

Scannell, P. (1991) *Broadcast Talk*, Thousand Oaks, London, Delhi: Sage.

Scheer, R. (2006) 'Now He Tells Us', AlterNet, 12 April, www.alternet.org/waroniraq/34861 (accessed 12 July 2009).

Schegloff, E.A. (1999) 'Whose Text? Whose Context?', *Discourse and Society* 8 (2): 165–87.

Schell, J. (2002) 'Introduction', in vanden Heuvel, K., *A Just Response*, New York: Thunder's Mouth Press/Nation Books.

Schlesinger, P. (2000) 'The Nation and Communicative Space', in Tumber, H. (ed.) *Media Power, Professionals and Policies*, London, New York: Routledge.

Schoonmaker, S. (1994) 'Capitalism and the Code: A Critique of Baudrillard's Third Order Simulacrum', in Kellner, D. (ed.) *Baudrillard: A Critical Reader*, Cambridge, MA, and Oxford: Blackwell.

Schubart, R. and Gjelsvik, A. (eds) (2004) *Femme Fatalities*, Goteburg: Nordicom.

Scraton, P. (2002) 'Introduction: Witnessing "Terror", Anticipating "War"', in Scraton, P. (ed.) *Beyond September 11th*, London: Pluto Press.

Searle, J.R. (1969) *Speech Acts: An Essay in the Philosophy of Language*, Cambridge: Cambridge University Press.

Semin, G.R. and Fiedler, K. (1992) *Language, Interaction and Social Cognition*, Thousand Oaks, London, Delhi: Sage.

Sengupta, K. (2008a) 'Taliban Factions May Be Using British Forces to Assassinate Rival Commanders', *Independent*, 25 July.

Sengupta, K. (2008b) 'Unmanned Spy Planes to Police Britain', *Independent*, 6 August.

Sengupta, K. and Macintyre, D. (2009) 'Israeli Cabinet Divided Over Fresh Gaza Surge', 13 January, www.independent.co.uk/news/world/middle-east/israeli-cabinet-divided-over-fresh-gaza-surge-1332024.html (accessed 30 January 2009).

Shepherd, L.J. (2008) *Gender, Violence and Security*, London and New York: Zed Books.

Sheriff, J.K. (1994) *Charles Peirce's Guess at the Riddle*, Bloomington and Indianapolis: Indiana University Press.

Simons, G. (2008) *They Destroyed Iraq and Called it Freedom*, Richmond, Surrey: Legacy Publishing.

Sipp, B. (2003) 'What is the Price of Freedom?', in Nuelken, A. (ed.) *The Liberator*, 7 (1): 2 (3rd US Infantry Division Public Affairs Office).

Slim, H. (2007) *Killing Civilians: Method, Madness and Morality in War*, London: Hurst and Company.

Snow, J. (2001) Report on World Trade Center Attack, Channel 4 News, 11 September.

Snow, N. (2006) 'Terrorism, Public Relations and Propaganda', in Kavoori, A.P. and Fraley, T. (eds) *Media, Terrorism and Theory*, Oxford and Lanham: Rowan and Littlefield.

Socialist Party (2005) Leaflet on Iraq, 19 March.

Sofsky, W. (2002) *Violence: Terrorism, Genocide, War*, London: Granta.

State of the News Media (2006) 'The State of the News Media', 2006 Annual Report, stateofthemedia.org/2006/printable_cabletv_economics.asp (accessed 22 January 2007).

Steele, J. and Goldenburg, S. (2009) 'What is the Real Death Toll in Iraq?', *Guardian* G2, 19 March.

Stiglitz, J. and Blimes, L. (2008) *The Three-Trillion Dollar War*, London and New York: Penguin, Allen Lane.

Stokes, R. and Hewitt, J.P. (1976) 'Aligning Actions', *American Sociological Review* 41 (October 1976): 838–49.

Stop the War Coalition (2009) 'Aims and Constitution', stopwar.org.uk (accessed 11 February 2009).

Stubbs, M. (1983) *Discourse Analysis*, Oxford: Blackwell.

Sun Editorial (2001) 'A Short Silence ... Then We Have a Job to Do', 14 September.

Sun Tzu (2002) *The Art of War*, New York: Dover Publications.

Sunday Times Insight Team (1990) 'Police Plan a "Shoot to Kill" Policy in Riots', *Sunday Times*, 8 April.

Swedberg, R. (2003) *Principles of Economic Sociology*, Princeton: Princeton University Press.

Swofford, A. (2003) *Jarhead*, New York: Scribner.

Tasker, Y. (2004) 'Women and Military Masculinities in *Courage Under Fire*', in Schubart, R. and Gjelsvik, A. (eds) *Femme Fatalities*, Goteburg: Nordicom.

Tebbit, K. (2007) 'Countering International Terrorism', in Hennessy, P. (ed.) *The New Protective State: Government, Intelligence and Terrorism*, London and New York: Continuum.

Therborn, G. (1980) *The Ideology of Power and the Power of Ideology*, London: Verso.

Thomas, E. and Barry, J. (2003) 'Now, Flexible Force', *Newsweek*, 3 March.

Thomas, E. and Hirsh, R. (2001) 'The Future of Terror', *Newsweek*, 3 to 10 January.

Thomson, A. (2004) Report from Fallujah, Channel 4 News, 9 November.

Thussu, D.K. (2006) 'Televising the "War on Terrorism"', in Kavoori, A.P. and Fraley, T. (eds) *Media, Terrorism and Theory*, Oxford and Lanham: Rowan and Littlefield.

Titscher, S., Meyer, M., Wodak, R. and Vetter, E. (eds) (2000) *Methods of Text and Discourse Analysis*, Thousand Oaks, London, Delhi: Sage.

Todd, E. (2003) *After the Empire*, London: Constable.

Tolson, A. (2006) *Media Talk*, Edinburgh: Edinburgh University Press.

Townshend, C. (2002) *Terrorism: A Very Short Introduction*, Oxford: Oxford University Press.

Travis, A. (2008) 'Revealed: Britain's Secret Propaganda War against al-Qaeda', *Guardian*, 26 August.

Traynor, I. (2009) 'US Outlines "New Realism" in Afghanistan', *Guardian*, 9 February.

Trefgarne, G. and Litterick, D. (2001) 'Recession Fear as Financial Markets are Hit by Chaos', *Daily Telegraph*, September 12.

Turner, G. (2008) *The Credit Crunch*, London: Pluto Press.

Turner, H.S. (ed.) (2002) *The Culture of Capital*, London and New York: Routledge.

United Nations Security Council (2002) Resolution 1441, 8 November, full text: www.guardian.co.uk/world/2002/dec/20/iraq.foreignpolicy2 (accessed 11 February 2009).

United Nations (2008) Resolution 63/95. Work of the Special Committee to Investigate Israeli Practices Affecting the Human Rights of the Palestinian People and Other Arabs of the Occupied Territories, 18 December, domino.un.org/UNISPAL.NSF/a06f2943c226015c85256c40005d359c/9ee939610361cc0c852575350057d134! (accessed 30 January 2009).

US Army/Marine Corps (2007) *Counterinsurgency Field Manual*, Chicago: Chicago University Press.

USA Today (2003) 'Bush: "Bring On" Attackers of US Troops', 7 February, www.usatoday.com/news/world/iraq/2003-07-02-bush-iraq-troops_x.htm (accessed 29 April 2009).

Usborne, D. (2009) 'Dawn of "Smart Power"', *Independent*, 14 January.

Vanaik, A. (ed.) (2007) *Selling US Wars*, Adlestrop: Arris.

vanden Heuvel, K. (2002) *A Just Response*, New York: Thunder's Mouth Press/ Nation Books.

van Dijk, T.A. (1998) *Ideology*, Thousand Oaks, London, Delhi: Sage.

Viner, K. (2000) 'Hand-to-Brand Combat', *Guardian Weekend*, 23 September.

Wade, R. (2008) 'Financial Regime Change?', *New Left Review* 53, September–October: 5–21.

Walczak, L., Crock, S. and Balfour, F. (2001) 'Winning the Peace', *Business Week*, 3 December.

Waldren, M.J. (2007) *Armed Police: The Police Use of Firearms Since 1945*, Stroud: Sutton Publishing.

Watt, E.D. (1982) *Authority*, London: Croom Helm.

Weil, S. (1988) *Oppression and Liberty*, London: Ark.

West, B. and Smith, R.L. (2003) *The March Up*, London: Random House.

Wheatcroft, G. (2009) 'How Israel Gets Away With Murder', *Independent*, 11 January.

Williams, M.J. (2007) 'Facets of Power in the "War on Terror"' in Berenskoetter, F. and Williams, M.J. (eds) *Power in World Politics*, London and New York: Routledge.

Wolin, S.S. (2008) *Democracy Incorporated: Managed Democracy and the Specter of Inverted Totalitarianism*, Princeton: Princeton University Press.

Wood, E.M. (2003) *Empire of Capital*, London and New York: Verso.

Woodward, B. (2002) *Bush at War*, New York: Simon and Schuster.

Woodward, B. (2006) *State of Denial*, London and Sydney: Simon and Schuster.

Woodward, W. (2006) '"Vast Bulk" of Foreign Prisoners to be Deported After Sentence, Blair Says', *Guardian*, 18 May.

Wright, E. (2004) *Generation Kill*, London: Corgi.

Wrong, D.H. (1979) *Power: Its Forms, Bases and Uses*, Oxford: Blackwell.

Yourish, K. (2003) 'Taking it to the Streets', *Newsweek*, 7 April.

Yunis, H. (1996) *Taming Democracy: Models of Political Rhetoric in Classical Athens*, Ithaca and London: Cornell University Press.

Zine, J. (2007) 'Between Orientalism and Fundamentalism: Muslim Women and Feminist Engagement', in Hunt, K. and Rygiel, K. (eds) *(En)Gendering the War on Terror*, Aldershot and Burlington: Ashgate.

Žižek, S. (2004) *Iraq: The Broken Kettle*, London and New York: Verso.

Žižek, S. (2005) *Interrogating the Real*, London and New York: Continuum.

Žižek, S. (2006) 'The Depraved Heroes of 24 are the Himmlers of Hollywood', *Guardian Unlimited*, 10 January, www.guardian.co.uk/media/2006/jan/10/usnews.comment (accessed 12 July 2009).

Žižek, S. (2009) *Violence*, London: Profile Books.

Index

Compiled by Sue Carlton